THE WELL-CONNECTED COMMUNITY

A networking approach to community development

Second edition

Alison Gilchrist

This edition published in Great Britain in 2009 by

Policy Press
University of Bristol
1-9 Old Park Hill
Bristol BS2 8BB
UK
t: +44 (0)117 954 5940
pp-info@bristol.ac.uk
www.policypress.co.uk

North America office:
Policy Press
c/o The University of Chicago Press
1427 East 60th Street
Chicago, IL 60637, USA
t: +1 773 702 7700
f: +1 773 702 9756
sales@press.uchicago.edu
www.press.uchicago.edu

© Policy Press 2009
Reprinted 2011

British Library Cataloguing in Publication Data
A catalogue record for this book is available from the British Library.

Library of Congress Cataloging-in-Publication Data
A catalog record for this book has been requested.

ISBN 978 1 84742 056 5 paperback

The right of Alison Gilchrist to be identified as author of this work has been
asserted by her in accordance with the 1988 Copyright, Designs and Patents Act.

Cover design by Qube Design Associates, Bristol
Front cover: image kindly supplied by www.corbis.com
Printed and bound in Great Britain by Marston Book Services, Oxford

This edition is dedicated to Keib Thomas, a key member of the Panel Study, who was an inveterate networker and died suddenly in the summer of 2007. The range of people at his memorial service was testimony to the incredible broadness of spirit that characterised his life and work.

Contents

List of tables, figures and boxes

Tables

Figure

Boxes

Preface to the second edition

'Tis true, there's magic in the web of it. (Shakespeare, *Othello*, Act 3, Scene 4)

This book is about connexity: the importance of connections and relationships within communities and society as a whole. Connexity is an old English word, revived by Geoff Mulgan (1997, 2004) to emphasise our mutual interdependence and the abundance of everyday interactions that characterise the modern world. There exists a plethora of means for contact and communication, from the almost imperceptible non-verbal expressions and gestures in face-to-face encounters, to the digital threads stretched between strangers in cyberspace exchanging information about calamitous events or simply sharing their favourite YouTube video clips.

In the five years since the first edition of this book was published, networking appears to be significantly more commonplace, deliberate and computer-mediated. It is now firmly acknowledged as essential to effective community development work. But the organisational and demographic environment in which community development workers and activists operate is becoming increasingly dynamic, complex and diverse. Practitioners need to be ever more versatile and willing to work across boundaries. In the UK integrated services and partnership working are well established as policy goals, with community empowerment proclaimed as a fundamental principle to achieving sustainable development and addressing profound inequalities in power and resource distribution.

Government and civil society alike recognise that being 'well connected' is a source of strength. However, less attention is paid to the practices and attitudes that foster these connections, nor the emotional ramifications that can nourish or corrode them. The 'web' referred to by Othello in the quote above is that of the fateful handkerchief that instantaneously fuels his jealousy and yet was woven long ago by an ancient sybil. It illustrates the need for both time and trust to build loving and respectful relationships. This applies equally to the development of community links and the arrangements that underpin partnerships across the public, private, voluntary and community sectors.

The theories and evidence offered in this book are rooted in *phronetic* knowledge: knowledge that is derived from practice and experience. The ideas have been distilled from action research, workshops, informal conversations, government reports and the academic literature. They are applicable to policy and practice, as well as intended to encourage critical reflection and further research.

This second edition incorporates developments in British government thinking, drawing on policy documents and the findings from recent research reports. There have been subtle, but contentious, shifts in the use of the term 'community development' which are hotly debated in the field. Accelerating globalisation has encouraged me to include more examples and lessons from development work with communities in and from the South. This has been aided by spending three months working on a Voluntary Service Overseas (VSO) special assignment in Sri Lanka, undertaking project development work for the Rural Development Foundation, a non-governmental organisation supporting the needs and aspirations of internally displaced people, whose lives have been disrupted by the tsunami and decades of civil war.

This experience gave me the opportunity and motivation to learn about community development in developing countries, through reading, direct involvement and discussions with colleagues in similar roles in Sri Lanka. In particular, I came to recognise that community development principles and processes are broadly transferable between different cultures and circumstances. My mind was sharpened in relation to key values of dignity, security, sustainability and human rights as I realised what matters to communities struggling to survive and recover hope for future generations. This made me all the more determined to present a model of community development that is transformative, empowering and challenging. Much of this second edition was drafted in sweltering heat, sitting on a hard chair under the whirr and click of a ceiling fan. Sri Lanka was once known as the Isle of Serendib, from the Arabic for jewel and island. Serendipity, discovering fortuitous opportunities by chance and coincidence, is an important aspect of networking.

I chose to work in Sri Lanka because it had been home to my mother and her forebears, members of the 'Ceylon' civil service during the colonial era. Community development can sometimes be seen as a form of colonialism; staff, resources and technical expertise imported often via middle-class professionals and project workers. The inequalities encountered are often steeped in tradition and cultural smokescreens, but the parallels are inescapable, even more so when I read through the reports from my grandfather, a government agent, outlining his work in dealing with problems very similar to those that I was writing funding bids to address. Our roles, status and power relations were formally different across the generations and after independence. Nevertheless

I could not help but reflect on a shared approach, especially in the face of ongoing problems arising from poverty, disease and inter-ethnic conflicts.

I hope therefore that this second edition reflects these insights and experiences as well as being substantially updated to take account of recent developments in theory, policy and practice. It affirms the continuing importance of networking for community development and the need for this to be grounded in core values of equality, empathy and empowerment. The fundamental purpose and structure of the book has not changed: my argument is that effective and inclusive networking is skilled, strategic and often serendipitous.

Chapter One begins with an exploration of how networks contribute to community life, individual well-being and collective survival strategies. The section on social capital has been considerably expanded to include a consideration of collective efficacy, community cohesion and integration, and the community dimensions of policy have been brought up to date. Chapter Two provides a historical account of different models of community development mainly as they have emerged in the UK but with reference to more global perspectives, as propounded by the International Association for Community Development (IACD) and the United Nations. Community development has become increasingly professionalised but still retains a strong activist base and focus on civil society. In Britain community development has to some extent been co-opted as a means of community engagement and empowerment, resulting in a delicate balancing act between the state agenda and community interests. This has proved a mixed blessing. In many ways it has highlighted the role of community practitioners, those who work at the interface between statutory bodies and citizens, in ensuring that the users of services can be involved in decision-making and the co-production of agreed outcomes, such as improved community safety or economic regeneration. This boundary-spanning role has long been a feature of community work but is given renewed prominence in government initiatives that seek to involve communities in cross-sectoral partnerships and service delivery.

Chapters Three and Four are concerned with the structure and functions of networks in society and in organisations. They examine how interpersonal linkages affect the flow of power and influence in decision-making, how community cohesion is enhanced through cross-community 'bridge building' and how emotions and shared understandings underpin strategies for collective action and political alliances. Networking is about communication, exchange, risk management and solidarity. The work of establishing and maintaining connections is a vital, but neglected, aspect of community development.

In Chapters Five and Six, I present the findings from research conducted for my PhD thesis (Gilchrist, 2001). These illustrate how community development workers use and support networks to achieve their aims of empowering communities and helping different agencies to work better together. Specific skills and strategies are identified as well as a number of valuable traits and attitudes. I argue that 'networking the networks' and actively nurturing the more difficult connections in communities is a distinctive contribution of community development work. I therefore introduce the term 'meta-networking' as a way of making visible this important role.

Chapters Seven, Eight and Nine consider why networking benefits communities and those that work with them. The concept of the 'well-connected community' is presented as a way of thinking about 'community' as the emergent property of complex and dynamic social systems. It is a means of managing chaos, building resilience and devising innovative collective solutions to intractable problems. Recent applications from the social sciences using complexity theory have been added, as have developments in information technology. The networking approach to community development poses a number of issues for practitioners, some of them already familiar, such as accountability, role boundaries, 'burnout' and so on. The book closes by examining the implications of this model for practice and policy, and makes recommendations regarding how 'good practice' (by which I mean ethical and effective practice) can be supported by funders, managers and policy makers.

Alison Gilchrist
Independent community development consultant
www.alisongilchrist.co.uk

Acknowledgements

I am grateful to colleagues at the Community Development Foundation (CDF), especially Jenny Fisher and Catriona May, for their support and encouragement. This second edition was supported by the CDF enabling me to take a sabbatical and to finish the writing in my final months before preparing to take up independent consultancy work.

Thanks to the International Association for Community Development for permission to use examples from their collection of case studies, 'What in the world?', and to the commissioning team at The Policy Press for their tolerance and advice during the rewriting process.

Members of the Panel Study: Frances Brown, Teri Dolan, Pete Hulse, Caroline Kay, Linda McMann, Susan Moores, Anne Pendleton, Gary Smith, Greg Smith, Keib Thomas, Chris Trueblood, and Mike Waite.

Bristol Festival Against Racism: Balraj Sandhu, Mike Graham, Rosetta Eligon, Ray Safia, Minoo Jalali, Steve Graham, Richard Jewison, Jane Kilpatrick, Lindy Clifton, Peter Courtier, Lil Bowers, and Batook Pandya.

Finally, I would like to thank friends and family for their continuing interest and providing occasional distractions.

ONE

Community networks: their significance and value

When the stranger says: what is the meaning of this city?
Do you huddle together because you love each other?
What will you answer?
'We all dwell together to make money from each other'?
or 'This is a community'?
(T.S. Eliot, *The chorus of the rocks*)

Introduction

Community development is fundamentally about the development of
'community' and it therefore makes sense to begin by examining what
we know and understand about the concept. This book is based on a
belief that the experience of community is generated by and manifest
in the informal networks that exist between people, between groups
and between organisations. Community provides a crucial dimension
to our lives and is a persistent theme within policy making. The idea
of community is generally regarded as a force for good: a means of
survival and progress. But without becoming cynical, it is important
to remember that references to community values and identities have
also been used to generate conflict and to resist change (Day, 2006).
Throughout history, people have lamented the 'decline' or 'eclipse' of
community (Stein, 1960) and the associated weakening of local social
ties. A recent consultation on present-day 'social evils' confirms this
yearning for community spirit and mutuality (Watts, 2008; Mowlam
and Creegan, 2008; Thake, 2009).

Surveys on the characteristics of a 'good' community consistently
reveal that people value a wide range of community and support
groups, alongside a set of residents who are good neighbours who
will help each other (Adams and Hess, 2006). Nearby networks of
family and friends contribute to feelings of community, sustained
through recurrent, often "mundane and everyday interactions between
people in localised settings" (Robertson et al, 2008). Most people
regard community as a 'good thing' that needs to be revived and

restored. Indeed, this has been the main rationale for community development in some quarters, especially where concerns about law and order have been raised. Bauman counterposes our nostalgia for community (with its cosy connotations of security and refuge) with the (post-)modern desire for freedom and autonomy. Community can be seen as 'liquid', taking shape to accommodate the lumps and bumps of existing circumstances and flowing with prevalent trends and discourses (2000, 2003). Some religious or ideological sects have established enclosed communities, intended to protect adherents from the perils of contemporary life (in whatever era) by rooting them in moral or spiritual certainties (Jones, 2007). But most of us belong to communities that are open to outside influence and continuously changing. Many have embraced globalisation, recognising that the networks of dependency and interactions that have emerged through migration and cultural exchanges represent a vibrant and enriching dimension of communities in the modern world (Mayo, 2005).

This chapter considers some of the benefits and limitations of community networks: for individuals, for society as a whole and for government programmes. It looks briefly at evidence and theories concerning community life from anthropology and sociology, and then considers the concept of 'social capital', before exploring the ways in which networks operate to the advantage of communities and, conversely, the ways in which they distort or suppress choices and opportunities. The model of the 'well-connected community' argues that community development has a role to play in helping people to make connections that are useful and empowering and, in particular, it addresses how to overcome or dismantle some of the obstacles that prevent people from communicating and co-operating with one another. First, however, how do networks contribute to community life? What have community studies revealed about people's everyday interactions and relationships? How is the term 'community' used and how does it compare to the idea of 'social capital'? What relevance does all this have for public policy and social well-being?

Anthropological research shows that community-type organisations characterise all human societies. Studies of humans and other higher primates suggest that we share an inherent sociability, a biological propensity to connect and to co-operate. Indeed it has been suggested that this ability to co-ordinate activities with people beyond the immediate family group was what gave Homo sapiens an evolutionary advantage over Neanderthals in the struggle for survival in the harsh climate of the European ice age over 30,000 years ago (Dunbar, 1996;

Gamble, 1999). Nevertheless, community has proved elusive and notoriously difficult to define and to study.

In his now classic trawl through definitions of community, Hillery (1955) identified a core feature to be regular, mostly co-operative, interaction among a set of people over time. Calling a set of people a 'community' generally implies that they have some common interest or bond (Taylor et al, 2000). It also raises expectations of loyalty, support and affirmation. Early sociologists such as Tönnies (1887) and Durkheim (1893) emphasised the emotional aspects of local life, arguing that common understanding, shared experiences and mutuality are what distinguish *Gemeinschaft* (community) from *Gesellschaft* (society). Tönnies contrasted community with the public, commercial sphere of society, while Durkheim argued that community represented a form of 'organic solidarity', based on resemblance and shared fate. In modern parlance, community comprises the informal interactions and connections that we use to co-ordinate everyday life. Personal, collective and organisational networks are clearly key to understanding how community operates, and how this differs from the more formal institutions of the state and civil society.

Aspects of community

This distinction inspired a whole research field known as community studies (see Nisbet, 1953; Bell and Newby, 1971; Crow and Allan, 1994; Day, 2006). Usually these involved detailed observations of "ordinary people's everyday lives" (Crow and Allan, 1994, p xiv), elaborated through conversations with community members in order to identify and analyse patterns of interaction and attachment. Interpreting the use of symbols, rituals and shared spaces has been of particular significance in understanding the functioning of different communities. Initially, community studies focused on specific localities, reporting on how institutions and traditions shaped community life.

The geographical dimension of community was paramount in defining the set of people studied, such as the residents of a particular neighbourhood, small town or island (Frankenberg, 1966). Locality was regarded as an important facet of people's identity and there was a strong emphasis in these studies on the positive aspects of community life – the solidarity, the mutual support and the ways in which people co-operated in their routine activities. Attachment to places, such as a neighbourhood or village, seems to be associated with strong social networks, and where there is high population turnover, for example due to migration, this tends to undermine feelings of trust, personal security and cohesion (Livingstone et al, 2008). This locality model of community still holds sway in many people's minds and has strongly influenced government area-based initiatives and some aspects of the 'place-shaping' strategies for community empowerment and local government in that they assume that people are more likely to become engaged in local decision-making processes if they feel they have a stake in the area where they live (Lyons, 2007; Sullivan and Taylor, 2007; Taylor, 2008).

However, people's social networks usually extend beyond geographical boundaries, often based around their work, faith or hobbies (Webber, 1963; Wellman, 1979). Communities are actively constructed by their members, rather than merely arising from local circumstances. Cultural traditions and symbols are used to assert community identity, expressed through ritual activities, music and flags, or their equivalent (Cohen, 1985; Back, 1996). This is about conventions and customs, often linked to religious or sporting occasions, but also about the ways in which people go about their everyday lives – their hairstyles, dress codes, language and so on. Such 'badges of belonging' reinforce community boundaries and can help identify 'friends' and 'foes' through multi-faceted 'webs of significance' (Geertz, 1973). These act as a social resource, reducing the stress of determining how to act and what to expect, but can sometimes constrain aspirations or choices (Green and White, 2007).

Informal networks enhance people's ability to cope with difficulties and disasters by keeping hope alive and bolstering well-being, even in the face of long-term social exclusion and sudden crises (Cattell, 2001). Sharing scarce resources during times of hardship is common among communities living in poverty or harsh environments, and can be crucial to the survival of some community members (Lupton, 2004). Studies of communities hit by catastrophe, such as a landslide (Miller, 1974; Erikson, 1979), heatwave (Klinenberg, 2002) or long strike action (Waddington et al, 1991), suggest that those with strong social networks are more likely to recover than those where networks are obliterated or non-existent. In Sri Lanka in the immediate aftermath of the tsunami in 2004, local networks mobilised to provide assistance to those affected on the coast. It is telling that these indigenous efforts were soon overwhelmed by the influx of well-meaning foreign aid agencies, some of whose activities have been criticised as undermining the capacities of surviving communities (Jirasinghe, 2007; Herath, 2008). Similarly, in the months after Hurricane Katrina caused widespread flooding in New Orleans, it was the informal neighbourhood associations that were most effective in helping communities to rebuild their shattered lives, rather than state agencies or non-governmental organisations. These networks mobilised flexible and efficient ways for delivering support and practical help where it was most needed (Coates, 2007). As well as communities appearing to crystallise from sudden disaster, they also coalesce around experiences of systematic discrimination and exclusion. This has been especially important in situations where communities have been disrupted by civil war or migration (Hall, 1990; Andrew and Lukajo, 2005). Work with refugees fleeing persecution and armed conflict emphasises the importance of helping people to rebuild social networks that are culturally specific, restoring personal and social resilience, to overcome trauma and literal dislocation (Miller and Rasco, 2004).

Sivanandan (1990) writing about the struggles of black and minority ethnic communities in Britain, calls these 'communities of resistance', similar in purpose to the array of self-help groups and buddying arrangements that sprang up within gay communities to cope with the HIV/AIDS crisis. They comprise communities of shared interest, which may take on a political purpose. Forming communities of identity or interest can thus be seen as a device for collective empowerment and is a familiar strategy for countering the dimensions of oppression associated with 'race', class, gender, disability, age and sexual orientation. As Weeks (2000, pp 240–3) writes, "the strongest sense of community is likely to come from those groups who find the premises of their collective existence threatened and who construct out of this a community of identity which provides a strong sense of resistance and empowerment".

Bauman (2001) refers to these as 'peg' communities, serving to protect people against fears of isolation or 'otherness'. This political dimension of 'community' articulates a particular perspective or 'consciousness' awakened through processes of reflection and debate. It finds expression in notions of 'pride' (such as Gay Pride or the Notting Hill carnival), the self-organisation of disabled people or through an exploration of historical 'roots' (Ohri, 1998). These actions provide opportunities for people to maintain a sense of collective identity in a hostile world by demanding that "difference not merely be tolerated and accepted, but that it is valued and celebrated" (Oliver, 1996, p 89). The resulting social networks reinforce a sense of community and provide a vital foundation for collective action, especially where this is risky or highly demanding, as is often the case when challenging injustice or exploitation. Solidarity in the face of adversity is an important facet of community, but this same sense of 'us' versus 'them' can lead to sectarian violence and the stigmatisation of minority groups.

The predominantly Western model of the free and independent individual seems strange to other cultures that have a more collectivist way of life and find great value in the web of relationships that connect people to places and to each other. For example, the Xhosa principle of *ubuntu* conveys the meaning 'I am because we are' (Shutte, 2001). As Archbishop Desmond Tutu explained, "It embraces hospitality, caring about others.... We believe a person is a person through another person, that my humanity is caught up, bound up and inextricable in yours" (cited in du Toit, 1998, p 89). Many people feel they belong to several communities simultaneously (Sen, 2006). Their networks are flexible and strategic, depending on the social and political context, as well as their personal circumstances and choices. In this post-modern view of social identity, community takes on a fluid, almost hybrid, form, containing contradictory and reflexive features that flow through people's lives, mingling different aspects of their experience and affiliations. The importance of diversity is well understood in southern and eastern cultures; as Gandhi asserted in his teachings: civilisation should be a celebration of differences. There is an African saying that 'It takes a whole village to raise a child' and an Akan proverb contends that 'in a single polis there is no wisdom'.

Within communities, diversity can be enriching and dynamic, but it also needs careful attention, particularly where inequalities and incompatibilities generate unease and misunderstanding. Strains and conflicts are inherent within communities, even where there is an appearance of unity (Brent, 2009). The reality of community life encompasses many different identities and allegiances making up a kaleidoscope of intersecting layers of experience and expectations that characterise people's real lives, their histories, current preoccupations, enthusiasms and future aspirations (Brah, 2007; Seidler, 2009, forthcoming). For children and young people moving beyond the parental sphere, their identities are initially shaped by interactions with siblings and peers in the community, negotiating opportunities, expectations, jeopardies and actual dangers. Neighbourhoods are characterised by 'encounter-space' in which children 'play out', quite literally, but also enact 'identity struggles' that enable them to define themselves in contrast to others (Percy-Smith and Matthews, 2001). Their networks allow them to build strategic alliances and tactical coalitions, that are shaped in part by family loyalties, ethnicity, class and gender (Edwards et al, 2006).

Community cohesion and integration

Differences are marked by terrain, fashion, jargon and other cultural signifiers. They become embedded in notions of collective identity or community belonging. Incompatibilities and rivalries sometimes flare up as inter-communal tensions, sparked off by trivial incidents that are fanned into incendiary significance by rumour and long-standing resentments (e.g. Black Radley, 2007). For young people, these networks are sometimes erroneously labelled as gangs, organised around estates or ethnicities (Alexander, 2000, 2007). Social cohesion is undermined in a twisting spiral of suspicion and competition for what are often scarce resources. In situations where communities feel aggrieved or under attack, they can become polarised and defensive, attempting to stem the tide of integration or to reclaim cultural traditions. The 'community' dimension of society can also be used as a mechanism for integration and cohesion. It creates arenas in which differences are acknowledged rather than feared or reviled. Ideally, community offers a simple affirmation of similarity and mutuality, in which individual relationships form and diversity can flourish. In Britain, however, research studies around nationality, citizenship and community cohesion have struggled to identify 'common values' and what constitutes 'belonging' (Rattansi, 2002; Modood, 2003; Buonfino with Thomson, 2007; Hudson et al, 2007; Mulgan and Ali, 2007; Seabeck et al, 2007; Flint and Robinson, 2008). The concept of social identity is recognised as an important, but fluid, facet of people's sense of their community (or rather communities), especially when faced with hostility or misconceptions (Bhavnani et al, 2006; Modood, 2007; Wetherell et al, 2007).

Evidence suggests that diversity is associated with reduced levels of social trust (Putnam, 2007), and is therefore undermining of community cohesion. This need not be about inter-ethnic antipathies, but can be explained in terms of cultural expectations and symbols which people use to interpret the behaviour and intentions of those around them. However, it would be wrong to assume that cohesion is only affected by ethnic or national differences, since other dimensions of diversity clearly shape community dynamics and disconnections at local levels, not least class and income differences (Hero, 2007; Flint and Robinson, 2008). We choose or are given multiple affiliations, reflecting our myriad interests and circumstances. As Sen wrote, "We are all members of several communities, and our ties with them can increase or decrease. It is both illogical and dangerous to corral people as if they could belong to only one community" (2006, p 160). When underlying inequalities and tensions are not addressed, or differences are not acknowledged, attempts to artificially generate (or, worse, to impose) a common (for example, national) identity tend to founder. One solution is to recognise the existence (and value) of a "community of communities", such as proposed in the report *The future of multi-racial Britain* (Parekh, 2000, p 56), and reiterated in the report of the Commission on Integration and Cohesion (CoIC, 2007). Strategies for managing diversity and promoting cohesion would benefit more than is generally realised from encouraging and facilitating 'bridge building' through inter-community activities that strengthen boundary-spanning ties in order to improve informal relationships (Gilchrist, 2004; Harris and Young, 2009). This might be termed the 'Velcro' approach to cohesion, enabling micro-interactions at community level to hook up with the tiny loops in people's lives (Richard Davies, personal communication). A recent analysis of the Citizenship Survey indicates that having friends from different ethnic backgrounds is positively related to perceptions of community cohesion (Laurence and Heath, 2008).

Social capital and community

As Williams (1976, p 65) noted, the term 'community' remains a "warmly persuasive word ... [that] never seems to be used unfavourably". It has similar connotations to the more modern, and currently popular, term 'social capital', first coined by Hanifan (1916), who described it as "those tangible substances [that] count for most in the daily lives of people: namely good will, fellowship, sympathy, and social intercourse among the individuals and families who make up a social unit". The idea of social capital was rediscovered several decades later, notably by Jacobs (1961), Coleman (1990), Bourdieu (1986), Putnam (1993, 2000) and Woolcock (1998, 2001). Jacobs (1961) referred to a "web of public respect [which constituted] a resource in times of personal or neighbourhood need". Social capital recognises that the relationships of everyday life between neighbours, colleagues and friends, even casual acquaintances, have value for the individual and for society as a whole (Dekker and Uslaner, 2001; Middleton et al, 2005). Coleman believed that social capital accumulates as a result of beneficial exchanges between people pursuing their own self-interest rather than as a deliberate investment strategy. For Coleman, the norms embedded in these community networks could counteract possible disadvantages associated with socio-economic background (Coleman, 1990), but he also acknowledged that pressures to conform, to save face and to avoid informal sanctions, could also act as constraints on innovation and dissent, as well as freedom and fun.

The French sociologist, Bourdieu, was more critical of the function of social capital in society because he was concerned with how inequalities in wealth and power were perpetuated through culture and connections (1986). His view was that social capital was a source of privilege that benefited the upper echelons, but had little relevance for other sections of society except to exclude them from opportunities for advancement. This notion of elite networks based on "who we know and how we use them" (Heald, 1983) will be explored further in Chapter Four. Hall's (2000) work on social capital in Britain suggests that there is a class factor, with middle-class people being more likely to be members of voluntary or civic associations while working-class households enjoy higher levels of informal sociability. Others have raised questions about gender dynamics and the well-documented contribution that women make to community life (Lowndes, 2000; Innerarity, 2003; Bruegel, 2005). The concept has been further refined to include structural and cognitive aspects, such that people's position in society interacts with their propensities to engage with others in co-operative action (Uphoff and Wijayaratna, 2000). This approach is particularly relevant for community development, acknowledging as it does emotional, political and practical factors in people's orientation towards collective or associative behaviour (Fraser et al, 2003).

Broadly speaking, social capital can be defined as a collective resource embedded in and released from informal networks (Lin, 2002). These are based on shared norms of trust and mutuality that bestow advantage on individuals and communities: "better connected people enjoy better returns" (Burt, 2000, p 3). The interest in social capital represents an attempt to "quantify a sense of 'community spirit' or altruism or indeed 'the conscious collective'" through assessing the "quantity and co-operative quality of a society's social interactions" (PIU, 2002). Measures of social capital have tended to focus on three different (and not necessarily causally related) aspects: levels of *trust* between people and social institutions; *participation* in social and civil activities; and *networks* of personal contacts.

Putnam is generally credited with popularising the concept of social capital and highlighting its implications for government (Harper, 2001; PIU, 2002). His more liberal approach has a particular resonance with communitarian models of social and family responsibility and therefore has wide appeal to politicians and policy makers. Putnam describes social capital as the "connections among individuals – social networks and the norms of reciprocity and trustworthiness that arise from them" (2000, p 19) that are created and maintained through voluntary associations, civic life and community activity. Putnam's research on levels of social capital appears to demonstrate strong correlations with economic prosperity, stable governance and social cohesion (1993, 1995, 2001). This has understandably attracted interest from a wide range of national and global agencies concerned with economic development and political stability.

The World Bank has been especially keen to invest in community empowerment and adult education programmes that build social capital in the developing world as a strategy for combating poverty and supporting regeneration (Narayan and Pritchett, 1997; Woolcock, 1998; Narayan, 2002; Alsop et al, 2005; Kane, 2008). Most international programmes for poverty eradication, for example sponsored by the World Bank or United Nations agencies, require forms of community participation as a means of building social capital, as well as ensuring some kind of contribution from the beneficiaries (Bowen, 2008; Kane, 2008). The British Department for International Development (1999, p 9) refers to social capital as "those resources inherent in social relations, which facilitate collective action. Social capital resources include trust, norms and networks or association representing any group, which gathers consistently for a common purpose".

Putnam acknowledges that social capital is closely related to our experience of community, reflecting levels of general trust and interconnectivity within society: "a well-connected individual in a poorly connected society is not as productive as a well-connected individual in a well-connected society. And even a poorly connected individual may derive some of the spill-over benefits from living in a well-connected community" (2000, p 20). Just like the concept of community, social capital reflects shared norms and values that are affirmed through sustained interaction and co-operation. Putnam and his followers, therefore, promote increased volunteering and active citizenship as the means to reverse an apparent decline in social capital in Western countries. In community development, we might argue that encouraging greater participation in community activities of all kinds would have the same effect, including involvement in civic associations, public partnerships and restorative justice schemes (e.g. Kurki, 2003).

Much of the literature on social capital emphasises trust as a component of "the ability of people to work together for common purpose in groups and organisations" (Fukuyama, 1996, p 10). Trust implies both an expectation of mutual commitment and a degree of predictability about other people's behaviour. It derives from experiences of others as reliable (delivering what has been promised), capable and accountable (giving an accurate explanation of what has happened). But trust is not just an aspect of social relationships; it is a vital component in our propensity to take risks, especially when it comes to co-operative exchanges with others (Boeck et al, 2006; Cohn, 2008). For communities, trust is a complicated process, requiring respect and an enduring capability on the part of leaders, partners and participants (Purdue, 2001). While the concept of trust has seen a welcome revival in discussions around policy and practice, it is perhaps most useful to regard social capital as "quintessentially a product of collective interaction" (Field, 2003, p 20). It is the value added through networking processes, and resides within the web of ties and linkages that we call community.

A recent study of social capital in different areas of Leicestershire (Boeck et al, 2007) came up with the intriguing finding that not only did levels of social capital vary between rural, deprived and affluent communities, but there seem to be two different kinds of people – those who were more trusting, but inward-looking in their networks (having strong bonding capital) in contrast with a different set of residents, who appeared to enjoy diversity more, but were more wary in their outlook. Trust is therefore context dependent, reflecting differential power and access to independent resources, as well as an ability (or not) to apply sanctions (Foley and Edwards, 1999). People who have been displaced by natural disasters or betrayed by torture and conflict may need specific interventions to help them rebuild their social capital in new surroundings (e.g. Zetter et al, 2005). Understanding how people perceive the different players in their social networks (as trustworthy, influential and accessible, or not) is an important aspect of devising strategies for communication and empowerment (Garland et al, 2002; Phillips, 2002).

Many theorists, notably Burt (2000), Cook et al (2001) and Lin (2002) argue that network structures are the key to understanding social capital and this is broadly the approach taken here. It is the nature and configuration of the connections, what Burt describes as the 'bridges' across 'structural holes', which are especially valuable. Of course, a web is only a metaphor and social networks are by no means uniform in their structure and configurations. As we shall examine more closely in Chapter Three, the filaments that connect people vary in strength, directionality and density. Woolcock (2001), building on Putnam's model and echoing Granovetter's (1973) distinction between 'strong' and 'weak' ties, suggested that there are different kinds of social capital:

- *bonding*: based on enduring, multi-faceted relationships between similar people with strong mutual commitments such as among friends, family and other close-knit groups;
- *bridging*: formed from the connections between people who have less in common, but may have an overlapping interest, for example, between neighbours, colleagues, or between different groups within a community;
- *linking*: derived from the links between people or organisations beyond peer boundaries, cutting across status and similarity and enabling people to gain influence and resources outside their normal circles.

These distinctions between types of social capital are not always clear-cut in reality since the boundaries and divisions within society are not themselves immutable or easily defined (Bruegel, 2005). Nevertheless it is useful as a theoretical model for thinking about the nature and purpose of different interactions. Each of these is necessary for strong and sustainable communities, but community development is primarily concerned with the latter two forms of social capital (Wakefield and Poland, 2005). Bridging capital can be seen as important for managing diversity and maintaining community cohesion (Gilchrist, 2004; Fieldhouse, 2008). Linking capital is needed for empowerment and partnership working. The networking approach used to develop the 'well-connected community' emphasises the role played by community development workers in helping people to build bridges and make links that they might otherwise find difficult.

As Arneil (2006, p 5, emphasis in original) argues in her 'multi-cultural theory of social justice', "the *nature* of the connections in any given community is what ultimately determines its capacity for justice". In societies where there are both inequalities and diversity, this cannot be overlooked (Evers, 2003; Wrench, 2007). Research investigating the relationship between social capital and well-being among poor people living in deprived communities in Colombo, Sri Lanka, and Durban, South Africa, revealed that the poorest people in society had rich networks that were highly localised, based on bonds with family, friends and neighbours that enabled them to survive through life crises or periods of extreme hardship. As one woman in KwaMasha township in the Durban study explained: "social capital is the fountain that the community drinks out of in times of crisis" (cited in Fraser et al, 2003). They were, however, lacking in the kinds of connections that would lift them out of poverty or enable them to influence decisions over how resources and opportunities are secured (Shankland, 2000; Shiva, 2002; Fraser et al, 2003).

This echoes findings by the World Bank that poor people use their networks to reduce risk and vulnerability to economic recession by managing their assets and pursuing a range of livelihoods (Narayan et al, 2000a; Moser, 2008). Research in the Philippines, Zambia, Ecuador and Hungary suggests that networks afford poor people access to job and trading opportunities, financial assets (such as revolving loan schemes) and inroads into supply chains. When poor people are asked about what they consider necessary for well-being, they identify connections with others as vital and judge families with the lowest well-being to be those that are isolated or excluded from networks that would allow them to improve their situation, such as mutual credit clubs (Narayan et al, 2000b). Networks are important channels for information about both opportunities and problems (Meikle, 2002). Inevitably they also represent ties of obligation and responsibility towards kin and others who may have helped out in the past and therefore have some moral claim on your assets in the 'good times'. The flow of resources and emotional support through networks is multi-directional and can serve to maintain poor people at subsistence level, rather than enabling them to participate in the wider community and take advantage of shared or self-help initiatives (May et al, 2000). For example, in rural areas of the South, the social necessities of bridewealth, dowries and funeral expenses can inflict severe debts on families to be repaid at extortionate rates unless they are members of local community-run insurance schemes such as burial societies (Chambers, 1983). Conversely, in many societies, the rich are compelled by customs of *noblesse oblige* to distribute sustenance and provide work opportunities to the 'less fortunate', a system of philanthropy which finds echoes in community volunteering and charity schemes, though often without the personal connection. Mapping informal networks has been seen as a way of measuring levels of social capital and somehow capturing the "myriad of inter-connected influences" (Adams and Hess, 2006, p 14) but the concept still suffers from an inherent difficulty in doing justice to the multi-faceted nature of community linkages (Boeck and Fleming, 2005).

The benefits of community networks

Although the idea of 'community as social capital' begs many questions (Taylor, 2003), community does seem to represent a significant collective resource. Many people get involved in community activities in order to meet people and gain a sense of belonging. For some, this is about self-help and survival, enabling people to cope during times of adversity and to secure a decent quality of life for themselves and their families (Burns et al, 2004). Community networks supply practical assistance with a variety of tasks (Williams and Windebank, 2000, 2003). They operate as a collective mechanism for sharing risk and resources in situations of scarcity and uncertainty (Stack, 1974; Werbner, 1988). The Pakistani clan-like *biraderi* offered similar networks of support to newly arrived migrants and continue to exert their influence on patterns of loyalty and exchange (Anwar, 1985), but perhaps to a diminishing degree (Shaw, 2002).

Transnational communities created by global migration rely on family and informal social networks to survive and these embryonic support groups are often the precursors of civil society organisations for those that settle (Theodore and Martin, 2007). These "networks of necessity" (Hunter and Staggenborg, 1988, p 253) are crucial mechanisms for the survival and sustenance of poor and other segregated groups. They are often based on kinship and community webs that support reciprocal arrangements for childcare, money-lending and similar exchanges, such as the pardoner system brought over by African-Caribbean communities and used to smooth their settlement in Britain (Kottegoda, 2004, p 103; Hanley, 2007). Small and routine acts of neighbourliness maintain loose and interdependent ties within localities, improving people's sense of safety and strengthening the sense of community spirit (Henning and Lieberg, 1996). Research in the Netherlands indicates that this is enhanced in localities with more than one meeting place, and where there are both opportunities and incentives for people to invest in local relationships (Völke et al, 2007).

Participation in community life takes many forms and is shaped by a variety of preferences and circumstances (Clarke et al, 2006). Such informal transactions retain a norm of 'generalised reciprocity' over time. A three-year initiative in England to empower community members by encouraging neighbourliness and breaking down the barriers between decision-makers and residents resulted in improved well-being and 'community spirit', defined as a 'local culture of support and volunteering'. This was attributed to the development of strong, wide-reaching social networks and an enhanced sense of local identity (Hothi with Bacon et al, 2008, p 47). As Sieh (2005, p 95) reminds us, "not all costs and benefits of social connections accrue to the person making the contact"; these flow through the social and neighbourly networks kept alive through small favours, casual greetings and exchanges (Cuff, 2005; Abrams, 2006; Harris, 2006). However, the quality of neighbourliness is obviously affected by levels of familiarity and reciprocity, which in turn reflect the opportunities for regular encounter. Evidence suggests that in industrialised societies there has been a decline in informal neighbouring, with such interactions becoming more discretionary, due to changing patterns of work, shopping, welfare and leisure (Blokland, 2003; Pilch, 2006; Buonfino and Hilder, 2007).

Local authority schemes, some using community development methods, have sought to establish good neighbouring or befriending projects but often these have not been self-sustaining and have withered away once funding has ceased (Northmore et al, 2006). There have been attempts in recent years to formalise arrangements for mutual support through community-based 'care and share' schemes, such as LETS (Local Exchange Trading Schemes) in which skills are swapped for tokens, or TimeBanks where the currency is measured in units of time (Williams et al, 2001; Seyfang and Smith, 2002; Smith, 2005). Proponents of these rather artificial mechanisms claim that they can be used to recreate community spirit and they have attracted interest (and some funding) from government regeneration and development agencies (Seyfang, 2001, 2003).

Health, well-being and care

The personal relationships and social networks established and nurtured through community or neighbourly activities appear to bring considerable benefits in terms of people's well-being and health (Gabriel and Bowling, 2004; Boyle et al, 2006; Helliwell and Putnam, 2006; Searle, 2008) and their general quality of life (Phillipson et al, 2004; Halpern, 2005; Harris, 2008). Informal conversations within trusting relationships provide information and advice on various matters. Community networks act as cheap and user-friendly referral systems, supplying informal help at times of crisis and are often resorted to before professional (sometimes stigmatised) help is requested from the appropriate agencies, particularly about embarrassing or risky problems (Godfrey et al, 2004). Having knowledgeable people within one's social network is generally useful, assuming of course that such enquiries will be treated in confidence and not form the basis for gossip or disapproval. Social networks supply informal care and a sense of belonging, although evidence suggests that family and friends provide different kinds of support compared to neighbours, a fact that was somewhat overlooked by 'care in the community' strategies (Barr et al, 2001; Evans, 2009). It has been suggested that in order to meet future needs within restricted budgets, a form of 'local care contract' resourced from social capital will be needed based on semi-formalised networks of support in every community (Brindle, 2008).

In addition to these practical benefits, social networks have an emotional impact. Social psychologists who have studied happiness have concluded that social interaction of almost any kind tends to make people happy, both in the short term but also in terms of their general disposition (Layard, 2005). It appears that it is not only the *quality* of social interaction that has this effect, but also the *quantity*. People with diverse networks (maintained through a variety of activities) seem to experience a higher degree of contentment than those with an intensely supportive, but homogeneous, set of relationships (Argyle, 1996; Young and Glasgow, 1998).

This also applies to reported health: individuals with robust and diverse networks lead healthier lives than those who are more isolated, lonely or whose networks consist of similar people (Szreter and Woolcock, 2004; Cacioppo and Patrick, 2008). They have stronger immune systems, suffer less from heart disease, recover more quickly from emotional trauma and seem to be more resistant to the debilitating effects of illness, possibly because of a generally more positive disposition or because they maintain a more active lifestyle (Kawachi, 1996). Mental health is similarly affected by people's level of social capital, especially in terms of their pathways to recovery (McKenzie and Harphan, 2006; Seebohm and Gilchrist, 2008). Strong social networks between providers and carers are also associated with good mental health programmes, especially where these prioritise self-help and community support (Coker, 2008). However, factors associated with poverty and social exclusion also contribute to ill-health and cannot be eradicated simply through the buffering effects of social capital (Cattell, 2001).

Influence and power

The concept of collective efficacy (Bandura, 2001; Sampson et al, 2002) has been developed as a way of explaining the shared belief that by working together, people can change situations and challenge injustices. Their combined experience, shared and reinforced through community networks, creates a virtuous spiral of learning, confidence and mutuality. Informal relationships make it easier for people to communicate and co-operate with one another. They create the conditions for collective action, enabling people to work together to achieve (or defend) common interests (Lowndes et al, 2006). Those communities that are 'well-connected' have an advantage when it comes to organising themselves for whatever purpose. Community networks enable people to mobilise for campaigns and events, pooling effort and resources for collective benefit and shared goals (e.g. Dale and Sparkes, 2008). Endogenous community action (that initiated by communities themselves) is more likely and more sustainable when people have strong social assets in the form of networks of relationships with others who share similar experiences (Burkett and Bedi, 2006).

Box 1.1: A village campaign

The residents of a small village on the outskirts of a city in south-west England learnt of plans to build a major housing development in the 'green belt' fields surrounding their homes. They rapidly mobilised through public meetings and used their personal networks to obtain information on what was happening, to make links with similar groups in the area and to acquire resources for campaigning. Using these links the village action group gained access to specific skills, materials, legal advice and political influence. Residents were able to develop a high-profile campaign in the local media and to involve most of their neighbours in taking some kind of action, whether this was petitioning the regional government office, writing letters to the council and MPs or planting a placard in their front gardens.

The village has no obvious space for informal interactions, having no village shop and straddling a busy road, so it was difficult for neighbours to get to know one another. The campaign to save the green belt provided opportunities for people to connect around a common concern and from that to develop informal neighbouring relations with a wider range of people along the street.

As a result of the regular gatherings and other activities, community networks have strengthened. People are noticeably more friendly; they know each other's names and circumstances, and are more likely to greet each other on the street. Several residents have taken on high-profile roles and one is planning to stand in the parish council elections.

See www.shortwoodgbc.co.uk

There is strong evidence from studies of community participation that behaviours such as helping neighbours or attending local events are the precursors for informal networks, which in turn result in strong governance and collective efficacy (Perkins et al, 1996; Wollebaek and Selle, 2002). Robust and diverse community networks are vital for effective and inclusive empowerment because they encourage a wider range of people to become active citizens and enable those who do take on civic roles to perform their roles as community representatives and leaders.

Problems of community

However, 'community' also has a downside and informal networks can be notoriously private and opaque (Taylor, 2003). Relationships are not universally beneficial, either for the individual or for society as a whole. Communities are sometimes elitist, 'tribal' and oppressive. The dominant norms associated with strong communities may damage the confidence and identity of anyone whose preferences or activities deviate from defined respectable behaviour. Consequently, people who cannot, or do not want to, fit in with what is deemed 'right and proper' either pretend to conform, are ostracised or they leave, hoping to find refuge and fulfilment in more tolerant settings. Community-based sanctions are used to uphold shared conventions and perpetuate stereotypes, including malicious rumour, 'sending to Coventry', and, at the extreme, vigilante activities and lynchings. In many countries, Gypsies, Romanies and Travellers still struggle to gain acceptance for their lifestyle and ethnic identity, despite being full citizens with a long-established community presence (Clark and Greenfields, 2006). Social networks are used to exert these pressures, causing misery as well as bodily harm.

Community ties sometimes work against wider integration and social inclusion, holding people back from pursuing their ambitions and restricting employment mobility. Peer pressure can outweigh scientific knowledge and personal belief systems, thwarting long-term benefits and aspirations. We see this in relation to the smoking habits of young people, and patterns of truancy or petty vandalism. Adults are also susceptible, finding themselves influenced by the ideas, choices and behaviour of friends, colleagues and neighbours, sometimes against their own better judgement. Criminal and paedophile rings operate in this way, justifying their activities only by comparison to other network members, rather than against wider social norms. Corruption likewise depends on closed networks and misguided loyalties. Communities that are closed to outside influence and scrutiny may become moribund and separated from the rest of society. Furthermore, networks often contain pockets of power that are difficult to unmask or challenge. Because networks can operate against opportunity and merit, a networking approach to community development must be proactive in countering and overcoming barriers set up through personal loyalties, cultural biases and prejudices.

Community as a dimension of policy

Despite these drawbacks, there has been a resurgent interest in the idea of community among academics, policy makers and politicians (Chanan, 2003; Raco, 2003; Taylor, 2003; Banks et al, 2007). This is true of Britain in the 21st century but has implications and a resonance way beyond this country (see, for example, Craig and Mayo, 1995; Burkett and Bedi, 2006). In the past the prefix 'community' has been used to soften the edge of state interventions, implying user-friendly, accessible services or partnership arrangements for the delivery of welfare to those sections of the population said to have issues that are particularly difficult to address. 'Community' is envisaged as both an agent, as well as an object, for interventions devised to remedy perceived deficits and alleviate deprivation (Day, 2006), or encourage adjustment to changed circumstances, as in the British coalfield communities (Francis et al, 2002).

Consequently, when used as a collective noun, 'community' tends to refer to people who are disadvantaged by poverty, oppression and prejudice. Communitarian thinking prescribes stable and well-integrated communities as a condition for progress and social inclusion, particularly when faced with complex and intractable problems (Henderson and Salmon, 1998). By promoting community involvement as a palliative (if not a cure) for 'disadvantage', governments may be seeking to avoid demands for significant redistribution of resources and opportunities (Henderson, 2005). It is by no means clear how much community participation, as a component of public policy, can be linked to either redistributive or market forms of social justice (see Craig et al, 2008). Indeed, it has been argued that communitarian strategies for building stable communities have exacerbated social exclusion, resulting in 'sink estates', slums and the same neighbourhoods consistently appearing towards the top of successive indices of deprivation. Community life can be seen as "a mechanism that arises to cope with lack of opportunity rather than one that creates opportunities" (Sprigings and Allen, 2005, p 398). The cynics might claim that community is more about chains than choices.

There are three conceptual struts that combine to triangulate government interest in 'community':

- social capital
- governance
- service delivery.

High levels of social capital appear to be correlated with several core policy objectives around improving health, reducing crime, increasing educational attainment and economic regeneration. Given the evidence linking social networks to these policy outcomes, it makes sense for the government to support interventions that strengthen networks and build trust (Halpern, 2005). More participative forms of 'governance' are being created that rely on multi-agency partnerships in which communities are strongly represented as stakeholders and local 'experts' (Stewart, 2000; Somerville, 2005). In Britain, this trend is typified by legislation and initiatives to promote active citizenship and community empowerment, such as the 2007 Local Government and Public Involvement in Health Act. Strategies are being implemented for improving the quality of engagement between state agencies and the communities they serve (Newman et al, 2004; CLG, 2008).

Equivalent programmes are appearing throughout Europe and the rest of the world and evidence is beginning to accumulate as to the benefits of community engagement (e.g. Rogers and Robinson, 2004). In terms of 'service delivery', community groups and voluntary organisations provide significant forms of self-help and informal support through self-organising and community action (Richardson, 2008). The voluntary and community sector, in particular, has been influential in pioneering welfare services tailored to the needs of specific sections of the population that have been overlooked by mainstream agencies. The recruitment and support of volunteers has also been a major function of the sector, running local and community activities in addition to providing auxiliary services in public institutions such as hospitals or schools.

Many current policies and programmes see 'community' as an arena of rights and responsibilities, expressed through individual acts of citizenship and volunteering, rather than a foundation for collective organising. The theme of community involvement, alongside communitarian notions of social responsibility, runs throughout modern urban and public policies (Chanan, 2003; Nash and Christie, 2003; CD Challenge group, 2006; Brannan et al, 2007). Increasingly, social networks are recognised as crucial to the capacity of communities to participate in, and even deliver, government initiatives (6, 2002; Taylor, 2003; CRU, 2005) but the explanations for this may be more complex than first realised (Brannan et al, 2006).

Community networks provide important infrastructure capacity within civil society. They have a particular relevance to policies and programmes seeking to promote democratic renewal, social cohesion, regeneration and public health. The current government's commitment to community involvement and partnership working represents a genuine and constructive attempt to transform public planning and service delivery (Tam, 2007). In order to turn the rhetoric of community empowerment and community leadership into a meaningful and sustainable reality, informal and formal networks must be developed and strengthened so that representatives can be supported and held accountable. Similarly, time and effort is needed to build relationships of trust and respect across different sectors and between partner agencies responsible for designing and managing the new plans or strategies.

Conclusions

The idea of community continues its hold on private sentiments and public imagination. It signifies a valued dimension of society and has become a preferred means of addressing policy problems, locally, nationally and even globally. However, communities take many forms and operate across various areas and levels. In addition to the more traditional models of local, geographically defined communities, we now need to consider the ways people connect with one another to form:

- communities of identity (to share cultural activities and experiences);
- communities of interest or passion (to pursue or resist shared fates);
- communities of purpose (to achieve a common goal);
- communities of practice (to exchange experience and learning);
- communities of inquiry (to collectively investigate an issue);
- communities of support (to provide mutual aid and encouragement);
- communities of circumstance (to deal with temporary, sometimes unplanned, situations).

Community development supports networks that foster mutual learning and shared commitments so that people can work and live together in relatively coherent and equitable communities. The purpose of community development is to maintain and renew 'community' as a foundation for the emergence of diverse initiatives that are independent of both the public and private sectors. This book aims to persuade policy makers and practitioners alike that networking is a necessary and effective method of boosting bridging and linking social capital, thus enhancing community cohesion and citizen empowerment. It goes on to argue that a core, but often neglected, function of community development work is to establish, facilitate and nurture the crucial, but more difficult, boundary-spanning ties that support collective action and empowerment.

TWO

Community development

There is no greater service than to help a community to
liberate itself. (Nelson Mandela, 2003)

Chapter Two provides an overview of community development,
focusing on its evolution as a form of professional intervention. It
traces the history of community development over the 20th century,
and examines applications of core methods and values in relation
to a number of government programmes. The role of community
development workers in supporting networks is briefly highlighted,
in preparation for a more detailed consideration in the following
chapters.

The term 'community development' is often used to describe
participatory interventions that promote self-help and service
delivery when the state is unable to satisfy community aspirations.
It is "about interacting with people to assist them to find ways to
build understanding and co-operation between individuals and
groups to enable them to make changes in their own lives and for the
greater good" (Bartley, 2003, p 186). The South African Community
Development Resource Association describes development practice as
"a conscious, facilitative approach to social transformation. Effective
development practice respectfully accompanies and supports people
and their organisations, communities and movements in their own
efforts to realise their aspirations, make their choices and access their
fair share of resources" (www.cdra.org.za). Whilst being explicitly
based on human rights, and therefore emphasising the political and
participatory aspects of interventions (Chambers, 1983), there is also a
strong emphasis on the creative achievement of dignity and freedom
as an aspect of well-being, ethics and emotions (e.g. Rahman, 1990,
1993; Ariyaratne, 1995).

In 1955 the United Nations referred to "Community development
[as] a process designed to create conditions of economic and social
progress for the whole community with its active participation" (United
Nations, 1955). This definition captured an approach to working with
people that can be used across all countries of the world. It recognised
the position of many underdeveloped nations that were on the brink of

independence and urgently needed to establish basic infrastructure for transport, health, welfare, water and so on. In the developed world the situation is different in that for most people these basics are available, even if access to services is not always straightforward or satisfactory. International statements, such as the Budapest (2004), Yaoundé (2005) and Hong Kong (2007) Declarations, have emphasised the contribution that community development as a people-centred practice makes to building the capacity of citizens and state institutions to work towards peace and democracy. Community development is described as:

> a way of strengthening civil society by prioritising the actions of communities and their perspectives in the development of social, economic and environmental policy.... It strengthens the capacity of people as active citizens through their own groups, organisations and networks ... to work in dialogue [and] plays a crucial role in supporting active democratic life by promoting the autonomous voice of disadvantaged and vulnerable communities. (Extract from Craig et al, 2004; Craig and Mak, 2007; Dorsner, 2008)

Community development in the UK has tended to emphasise a more general approach to strengthening community capacity and tackling broader issues around equality and social justice. Processes and principles are regarded as paramount and this is reflected through an emphasis on working *with*, rather than *for* or *on behalf of*, people. The current position of community development within government policy and programmes, focused primarily on community empowerment, health and cohesion, is a continuation of past attempts to promote participation and partnership in public decision-making and service delivery (CLG, 2008).

A brief historical overview

In the UK, community development derives its inspiration and rationale from three traditions each of which dates back to at least the 19th century. The first of these is *informal self-help and solidarity*, the reciprocal support and sharing that characterise small-scale forms of social organisation, for example the kind of neighbourly help that is routinely available or that emerges in times of adversity (Crow, 2002). The second strand represents a more organised form of *mutual aid*, whereby formal associations were established to provide assistance and shared resources across a defined subscriber membership. Collective organisations such as the early craft guilds, friendly societies and trades unions are examples of these, many of which also had a campaigning role. The third strand differs from the others in that it is based rather more on notions of *philanthropy and voluntary service*, expressed as a desire to improve the lives and opportunities of others deemed 'less fortunate'.

Some aspects of community development were explicitly remedial, devised to tackle what were seen as deficits in poor communities preventing residents from achieving their potential or participating in opportunities for personal advancement and democratic engagement. The work of the former University Settlements is representative of this approach, combining adult education with 'character-building' activities and a somewhat condescending approach to the relief of hardship (Barnett, 1888; Clarke, 1963). Although the pioneers of the Settlement movement clearly stated their belief that people living in the Settlements (usually university students on temporary placements) would learn as much from local residents as vice versa, the underlying ethos was patronising and management of the Settlements' resources (buildings, workers and funds) remained in the hands of well-meaning outsiders for many decades.

Community development has also been used as a preventative strategy, intervening in situations to avert potential crises or to address issues before they become conflicts. During the re-housing programmes after the two world wars, whole communities were fractured or relocated causing widespread disruption and alienation. Community development workers were employed in the New Towns and on peripheral estates to arrange events that would foster a sense of community and to encourage residents to organise activities for themselves (Goetschius, 1969; Heraud, 1975). These workers were frequently employed by social services or housing departments and saw themselves as 'agents' of the state, acting on behalf of the relevant authority rather than the local residents. Nevertheless they played an important role in managing the links within and between groups and external bodies to improve social welfare through the establishment of autonomous voluntary groups.

During the 1950s and 1960s community work saw itself as a branch of social work, emphasising both individual development and collective benefit. The 'community' was seen as offering some protection from the impersonal institutions of the modern welfare state and providing opportunities for social participation. Early writers advocated non-directive methods of intervention (Batten, 1957; Biddle and Biddle, 1965; Batten and Batten, 1967) and a new profession gradually emerged that combined two related approaches. The first saw the community as a resource, a partner, in the provision of services. Problems could be addressed by involving local residents in developing collective solutions. As well as supplying volunteer staff, community associations and other locally based voluntary organisations were seen as potential managers of projects delivering social care for older people, health education, benefits advice and childcare. The second approach was similar, but placed more emphasis on personal fulfilment, regarding community involvement as a vehicle for self-advancement. Taking part in community activities was seen as therapeutic (staving off mental health problems), morally worthy (encouraging mutuality and social responsibility) and educational (promoting the acquisition of skills and new understandings). Adult education classes and cultural societies were seen as 'improving' in themselves, while recreational activities such as youth clubs and sports associations were encouraged as a means of diverting people from a life of crime, idleness and social isolation.

In the 1970s and 1980s community development was strongly influenced by a radical model that saw community activism as an extension of the class struggle. Some community development workers sought to build alliances with the labour movement through trades councils and a chain of resource centres, specifically set up to support local campaigning. The radical model favoured a more adversarial approach; for example, collective action against some kind of threat or to achieve a positive change that is opposed or obstructed by those with the money and power. Citizen–led action models, such as Alinsky's community organising approach, tried to challenge existing power structures by mobilising residents around issues that brought them into conflict with economic interests or state institutions (Alinsky, 1969, 1972; Smock, 2004). They work on the principle that "empowering individuals also empowers the communities to which they belong" (Demos, 2003, p 15).

A Marxist analysis of the impact of modern capitalism on working-class neighbourhoods became highly influential in Britain in the 1970s, mainly through the fieldwork and research reports of the Community Development Projects (CDP, 1974, 1977), supplemented by a series of essay collections published by the Association of Community Workers (ACW, 1975, 1978). For those on this radical wing, community work was seen as contributing to the fight for socialism, through local, militant community action. Community development workers were active on issues concerning the level and distribution of the 'social wage', through campaigns to defend or increase the quantity and quality of state welfare provision (for example, O'Malley, 1977; Corrigan and Leonard, 1978). There were increasing demands for the democratisation of the 'local state' (Lees and Mayo, 1984) and this led to a belated recognition that the role of the community development worker as an agent of change was both 'in and against the state' (LEWRG, 1979). The call to pursue confrontational and subversive tactics required an explicit rejection of the idea that the community development worker was a neutral agent even when employed by the local council (Cowley, 1977; Loney, 1983).

The more radical workers saw community politics primarily as a means for raising 'class' (and subsequently gender) consciousness outside the workplace. Community organising was about laying the foundations for a revolutionary grassroots democracy (Tasker, 1975). This involved equipping people with the skills, knowledge, confidence and political 'nous' for challenging the root causes of poverty and discrimination. More recent versions of this approach have asserted the transformative nature of democratic participation as a form of radical empowerment (Ledwith, 2006; Pitchford, 2008) and the means by which many different forms of oppression and inequality can be overcome (Dominelli, 2006). Shaw and Martin regard actions by people in their communities as the "essence of democracy" and consider community development workers as "key agents in re-making the vital connections between community work, citizenship and democracy" (2000, p 412). Shaw (2008) reasserts the importance of political analysis and motivation in critiquing the state's adoption of community development, arguing that, as an occupation, community development workers must continue to create spaces for opposition as well as participation. Modern broad-based organising strategies have adopted this approach but are often highly critical of the role played by community development professionals and partnerships with government agencies (Demos, 2003; Traynor, 2008).

Alongside the radical community work that was undertaken in the 1970s and 1980s, a more liberal approach continued, preferring to win small gains that improved life for some people rather than taking on the whole world (Twelvetrees, 1982). This model assumes a pluralist model of society in which competing interests vie with one another to persuade decision-makers to support their cause. The 1970s witnessed a strong commitment from national government to public participation, ushered in by several official reports published at the tail-end of the previous decade urging greater citizen involvement in the planning and delivery of public services (for example, Plowden, 1967; Seebohm, 1968; Redcliffe-Maud, 1969; Skeffington, 1969). Many community development workers and activists saw this as an opportunity for marginalised people to find a voice, to articulate their concerns and to have some influence over decisions that affected their lives (for example, Symons, 1981). Community work was defined as having a fundamental role in promoting participation and increasing people's capacity to influence the decisions that affect them (ACW, 1978).

For those with a radical analysis, removal of the economic and political barriers to participation constituted a core, but long-term, goal of community development. Consequently, there was broad agreement that community work was concerned with social change and active citizenship, but that it had a primarily local dimension (Younghusband, 1968; Thomas, 1976). Influential community work 'texts' published around this time focused on the neighbourhood as the most appropriate level for community work interventions (Henderson and Thomas, 1980; Twelvetrees, 1982). During this period, community development work was seen as localised and generic, having an overarching purpose of creating integrated and 'harmonious' communities, based on neighbourhood identity and a notional egalitarianism. The aims of the community development worker were intertwined: on the one hand, to enhance a community's internal democracy by assisting local people in developing and managing their own organisations, and, on the other, to enable the (preferably consensual) views of the community to be expressed to relevant decision-making bodies through representative leadership or participation in public consultation exercises.

Recognising and respecting differences

As Popple (1995) has observed, this 'golden age' in the late 1970s and early 1980s, with its relatively stable understanding of the main objectives of community work, was soon to be shaken by the appearance of identity politics and separatist strategies for achieving social change. Drawing on the experiences of the women's and black movements of earlier decades, community work was forced to engage with the debate around different dimensions of oppression (Mayo, 1977; Ohri and Manning, 1982). Marxist and feminist models of society were extended and challenged by the experiences and demands of gay men and lesbians, disabled people and black and minority ethnic communities. The different expectations and demands of older and younger people were also being increasingly acknowledged. Communities based on political identity or ethnic origin organised themselves separately, setting up parallel community projects and representative organisations. Within community development and the more radical parts of the voluntary sector, these strategies of resistance and emancipation were regarded as legitimate and necessary means of developing services and campaigns that asserted *specific* (sometimes competing) perspectives on a range of issues (Shukra, 1995). In more progressive local authority areas (mainly the Greater London Council and metropolitan boroughs), they received controversial recognition through grant-aid and political status on advisory forums or liaison committees. By constructing their own collective identity, 'communities of interest' achieved hitherto unknown levels of political influence. This was earned through contributing particular expertise and experience to decision-making processes while simultaneously attempting to shift the balance of power and resources within society.

A key political development over the past few decades has been the growth of self-organised movements around different forms of discrimination and oppression. Alongside demands for equal rights and equal treatment has developed a recognition that this does not mean treating everybody the same, or expecting people to conform to prevailing cultures or social expectations. There emerged a growing understanding that many people, perhaps the majority, experience multiple, interacting oppressions. Strategies and measures are needed to meet people's practical and psychological requirements by working simultaneously with a range of self-organised communities. As a consequence of these struggles, a majority view gradually emerged within mainstream community work that anti-oppressive strategies and positive action measures should be incorporated into notions of 'good practice'. While this somewhat 'top-down' approach was contested in some quarters as being heavy-handed, 'politically correct' and ineffective, it did ensure that organisations were forced to consider issues around discrimination and access. By the 1990s equality had secured its position as a core value of community development. Funding for community-based projects became increasingly dependent on satisfactory equal opportunities policies, and equality perspectives became a powerful driving force within community development, underpinning its other commitments to participation and empowerment.

Achieving this required interaction between communities on the basis of equality, tolerance and mutual learning. In this respect, community development work has two contributions to make. The first is to provide the initial spans for building bridges across divides of prejudice and ignorance. The second role is more challenging and involves an acknowledgement that equality must be actively constructed, tackling power differentials, disagreements and animosity. Models of anti-oppressive practice became incorporated into community work training and thinking. This involves working with those who are oppressed; developing confidence, esteem, skills and awareness. It also requires work with those who are either benefiting from the inequality (for example, through privileged access to resources or assumptions of normality) or actively defending it (Gilchrist, 2007).

During the 1980s and 1990s the basis for community development shifted from long-term state funding of generic posts, such as neighbourhood development workers or community centre wardens, to relatively short-term project-oriented activities. Earlier, community development workers had been able to articulate and respond to local issues as they became evident, helping residents to organise campaigns around, for example, the closure of a nursery, sources of pollution, or unwelcome planning decisions. However, these posts gradually disappeared in a welter of local authority budget cuts, with community and voluntary organisations being particularly hard hit. Between 1979 and 1997, under successive Conservative governments, community development became oriented more towards self-help, training and service provision. The funding regimes of the 1990s meant that many community development workers were employed on temporary contracts and had to concentrate their efforts on government priorities (homelessness, drugs, mental health and so on), by running community-based welfare services for specific 'client groups'.

Projects were required to set and meet targets, which were bureaucratically monitored and checked by external scrutineers. In the voluntary sector generic community development was largely replaced by issue-based work, carrying out government policies, and became tightly constrained by contracts or service agreements containing predetermined performance criteria and mechanistic auditing procedures. At the same time local authority community work became increasingly directive and less concerned with processes of education and empowerment. Instead, job descriptions tended to emphasise responsibility for grants administration, consultation exercises, service delivery, partnership arrangements and bidding procedures for regeneration funding (AMA, 1993). Consequently, work programmes were delivered and evaluated around much more rigid objectives, necessitating a greater degree of formal record-keeping and accounting. Business language of inputs, outputs, costs and benefits appeared and the pressure was on for more rigid forms of evaluation and accountability.

Community involvement

More nebulous activities that promoted community spirit and created community-based assets, but did not lead to predictable (and measurable) outputs, were severely constrained or abandoned altogether. An early casualty was the provision of effective support for communities to develop their own ideas, skills and enthusiasm. The community development worker's role in helping to organise community-led collective action all but disappeared, although campaigning itself did not. The radicalism of earlier decades became muted and a new approach to working with communities was fashioned, termed 'community practice' (Butcher et al, 1993; Banks et al, 2003; Banks et al, 2007). Community practice refers to a relatively new, but rapidly expanding, approach based on community development principles and located usually within an institutional structure but with a remit for managing the interface between communities and statutory institutions, such as local government, the police or health agencies (Banks and Orton, 2007). Community practitioners are responsible for communication across this increasingly blurred boundary, and often play an important role in facilitating community empowerment in strategic decision-making, for example through representation on inter-sectoral partnerships or community planning exercises. Community practitioners might be responsible for outreach strategies, consultation exercises, partnership work and participation mechanisms such as neighbourhood forums and developing community leadership.

Frontline workers in a variety of services are finding that they are expected to work with communities in ways that are empowering and inclusive. For many this will require changes in their attitudes and professional skills as they learn how to share expertise, invite and deal with differing opinions, and involve the least heard groups in society. Increasingly, government programmes are managed through cross-sectoral partnership arrangements, with a requirement that the voluntary and community sector is represented not just by paid professionals, but through representatives from the target communities themselves. Community representation is seen as essential to their success and yet the people responsible for this new approach rarely have the skills or knowledge to engage effectively with the relevant communities, especially in the most disadvantaged areas. Nevertheless, evidence accumulated from UK government programmes suggests that the higher costs of community involvement were negligible when offset against the gains of better decision-making and improved outcomes (Andersson et al, 2007).

Promoting participation

The emphasis on participatory governance has been criticised on political grounds (e.g. Cooke and Kothari, 2001), as well as for difficulties around implementation (Andersson et al, 2007; Barnes et al, 2007). Government initiatives tended to focus on the role of individuals in communities, with funding schemes to support 'community champions', 'social entrepreneurs', neighbourhood wardens and the like. Capacity building was provided for individuals prepared to take up these roles, but there was little recognition that community leaders needed mechanisms for support and accountability in order to carry out their role effectively (Gilchrist, 2006a; Skidmore et al, 2006).

Community members who did rise to the challenge became unfairly branded as the 'usual suspects', and the pressure of partnership work often led to them becoming isolated and 'burnt-out', or simply disillusioned by the whole process (Anastacio et al, 2000; Purdue et al, 2000; Purdue, 2007). Disappointment and frustrating experiences of participation can exacerbate feelings of disempowerment, especially for black and minority ethnic communities (Rai, 2008), damaging community well-being and resulting in personal stress (Dinham, 2005, 2007; Kagan, 2006). Similarly, initial attempts to 'consult with the community' were met with cynicism and 'apathy', often eliciting views only from a dominant minority or outright opposition. Non-participation may well be a rational survival strategy among populations that have other priorities and tactics for coping with long-term disadvantage (Mathers et al, 2008).

Until relatively recently, there has been a failure to understand that community empowerment requires a longer-term approach that:

- is sensitive to differences within communities;
- manages tensions and expectations;
- includes a variety of ways for people to contribute their ideas.

Communities are not homogeneous, rarely speak with one voice and are often sceptical about the motives of local officials. The requirement for democratic representation is a challenge for even the most well-organised and articulate community (Prendergast, 2008). For civic capability to be sustainable and inclusive, a wider and larger set of people must be recruited and supported to take on governance roles and participate in public decision-making. This means increasing the numbers of individuals with sufficient 'resourcefulness, connectedness, confidence and effectiveness' to become local leaders and community representatives (Cox, 2006). Those who have experienced years of deprivation often feel deeply disenfranchised and angry. A necessary first step is to acknowledge these feelings and to help people to learn from their emotions and experience, channelling them into constructive and feasible strategies that can really transform the quality of life and open up new opportunities. However, participatory strategies are only really effective over the longer term if they acknowledge the political dimensions of these arrangements, actively tackling differentials in power and status (Hickey, 2004; Taylor, 2007; Ledwith and Springett, 2009).

Democratic renewal

The revival of interest in community participation has been accompanied by an explicit commitment from government to promoting cohesion, diversity and social inclusion. The skills, values and understanding that exist within the community development field are vital to the success and sustainability of government programmes around regeneration and empowerment. In particular, community development has much to offer in relation to strategies for:

- tackling social exclusion (Henderson and Salmon, 2001; Henderson, 2005);
- increasing community participation (Burton, 2004);
- building community capacity (Eade, 1997; CRU, 2005);
- promoting community cohesion (Commission on Integration and Cohesion, 2007; James, 2007; Spratt and Miller, 2008);
- integrating refugees and asylum seekers (Andrew and Lukajo, 2005; Navarro, 2006);
- conflict resolution and peace-building (Gilchrist, 1998a; Murray and Murtagh, 2003);
- supporting social–economic development (Mubangizi, 2003; Korsching and Allen, 2004; Kay, 2006);
- improving multi-agency working through partnerships (Mayo and Taylor, 2001; Chappell et al, 2006; Datta, 2007).

Community development workers have become adept at working in many organisational cultures and social environments. This is important for developing co-operation across boundaries and for reaching out to sections of the community that are disaffected or appear difficult to engage for practical reasons. This focus on working with voluntary groups and marginalised communities acknowledges that these groups probably need additional support if they are to operate effectively within organisational environments dominated by powerful private and statutory interests. A key role for community development workers is to provide and maintain communication channels between different sectors by linking different agencies and population groups. This is especially important where community representatives are involved. The latest survey of community work in the UK indicated that the number of such posts had increased since the 1990s but that these were often short term, focused on specific tasks and managed by people with only limited understanding of community development (Glen et al, 2004). This situation makes it more difficult to build effective networks within the community and undermines the sustainability of such programmes. A networking approach needs a long-term perspective based on job security and relatively stable funding arrangements guaranteeing at least core costs.

The apparent support for community development at central government level and in some local authorities (Henderson and Glen, 2006) poses a number of challenges for state and non-state actors, and for community development advocates (Archer, 2009). In the UK, a group of leading professionals, academics and community development organisations, known as the CD Challenge group, identified the distinctive contribution of community development as the 'combined effect' of 'six progressive components' set out in Table 2.1.

The CD Challenge report, endorsed by government and widely debated within the field, also called for a more strategic investment in community development resources enabling interventions to be better co-ordinated and to be sustained over the long term. However, there is still widespread misunderstanding of the contribution that community development can make to strengthening civil society, encouraging active citizenship and tackling disadvantage.

An emerging profession

Community development is distinguished from social work and allied welfare professions through its commitment to collective ways of addressing problems. Community development helps community members to identify unmet needs, to undertake research on the problem and present possible solutions. Initially this may be on a self-help basis, pioneering different ways of addressing a particular issue. If this is successful and demand grows, the worker might assist group members to establish the initiative on a more secure footing, with a formal management committee, constitution, funding arrangements

Table 2.1: Six components for community development

Role	Outcome
1. Help people see that they have common concerns about local or other public issues that they could benefit from working on together under their own control	• Reduction of isolation and alienation • Increase in social capital and co-operation
2. Help people to work together on those issues, often by forming or developing an independent community group, supporting them to plan and take actions and encouraging evaluation and reflection as a way of improving effectiveness	• Creation or improvement of bona fide community groups • Increase of opportunities for activity in the community • More effective community activity
3. Support and develop independent groups across the community sector, not directively but within an ethical framework, and increase networking between groups	Increase in: • Community sector • Volunteering • Mutual aid and autonomous services • Learning between groups • Improvement in conditions in the locality
4. Promote values of equity, inclusiveness, participation and co-operation throughout this work	Increase in: • Participation • Social capital • Co-operation • Community cohesion
5. Empower people and their organisations to influence and transform public policies and services and all factors affecting the conditions of their lives	• Community engagement and influence • Improvement in dialogue between community and authorities • Improvement in coherence and effectiveness of public policies
6. Advise and inform public authorities on community perspectives and assist them to strengthen communities and work in genuine partnership with them	• Increased capacity of agencies, authorities and professions to engage with communities • Improvement in delivery of public services • Increased resources for the community sector

Source: CD Challenge group (2006, p 17)

and paid staff. This transformation of a community-run activity into a voluntary organisation will be familiar to most community development workers but is not always a straightforward process and may take place over several years. It will involve direct support of individuals as well as help with managing group dynamics and developing appropriate organisational structures.

There may be times when the worker takes on a role as advocate, occasionally even running the organisation, but mostly their function will be to support and guide community members, helping them to achieve their goals in the way that they have chosen. Community development is primarily concerned with meeting the needs and aspirations of community members whose circumstances have left them poorly provided for, often without adequate services, with limited means to organise and excluded from mainstream opportunities to participate in activities or decision-making. Community development seeks to build collective capacity by improving skills, confidence and knowledge for individuals and the community as a whole. Community development nurtures community infrastructure by supporting informal networks as well as formal organisations.

The Community Development Exchange, the umbrella body for community development in the UK, describes community development as "an occupation (both paid and unpaid) which aims to build active and influential communities based on justice, equality and mutual respect" (CDX, 2006, p 1). This is accomplished by working with individuals, groups and organisations on the basis of the values and commitments shown in Table 2.2.

The UK framework for national occupational standards for community development work gives the following definition:

> Community Development is a long term value based process which aims to address imbalances in power and bring about change founded on social justice, equality and inclusion. The process enables people to organise and work together to:
> - identify their own needs and aspirations
> - take action to exert influence on the decisions which affect their lives
> - improve the quality of their own lives, the communities in which they live, and societies of which they are a part. (FCDL, 2009)

Table 2.2: The values and commitments of community development

Collective working	• working together towards common goals • forming networks and making connections to help people collaborate and come together in groups
Equality and justice	• challenging discrimination and working alongside those who are powerless • raising awareness about inequality and how things can be changed
Learning and reflection	• recognising that everyone has skills and knowledge • learning from mistakes as well as successes
Participation	• helping individuals to get involved and sharing power throughout communities • increasing people's influence over decisions that affect their lives
Political awareness	• raising awareness of communities' concerns • linking local concerns to the bigger picture
Sustainability	• working with and investing in the capacity of people and groups so that change lasts • using environmental resources responsibly

Source: CDX (2006)

The use of networks and networking are seen as central to working with communities and building partnerships with statutory bodies.

Both these models describe the processes, skills and outcomes that are involved in community development work. In order to distinguish this from community activism or voluntary work, it is useful to think about the role that the community development worker plays in:

- *enabling* people to become involved by removing practical barriers to their participation;
- *encouraging* individuals to contribute to activities and decision-making, and to keep going when things get difficult;
- *empowering* others by increasing their confidence and ability to influence decisions and take responsibility for their own actions;
- *educating* people by helping them to reflect on their own experience, to learn from others and through discussion;

- *equalising* situations so that people have the same access to opportunities, resources and facilities within communities and mainstream services;
- *evaluating* the impact of these interventions;
- *engaging* with groups and organisations to increase community involvement in partnerships and other forms of public decision-making.

These seven 'E's of community development make it clear that the community development worker is concerned not with their own interests and needs, but instead supports community members and activists to organise activities, take up issues and challenge unjust discrimination.

Power is a dominant theme within community development, and in this respect, the role is fundamentally about working with people in communities so that they have more influence over decisions that affect them, whether this is about their own lives or about what happens in the world around them. Community development addresses and seeks to change relations of power within communities and society as a whole, and, as such, it inevitably has a strong political dimension. However, this has become less about confrontation and more about compromise and negotiation, especially since the advent of partnership working.

Models of community development in the UK

Compared with law, medicine or even social work, community development is a relatively new profession. To some extent, it has become an instrument of state policy, designed to address perceived problems

Table 2.3: Models of community development

Model	Political framework	Typical activities
Consensus	Conservative Communitarian	Social planning Self-help groups Volunteering
Pluralist	Liberal Social-democratic	Community engagement Partnership working Lobbying Community capacity-building
Conflict	Radical Socialist	Community organising Campaigning Advocacy work

of what we now call 'social exclusion': poverty, discrimination and an apparent breakdown in public order. Community development makes an appearance under several auspices, including health, regeneration, crime reduction and so on, where there is a shared belief that 'community participation' and/or 'citizen involvement' are necessary and desirable prerequisites for social improvement (Henderson, 2000; Taylor, 2000, 2008). However, behind this apparent agreement lie three different models of community development, each related to contrasting political analyses of society and the state (see Table 2.3).

The first approach assumes that there is a broad *consensus* about social issues, how they can be tackled and how society in general should be organised. Within this model, state-sponsored community development projects have been devised to:

- encourage local responsibility for organising self-help activities;
- facilitate the delivery of welfare services, particularly to marginalised sections of the population;
- enhance community liaison and partnership working;
- support community ('user') participation in 'democratic' processes of consultation and engagement.

Community development workers have been deployed to foster community spirit, for example through cultural activities, and to work with statutory agencies to ensure that services provided match local needs. The goal for this model of community development is social harmony through the provision of a welfare 'safety net' to those most in need, but with pressure to conform to prevalent norms of behaviour. Communitarian ideas around family and social responsibility underpin this approach, especially in relation to volunteering, parenting and active citizenship, as the embodiment of civil society, expressed through collective self-help and voluntary forms of association (Etzioni, 1993; Blunkett, 2001). Although communitarian approaches have found their advocates within community development, there have also been criticisms of their reliance on moral authoritarianism and their consequent failure to effectively understand and counter structural inequalities and power differentials (Henderson and Salmon, 1998; Henderson, 2005).

The *pluralist* or *liberal* model contains a stronger sense that society consists of different interest groups and that these compete to influence decision-making. This approach acknowledges that some sections of the population are disadvantaged in this struggle and community development is seen as enhancing public decision-making by enabling them to be heard. The task of the community development worker is to assist communities to organise themselves, to find a collective 'voice' and to put pressure on the policy makers to pay more attention to *their* needs. The pluralist model of community work is often found in the job descriptions of neighbourhood workers, community engagement officers, tenants participation officers and equalities officers, developing and supporting local or identity-based communities to participate in advisory forums and consultation exercises. The Community Empowerment Networks, set up to select and support community representatives on Local Strategic Partnerships, benefited from community development support especially in the functioning of themed forums and the articulation of minority perspectives (e.g. Blake et al, 2008).

The more *radical* version of community development explicitly identifies 'conflicts of interest' within society and aligns itself with the poor and other oppressed groups (for example, Baldock, 1977; Mayo, 1979; Ledwith, 1997, 2006; Shaw, 2008). It argues that the causes of poverty and disadvantage are to be found in the economic system and reflect historical patterns of exploitation embedded in social and political institutions. It aims to reduce inequalities by addressing issues around discrimination and prejudice. Radical community work emphasises people's civil rights and strives for social justice, seeking to develop political consciousness and powerful forms of collective organising to effect social change through a redistribution of power and resources. At local levels, for example within communities and organisations, this might involve the development of 'anti-oppressive strategies' by helping people (individually and collectively) to challenge the roots of their disadvantage and to demand better or fairer treatment.

Community development workers using this model see themselves as advocates and organisers, helping communities to organise themselves effectively around issues they identify for themselves, in order to challenge the poverty and discrimination they experience. This approach was a feature of community work during much of the 1970s and 1980s and has been resurrected more recently as 'critical community practice', broadly defined as transformatory work with communities (Banks et al, 2007). It continues to guide those broad-based organisations affiliated to the Citizens Organising Foundation, such as the ongoing London Citizens (formerly TELCO) campaign for a living wage for London (Demos, 2003). Community organising uses 'one-to-one' interviews with community members and leaders to identify emerging issues and undertakes a detailed power analysis as part of its approach to building alliances for political leverage. These were the methods used by the young Barack Obama in his days as a community development worker in Chicago's South Side district in the 1980s, and which to some extent informed his strategy in the campaign to win the US presidency (Obama, 2005).

Many current definitions of community development work assert a radical model striving for social, environmental and economic justice (e.g. FCDL, 2009) but it can prove more difficult to implement in practice, mainly because workers find themselves in situations where their best intentions are constrained by the expectations of employers and external funders. Many practitioners lack the consciousness, the confidence and the skills to undertake radical practice and, in reality, a community development worker or project might combine these models, adopting different approaches depending on circumstances and competence.

Networking for community development

A key principle of community development is to ensure that participation in decision-making is democratic and inclusive, enabling people to contribute as equal citizens and to learn through their involvement. Interaction with others is an inevitable and necessary aspect of this, and community development workers play an important role in helping people to work together, to communicate effectively and to deal with the inescapable tensions and disagreements that arise from this work. Networks that connect individuals and different sections of the local community are an invaluable resource, functioning as communication systems and organisational mechanisms. The development of 'community' is about strengthening and extending networks between individuals, between groups, between organisations and, just as importantly, between different sectors and agencies. "Community development is ... instrumental in setting up groups, supporting forums and networks, and organising events and activities that enable people to work together across organisational and community boundaries" (CD Challenge group, 2006, p 10). Working to establish and maintain these networks is fundamental to effective community development work.

The idea that the 'essence' of community is to be found among relationships, rather than within the physical environment of 'place', is not new. The early studies of 'community' were very much concerned with describing the patterns of interaction and connection among residents. Almost regardless of ideology or context, community development has been concerned with developing and negotiating relationships. In particular, some early writers on the skills and methods of community work recognised the importance of contact-making, communicating, and convening and coordinating activities (Klein, 1973; Leissner, 1975), although the term 'networking' appeared only in the early 1980s (Symons, 1981).

From the first stages in the development of community work as a professional activity, writers and trainers have identified the role of helping people and organisations to co-operate and communicate across boundaries as a significant, perhaps unique, aspect of the job. The existence of "informal, co-operative links" within the community sector has long been recognised, described as "all kinds of networks whereby members of different groups know each other" (Dharamsi et al, 1979, p 136). A pamphlet published as part of the debate on community work training described the job as a "general purpose facilitator of local initiative networks" (Griffiths, 1981, p 14) and Francis et al's (1984) survey of the community work occupation concluded that the community development workers themselves represented a "significant network of skills and commitment" (p 14). Liaison had already been identified as a key function in building multi-agency organisations such as "alliances, federations, standing conferences and more modest working groups at local level" (Thomas, 1983, p 159). Thomas emphasised the linkages between people within neighbourhoods and the need to "strengthen", "renew" and "nurture" existing networks (Thomas, 1983, pp 171-3). These were seen as supporting processes of sharing and dialogue. Fostering informal interpersonal and inter-organisational linkages within communities requires particular expertise and a strategic approach.

Attitudes and relationships underpin organisational functions, such as communication and co-operation, especially in dealing with "some of the uncertainties and blurred boundaries which arise in community work" (Payne, 1982, p 133). Milofsky (1988a, p 7) wrote that "community development requires network-building" and Bell, in his evaluation of a community development project, refers to networks as "the crucial steps which take community work on the road to community development" (1992, p 32). Bell emphasised the need for unforced opportunities for people to meet and work together, building mutual recognition and confidence. He also saw community networks as creating "a new stratum in the power structure which offers the possibility for long-term and important change" (1992, p 32). The debates around community work training in the early 1970s identified a role in fostering social cohesion through community activities and inter-organisational work. To do this, an understanding of local social systems and skills in informal communication and contact-making was needed (ACW, 1975).

In these early accounts the role of the community development worker was described as discovering and utilising existing networks. Networks were regarded as something community development workers needed to know about and could work with, but the idea of intervening to change or develop these came later. A more proactive approach was gradually adopted that recognised that the formation and transformation of networks was a legitimate (and desirable) focus for professional interventions. In the second edition of their book on *Skills in neighbourhood work*, Henderson and Thomas devote an entire chapter to the skills and strategies of helping people to associate and maintain contact with one another, describing neighbourhood development as:

> about putting people in touch with one another, and of promoting their membership in groups and networks.... In the act of bringing people together, neighbourhood workers are performing an essential role. (1987, p 15)

Within patch-based or community social work, there was a growing interest in networking across agencies and role boundaries, a trend reinforced in the 1990s by care in the community and user involvement strategies. A modern version of this approach, co-production, appreciates that relationships between the public and professionals can be more respectful and more reciprocal (Stephens et al, 2008). Edgar Cahn (2000), who developed the original concept from an idea by Elinor Ostrom, refers to a 'core economy' of family, neighbourhood and community networks, undertaking the 'hidden work' of mutual support and solidarity within society (Boyle et al, 2006). For people who have traditionally been regarded as dependent 'clients' this approach is potentially liberating, enabling them to contribute on an equal basis to their own welfare and make choices about the help they receive. This prevents ostracisation and recognises the assets and expertise that each brings to these situations. This is the approach taken by asset-based community development, which uses community strengths as its starting point rather than focusing on perceived deficits and disadvantage (Kretzmann and McKnight, 1993).

On a collective level, communities can lead initiatives that result in the co-production of services (such as children's play groups) as well as the less tangible outcomes of well-being, community spirit and civic engagement (Skidmore and Craig, 2005). Trevillion, an early proponent of networking for social care, argues that it promotes a 'culture' of community through:

> activities which enable separate individuals, groups or organisations to join with one another in social networks which enhance communication and/or active co-operation and create new opportunities for choice and empowerment. (1992, p 4)

Community development workers are expected to be in touch with a sometimes bewildering range of individuals and organisations. Their role in facilitating communication and co-operation within communities is alluded to in much of the early community work literature, in the guise of, for example, community newsletters, liaison meetings, tenants' federations, festivals, resource centres, social gatherings and forums that were often serviced, managed or entirely run by community development workers. These were, and remain, excellent vehicles for networking, enabling people to meet to share ideas and to gain experience in working together. As we shall see in later chapters, community development workers often find themselves in key positions within formal and informal networks, co-ordinating the organisational arrangements as well as managing a complex array of interpersonal relationships.

Networking becomes a core competence

Since the 1990s networking has increasingly become recognised as an important aspect of community work (Gilchrist, 1995; Henderson and Thomas, 2002) and a necessary aspect of building partnerships generally. The Standing Conference for Community Development (SCCD; now CDX) strategic framework recognises networking as a significant aspect of the work, arguing that it "depends on establishing and maintaining both organisational links and personal relationships" (SCCD, 2001, p 20). The revised version of the framework for occupational standards for community development work, published in draft form at the beginning of 2009, asserts that community development practitioners need to understand "The role and functions of networks and networking" (K6) in order to "Review and evaluate your contacts and identify gaps in your networks" and then "Actively seek contacts and links with excluded communities and marginalised groups" (FCDL, 2009).

What has not been so generally recognised is the more hidden work of assisting people to make connections and sustain relationships where there are cultural differences, practical obstacles or political opposition. This requires political awareness, emotional sensitivity and advanced interpersonal skills (Hastings, 1993, p 76). Community development workers operate within complex multi-organisational environments so they need to be strategic in making links and building relationships among a huge variety of potential and actual collaborators, including people from all sections of the community. In particular, community development often works best by identifying and supporting the 'linkers' (Fraser et al, 2003) or 'moving spirits' (Gibson, 1996): those individuals who are not community leaders as such but who work, often invisibly, at the grassroots level to connect people with the more visible institutions, bringing about change in very subtle ways.

Community development workers are themselves a resource or a tool in this process, but do not usually have a 'stake' in what happens as a result of those connections. They act as guardians or custodians of the networks, rather than using them to promote their own interests. Responsibility for network development and management is increasingly recognised as a job in its own right. Indeed, it is gratifying to find that the networking approach has been explicitly incorporated into some models for community engagement, for example, in Aberdeen, Scotland (Aberdeen City Council, 2008), and for strengthening local leadership (Hay, 2008). The government's Office of the Third Sector's recent review (2007) recognises 'connectedness' as a feature of strong communities, and therefore the legitimate focus for funding support. Community development organisations need networking capacity in order to form partnerships and coalitions for campaigning. This helps them to connect members of different communities, to access resources and power in external institutions and to manage tensions with other stakeholders.

Conclusions

This brief review indicates how, for over a century, communities have experienced the well-meaning intentions of community development workers coming from different ideological positions and government programmes. Community development continues to be contested, despite some evident continuities in definition and application (Craig, 2007; Mayo, 2008). Is it a social movement, a distinct profession or an approach that can be adopted by anyone working on the front-line of the state–community interface (Shaw, 2008)? Where it has been successful, community development has sought to strengthen connections between individuals, groups, agencies and sectors so that the needs and aspirations of communities can be effectively met through collective action and improved services. The work involved in establishing and maintaining these boundary-spanning linkages has come to be known as networking but has often been hidden from public view. The following chapters aim to make the skills and strategies that underpin networking more explicit and, hopefully, better recognised by managers and funders.

What is it about networks that makes them figure so prominently within the community and voluntary sectors? This question will be considered in the next two chapters, which explore specific features of networks as a form of organisation and their relationship with wider social environments, particularly looking at informal voluntary activity. Studies of the community sector and the emergence of community activities over time suggest that community groups, forums and semi-formal networks provide the seedbed for the growth of more formal voluntary associations and campaigns (see Milofsky, 1987). The networking approach to community development described in this book recognises the significance of informal networks in gathering the energy, motivation and resources needed to organise collective activities and address crucial issues around equality and social justice.

THREE

Network theory and analysis

How do you hold a hundred tons of water in the air with
no visible means of support? You build a cloud.
(Cole, 1984, p 38)

Introduction

In recent years the concept of networks as a form of organisation has
gained in currency both as a metaphor and as an explanatory tool. The
term 'network' seems to have been first used in academic literature
by Radcliffe-Brown in 1940 and early sociologists recognised its
significance as an aspect of social living (Warner and Lunt, 1942). It
offers a useful model for examining the interactions of daily life and
thinking about community dynamics. Within community development,
networks are increasingly seen as the means for co-ordinating collective
action, supporting the activities of practitioners and providing important
means of communication through various technologies as well as face-
to-face interaction.

This and the following chapter provide an introduction to network
theory specifically examining form and function. This chapter reviews
analytical models developed from group and organisational studies
and identifies key features often associated with effective networking.
Networks are presented as an effective mode of organising in
complex, turbulent environments. They play an important role in the
development of successful coalitions and partnerships. Networks can
be described as either 'organic' – sustained as a natural result of the
interactions between members – or they can be seen as 'engineered'
– devised and established by an external agency for a specific purpose
(Liebler and Ferri, 2004).

Chapter Four focuses on networks as informal knowledge
management systems and as vehicles for supporting collective action
in communities and social movements. A networking approach to
empowerment is developed using a 'circuits of power' model that
emphasises the value of boundary-spanning work in promoting
cohesion and managing diversity. Community development work

supports formal organisations and groups, helping them to set up, grow, evolve and occasionally dissolve. These often emerge from and are sustained by networks of volunteers, activists and professionals that are constantly changing. Community development workers, therefore, need to understand how networks operate, what functions they perform for individuals and communities, and how they can be supported.

The word 'network' can be applied to a whole variety of multi-agency configurations, but it is useful to begin by thinking about what distinguishes networks from other forms of organisation. Essential characteristics of networks are a web of lateral connections and avoidance of formal bureaucratic structures. As shown in Figure 3.1, a network comprises:

- a set of *nodes* (where connections are made either through individuals or organisational units);
- the *linkages* between them (Wasserman and Faust, 1994).

Figure 3.1: Diagrammatic representation of a network

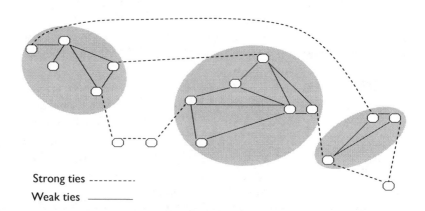

Strong ties ----------
Weak ties ————

The significant thing about network ties is that they enable the nodes to influence one another. Some nodes are more critical than others to the overall functioning of the network, depending on their current state and specific pattern of linkage. Pressure placed on these 'soft spots' can have a profound effect on the whole system and community development workers do well to seek out these especially sensitive or influential people within communities and organisations. A nudge in the right direction, through encouragement or information sharing, can result in far-reaching changes in collective understanding or commitment.

In so far as networks have structure, they can be represented as polycentric and dynamic patterns of interaction, which are neither random, nor explicitly ordered. Networks operate on the basis of informal relationships rather than formal roles, and membership tends to be voluntary and participative. The existence and vitality of the linkages are determined by personal choices, circumstance or occasionally sheer coincidence. Co-operation between members relies on persuasion and reciprocity rather than coercion or contracts. There are often no clear affiliation mechanisms and membership itself is a fuzzy category with constantly shifting boundaries and allegiances. The tenuous nature of network connections makes it awkward to refer to network membership as if this were a defined category. Perhaps 'participant' is a more appropriate term, conveying the idea that networks are actively constructed and maintained, even though 'affiliation' may sometimes be unplanned or unwitting. The most important and useful aspect of a network is its pattern of connections, which often reflects an underlying value base, a shared interest or simply the geography of overlapping lives.

Broadly speaking, a network can be regarded as a complex system for storing, processing and disseminating information. It is usually non-hierarchical with a range of access points and a multitude of transmission routes. This means that information can be obtained and transmitted between any number of different nodes without being monitored or censored. This multiplexity is a major factor in the resilience of networks to structural flaws, disruption or attempts to control the through-flow of information. Network-type structures are particularly useful in situations when information is ambiguous or risky, since contradictions can be clarified by turning to alternative sources for comparison and checking.

Dialogue and debate within networks transform information so that it becomes intelligence (about the current situation) and knowledge (about the wider context). This is vital for solving immediate problems and for adapting to a changing world. Community connections are like the neural networks made of axons and dendrites in the brain, integrating and transmitting information across linguistic and cultural boundaries like some kind of supercomputer constantly revising a shared but dispersed model of the world (Dunbar, 1996).

Network analysis

Networks are neither groups nor organisations although they create the conditions for these to emerge. Networks enable members to form clusters that undertake specific activities, focused around a common goal or function, and co-ordinated on a semi–autonomous basis. This mode of organising is termed 'flexible specialisation' and is a feature of many complex systems, especially where innovation and creativity are at a premium. Early attempts to investigate the structure and function of networks originated in the *Gestalt* approach to human psychology, which recognised that in order to understand individual behaviour, it was necessary to study the 'whole' context, including interactions with others in the social landscape (Scott, 2000). *Gestalt* methods were applied to 'real life' situations and produced results that had the appearance of scientific rigour reinforced by an intuitive familiarity. Early studies of community relations carried out by the Chicago and Manchester schools of network sociology (for example, Park, 1925, 1929; Warner and Lunt, 1942; Mitchell, 1969) used both observation and interviews. The researchers noted patterns of interaction and also asked people about their personal affiliations. Rather than studying just individual actions, social network analysis (as it became known) was concerned with the array of informal relationships as a means of understanding the organisation or community as a whole. Deconstruction of the overall structure used the ties between people to map patterns of communication that could be used to identify decision-making and alliances (Laumann and Pappi, 1976).

Network analysis generated a number of useful theoretical developments in the social sciences, notably in sociology, anthropology and organisation theory. These include ideas around leadership, trust, decision-making, coalitions and creativity, all of which are relevant to community development. Early network approaches to social behaviour explored the emergence of social clusters, such as acquaintance (Newcomb, 1961); friendship cliques (Boissevain, 1974); dissemination of rumours (Allport and Postman, 1947); the operation of prejudice (Allport, 1958); shifts in attitude and affinity (Homans, 1950); the management of conflict (Gluckmann, 1952); and the operation of power blocs within democratic societies (Hunter, 1953; Miller, 1958). The social psychologist Milgram (1967) used the idea of interpersonal connections to explain the global reach of social networks in what has become known as the 'small-world effect', also popularised as the notion of 'six degrees of separation'. Experimental studies to replicate and explain this phenomenon have consistently demonstrated that people are able to use tenuous connections and informed guesses to reach a total stranger on the other side of the world within just a few steps (Buchanan, 2003; Watts, 2003, 2004).

Of particular relevance is Granovetter's research on the strength of 'weak' ties. Granovetter (1973, 1974, 1978, 1985) investigated how people used personal connections to obtain information and share ideas. He identified the importance of the 'weak ties' between acquaintances in 'bridging' the gaps between different social clusters, and maintaining social cohesion in modern urban life. This was a useful counterbalance to earlier studies that had focused on networks based on the 'thick ties' of kinship and friendship operating within neighbourhoods and villages (Bott, 1957; Young and Willmott, 1957). Community development is mainly concerned with strengthening and extending the 'weak ties' or, in social capital terms, the 'bridges' and 'links', particularly in situations where people find it difficult to meet and make connections.

But bridges need support mechanisms, either in the form of sturdy structures at each end or a securely anchored suspension, especially when the ground is uneven or friable. The bonding capital of strong communities is crucial in supplying these foundations and also needs attention in the form of support to single-identity groups, for example, based on a common culture or origin (Butt, 2001; CDF, 2008a). This is particularly pertinent to strategies for building community cohesion in towns and cities that have been fragmented by ethnic, sectarian and other social fissures (Morrissey and Smyth, 2002; Gilchrist, 2003, 2004; Chauhan, 2009). In Northern Ireland, Hewstone and colleagues found that relations between Catholic and Protestant young people were better where they shared common experiences (through school or mixed residence) and *also* had pride in their own cultural traditions. Contact between groups *and* recourse to valued identities seem to be more effective than requiring allegiance to some overarching, unifying identity that is artificially imposed rather than emerging from more naturalistic interactions (Gaetner and Dovidio, 2000; Hewstone et al, 2007).

Several of the studies using techniques of network analysis generated some interesting observations regarding the operation of power in society (Knoke, 1990a, 1990b), and the importance of informal interactions within organisations (Emery and Trist, 1965). The methods of investigation were, however, fairly crude compared with the inherent complexities of most real networks and, unsurprisingly, network analysts tended to gather evidence in situations that were relatively stable, bounded and integrated. They largely failed to capture the intricacies and dynamics of personal relationships, especially where these involved tensions and negative attitudes.

In recent years, network analysis has developed more sophisticated techniques of mathematical modelling that use computer programs to calculate statistical algorithms and display them in diagrammatic or matrix form (for example, Stephenson, 1999; Freeman, 2000). Software packages such as UCINet, Payek and Netdraw have made it considerably easier to statistically analyse and visualise the pattern of connections between interacting agents (Scott, 2000; Borgatti et al, 2002; Huisman and van Duijn, 2005). These have the capacity to monitor changes over time, an important potential application for measuring the impact of this networking approach to community development as well as other interventions. An alternative approach is to use the Erdős–Rényi model for random graph analysis which uses vertices (nodes) and edges (links) to understand the shape and dynamics of a network (Bollobás, 2001).

Network analysis has found practical applications within organisation development and some welfare professions (Baker, 1994). Although in its preliminary stages, there have been moves to evaluate the effectiveness of community development by tracking changes in the connectivity between people and organisations. For example, Community Evaluation Northern Ireland (CENI) have used social capital mapping to assess the strength of local community infrastructure and to develop toolkits for setting baselines and progress measures for community development (McDonnell, 2002; CENI, 2006; Morrissey et al, 2006). Promising developments in producing instruments that are valid for assessing the effectiveness of networks need to be followed up (e.g. Karl, 1999; Ashman, 2003). Network analysis offers a potentially fruitful avenue for community action research and participatory appraisal methods, which explores the interactions and perceptions within whole systems, such as communities and the partnerships that serve them (Burns, 2007).

Network or organisation?

Networks have been variously described as a new, intermediary or hybrid form of organisation. Early organisation theorists believed that economic and social regulation takes place either through 'market' or 'hierarchical' mechanisms (Williamson, 1975). The network model was originally proposed by Ouchi as a form of organisation that was distinct from markets and hierarchies (1980) and Powell described networks as primarily based on relationships and reputation that form "an intricate lattice-work of collaborative ventures [that] are especially useful for the exchange of commodities whose value is not easily measured" (Powell, 1990, pp 269–72). The majority of organisation theorists adopted a combined approach acknowledging that the three forms probably co-exist within most organisations (Frances et al, 1991). Some considered networks to be an entirely novel form of organisation, suited to post-modern conditions, while others saw networks as encompassing all kinds of organisation, weaving a complex web of informal relationships in and around the formal structures.

True networks have no central organising or control mechanism. Function and authority is distributed across the nodes and linkages, such that decision-making and implementation are conducted through informal and temporary coalitions of actors and resources. Within networks, influence operates predominantly through informal connections based on trust, loyalty, reciprocity, civility and sociability (Misztal, 2000). Network enthusiasts tend to emphasise their 'flatness' and flexibility, assuming network members enjoy a nominal equality and ignoring issues around elitism and exclusivity. In reality, networks also include relationships based on fear, jealousy, animosity and suspicion (Fineman, 1993).

Some have argued that the network concept is only valid in the context of formal modes of organising, suggesting that the metaphor of a 'circle' is more appropriate to describe the pattern of informal connections operating within communities (Giarchi, 2001). However, this distinction does not allow for the inherent complexities and blurring that characterise many situations where formal organisations and informal webs of relationships co-exist. Networks have been described as "an environment of connectivity" that is value-driven and self-generating (Traynor, 2008, p 222). They offer a mode of organising through informal co-operation and exchange between autonomous and disparate bodies without formal procedures or structures. They enable resources and information to be shared across boundaries without the necessity (or authority) of explicit contracts.

Organisations, on the other hand, exercise control over jointly owned resources through protocols and explicit decisions. They function through roles and regulations that exist independently of who might be occupying or implementing these. In contrast, networks operate through connections between specific individuals whose attitudes and actions shape interpersonal interactions and incorporate local conventions. Organisations use rules and protocols to co-ordinate activity. Networks need relationships to influence behaviour and change minds. They are more flexible, less hierarchical and therefore more responsive to unexpected shifts in the environment. Networks live within and around organisations linking people in different departments and external bodies. Networks may well improve an organisation's performance, providing a hidden resilience and flexibility, but they

Table 3.1: Key differences between networks and organisations

	Network	Organisation
Nature of connections	Interpersonal relationships	Formal procedures and lines of accountability
Membership	Fuzzy category, depends on ongoing participation and interaction	Clearly defined by affiliation, subscription, employment
Nodes	Individuals/organisational unit	Roles/posts/units/teams
Type of structure	Non-centralised web of connections	Usually bureaucratic arrangement, with central control from the top
Boundaries	Unclear, permeable; many boundary-spanning links	Defined and maintained, often through constitution or written protocols
Mode of interaction	Based on custom, personal history and mutual affinity	Rules and regulations
Basis of exchange	Trust and favours	Contracts and directives
Common bond	Shared values and interests	Agreed aims and objectives

can also sabotage its democratic structure and mission, undermining authority and circumventing official procedures.

These distinctions are summarised in Table 3.1, but are not always clear-cut. They provide a rough guide as to whether a network or an organisation is the most appropriate term to describe a conglomeration of people working together. This is not just a semantic issue, as we shall see later. Expectations are different for networks, and for some purposes these are not the most suitable mode of organising. Yet people often choose to set up loose networks when a more formal structure would do the job better and more democratically. Sometimes both types are needed and what starts life as a network may transform itself into a formal organisation as its function and environment change. Community development is often concerned with developing organisations and working to challenge the policies of institutions. In particular, the routes through which information reaches people can crucially affect how new ideas are received in that we are more inclined to listen to and accept the opinions of those we know, like or admire. Similarly, it is important to recruit potential allies and helpers who will be supportive rather than block change or innovation.

A primary function of networks is to facilitate boundary-spanning co-operation, co-ordination and communication. The value of lateral connections within and between organisations has been noted for some time. Decentralised networks, founded on norms and trust (rather than administrative edicts) have an advantage over formal organisations in what Emery and Trist termed 'turbulent environments' (1965). By this they meant situations where there is rapid change and unpredictability. Benson (1975) took this one step further by introducing the idea of the 'inter-organisational network' needed to cope with changing conditions by being more responsive, more connected and more creative. Informal patterns of interdependency among organisations have been identified as an important source of stability and coherence within complex fields. In a network-type organisation, members are generally loosely connected through a variety of formal and informal linkages that enable them to share information or to trade with one another.

It has been suggested that network configurations reduce transaction costs (Williamson, 1975), primarily through bonds of trust which are said to minimise risk and enhance mutual commitment (Perrow, 1992). But there *are* costs associated with networks, usually absorbed within informal (usually pleasant) social and quasi-professional activities. These costs accumulate outside the organisation's normal accounting procedures, through the invisible and un-audited trading of resources, ideas and favours.

For several years within the voluntary and community sector the network form of organisation became the favoured alternative to hierarchy and competition, encapsulating (it was thought) egalitarian and democratic values often associated with the feminist and anarchist left (Ward, 1973; Ferguson, 1984). Somewhat paradoxically, and despite acknowledged examples of elitism and secrecy, many working on the radical wing of community development embraced the network model wholeheartedly. During the 1980s a host of 'network'-like organisations appeared to displace (in name at least) the federations, councils, associations and similar multi-agency consortia that had previously brought together diverse groups. Networks were assumed to operate according to principles of collective decision-making and mutual accountability rather than bureaucratic control. However, as Miller (2004) has observed:

> accountability is often messy in networks, not easily corresponding to conventional ideas of due process and democracy. The qualification for inclusion in a network is enthusiasm and a willingness to work with others, but

> this can develop to a point where the people who are the
> most enthusiastic and most connected ... can dominate.
> (p 214)

Networks are not always the organisational panacea that many envisage, often failing to fulfil their intended function. They contain patterns of prejudice, preference and power because they are based largely on personal choices that are both "tactical and strategic" (Chambers, 1983, p 216). Networks have limited ability to reach and carry out consensual decisions and this makes it difficult to deal with internal disputes, resulting in hidden power elites which are difficult to challenge. As Freeman (1973, p 1) noted in her book on *The tyranny of structurelessness* within the women's liberation movement, informality can become a "smokescreen for the strong or the lucky to establish unquestioned hegemony over others". Inequalities between network members can undermine the reciprocity that is needed to sustain relationships and may provide a systematic advantage for a specific clique. This is both unjust and inefficient because it fails to harness or fairly reward ability. An audit of who gains and who loses as a result of proposed changes (or maintaining the status quo) may uncover a political economy within a network, which should lead to more transparent decision-making and reveal potentially more equitable settlements.

Networks retain their popularity, perhaps because the voluntary and community sector can itself be characterised as a turbulent environment, inhabited by interacting organisations that often compete for resources (members, funding, status). And yet informal relationships based on trust and shared values enable voluntary and community organisations to co-operate around matters of principle. These interpersonal connections form a network of like-minded and dedicated individuals who serve on each other's management committees and are able to work together to co-ordinate activities and develop new organisations to meet emergent challenges.

Box 3.1: Uganda Rwenzori region

The Kabarole Research and Resource Centre (KRC), operating in the Rwenzori region of Uganda, has supported communities to develop networks, specialised around particular themes, such as sustainable agriculture, microfinance, sexual health, corruption and human rights. The networks allow a 'critical mass' of individuals and groups to work together on the issues they have in common: sharing experience and information, undertaking joint training and targeting their efforts to campaign on common problems, for example against the use of DDT in farming or for the abolition of the bride prize system which can lead to domestic violence against women.

The KRC's role has been to build capacity in civil society by facilitating the emergence of autonomous networks, supporting people to make connections and continually to reflect on their experiences. The Centre acts as a catalyst, initially servicing many of the functions of the networks but withdrawing as these became stronger and more self-reliant. In recent years, the various specialist networks and non-governmental bodies have been brought together under the umbrella of RANNET (Rwenzori Association of NGOs and Networks), to provide a collective voice for communities across the whole region.

Contact: Alex Ruhunda, Director, KRC. ruhundaalex@yahoo.com

The sector thus achieves both coherence and creativity without sacrificing the autonomy of separate organisations, or its ability to act in consort where necessary. However, many of the arrangements which support co-operation within the community and voluntary sector become disadvantageous when these positive links and affiliations prevent organisations from dealing with difficult situations, such as fraud, incompetence or discrimination. Improprieties and conflicts of interest may be deliberately hidden or simply underplayed in order to avoid explicit disagreements. This collusion is damaging and, if unchecked, can seriously erode the credibility of the whole sector.

Partnerships and cross-sectoral working

The present policy imperative for partnerships means that networking processes are even more necessary, and need to be adequately resourced. In the public sector, local government services have been gradually coaxed into complex area-based partnerships where cross-sectoral networks play an important role (Balloch and Taylor, 2001).

The emphasis on 'joined-up' working, especially within government programmes, reflects two parallel concerns. Partnerships are seen, on the one hand, as enabling coherent and efficient delivery of policy and services, and, on the other hand, as a way of renewing local or 'everyday' democracy by involving players from outside the state system in new forms of governance that sit alongside traditional forms of representative democracy (Barnes et al, 2004; Bentley, 2005). In development practice, international aid agencies are increasingly keen to work in partnership with governments and local non-governmental bodies rather than perpetuating the old donor–recipient relationship of control and dependency.

Partnerships formalise arrangements for joint ventures through the sharing of resources and responsibility between multiple stakeholders. Issues around public participation, power, trust and accountability are key to understanding and improving partnership working (Lowndes and Sullivan, 2004; Åkerstrøm Anderson, 2008). Human relationships are critical to the effectiveness of partnerships, emerging from 'a complex reciprocal process' of working and learning together as set out in the Warnwarth model of the 'good enough partnership' (Warne and Howarth, 2009). Networks are often the precursors to these arrangements and continue to be important in maintaining commitment, dealing with tensions and ensuring proper representation. Inclusive networks enable information and resources to be shared across group and organisational boundaries. They provide the means to compare, challenge and contradict different versions of the world, and in doing so discover new ideas (Agranoff and McGuire, 2001).

Trust is a key ingredient of such arrangements, although it can be an ephemeral and disarming virtue, evoked and revoked to suit the continuing power of professionals. In their study of community leadership, Purdue et al (2000) observed that feelings of trust and empowerment are linked, but that the power dynamics of the partnerships often oblige community representatives to trust the authorities because they have no sanctions and limited access to independent technical expertise. The legitimacy of community representatives is sometimes questioned when they challenge prevailing assumptions and aims. This can lead to antagonism and withdrawal of co-operation from some partners.

For communities to feel genuinely represented and empowered in these situations, they need to be able to trust their representatives, and to know that these in turn are trusted within the partnership structure (Lowndes and Sullivan, 2004). Networking contributes to this by building mutual commitment, generating trust and enabling accountability (Gilchrist, 2006a). Without community networks supporting local leadership on these partnerships, state and market forces become much more significant in regulating social behaviour because the voices of users, residents or other potential partners/ beneficiaries are distorted or suppressed altogether.

Members of black and minority ethnic communities in the West Midlands identified the need for strong effective leaders who were connected with (and therefore accountable to) the communities they served, but also able to build relationships between cultures and sectors (Rai, 2008). In studies of urban partnerships in Nairobi, Rio de Janeiro and Colombo, Riley and Wakely (2005) found that misunderstandings, mistrust and prejudices were rife, but could be mitigated through improvements in communication between communities and the various partners. Similarly, Schilderman and Ruskulis (2005) found slum dwellers in developing countries used their informal community networks to share knowledge and to access external information sources, so that they could be more influential.

In order to restore the credibility of community participation it is necessary to build formal infrastructures, as well as encouraging informal communication. Face-to-face interactions are vital to both of these, and networking within and across the sectors provides an effective means of building new forms of trust and accountability. Accountability issues arise whenever people are engaged in joint endeavours and permitted to act with discretion within a broad framework of agreed aims. This takes three forms:

- giving an account of what was done and why;
- taking into account the interests of different stakeholders;
- accounting for the use of resources, especially finances.

In formal terms, accountability operates through systems of contracts, audits, scrutiny exercises and complaints procedures in ways that are usually transparent and quantifiable. Face-to-face interactions tend to increase 'felt' accountability, with a consequent partiality towards familiar (and presumably liked) stakeholders. In this respect, informal networks constitute hidden and irregular policy communities, searching out opportunities to influence or subvert formal decisions (Laguerre, 1994). Voluntary organisations are particularly prone to these influences, tending to be accountable to several constituencies, including a range of funders and users. Without strong community networks holding leaders to account and providing them with support, there is a high risk of power tarnishing individual motives and integrity. Arrangements are needed that place a "premium on transparency and communication" in order to manage the multiplicity and diversity of expectations (Taylor, 1996, p 62).

Conclusions

An understanding of how networks operate within and between organisations is essential when it comes to helping communities to develop their own ideas and infrastructure. Many voluntary organisations and community groups evolve to meet a perceived need within communities. As we shall see in the next chapter, networks provide the conditions from which these initiatives spring. 'Well-connected' communities (with established voluntary associations, community groups, forums and robust informal networking opportunities) are well placed and well equipped to make a major contribution to multi-agency developments around many issues and at all levels. This was recently recognised in the British government's review of the third sector, which acknowledged 'connectivity' as an important community strength (Office of the Third Sector, 2007). Community development workers, as individuals, often bear the hidden costs of networking through personal, 'out of hours' investment of time and emotion in relationships which benefit their paid work. This has become more significant in recent years with the increased demands on communities (often supported by community development workers) to engage in inter-agency arrangements where boundary-spanning links are particularly helpful (Hoggett et al, 2008). Networks within communities, among people carrying out their normal, everyday activities, are also a vital source of social capital and community cohesion.

FOUR

Network functions

In life, the issue is not control, but dynamic inter-connectedness. (Jantsch, 1980, p 196)

Perhaps the most important, although somewhat tautological, function of networks is their capacity to support networking: enabling people to share ideas, consolidate relationships, exchange goods and services, and co-operate. Networks generally operate on the basis of shared values and informal connections that are maintained by a general reciprocal commitment. They differ from formal organisations in being less dependent on structure and tend to function through personal interaction between people who know (or know of) each other. For community development purposes, networks are important because they:

• provide robust and dispersed communication channels;
• facilitate collective action;
• underpin multi-agency partnerships;
• support citizen engagement;
• promote community cohesion;
• create opportunities for reflection and learning.

Conversation and communication

A huge amount of information and 'common sense' is communicated via informal networks. Conversations among friends, acquaintances, colleagues and neighbours convey rumour, opinion, local knowledge and news, allowing constant revisions to our understanding of the immediate and changing world in which we live (DiFonzo, 2008). The networks themselves become a repository of local knowledge, acting as a source of wisdom, information and 'gossip'. As Smith recognised:

Experienced community development workers develop the art of 'jizz' over time and find it invaluable. Intimate knowledge based on networking covers such areas as who gets on with whom, who used to work for which organisation and why the director of one local organisation has the ears of the chair of social services. Gossip is among the most precious information in community work. Such material is too sensitive and too complex to store on a computer ... what a competent community development worker carries in her head is a highly sophisticated relational database. (1999, p 13)

Maintaining connections with different sources within and beyond the community allows a form of intelligence gathering, enabling people to gain access to advice, services and resources that they might not otherwise know about or be able to influence. Gossip is also a way of learning from different experiences, generating new ideas and insights. Networks can be used to suppress views that question prevailing assumptions and customs, but they are also the mechanisms by which subversive ideas circulate, gather momentum and finally surface to challenge the status quo (Laguerre, 1994). People use their informal networks to develop controversial or critical opinions, often initially through muted debates among known allies or conversations with strangers that allow them to reveal risky thoughts and rehearse arguments. The 'off-stage' nature of these discussions allows alternative versions of the world to be constructed and for a new consciousness to emerge. Reflective conversation and 'critical dialogue' underpin several radical models of community development and informal learning (Ledwith, 1997, 2006; Stephenson, 2007).

As Alinsky (1972, p 69) noted, "happenings become experiences when they are digested, when they are reflected upon, related to general patterns and synthesised". The fact that much of this occurs in settings where formal accountability and scrutiny are minimal or non-existent allows such conversations to be opportunities for exploring ambiguity, contradictions and dissent. Knowledge dispersed through networks does not become 'thinner' but rather provides a collective wisdom that is empowering because it creates a "people's praxis" based on direct experience and empathy (Rahman, 1993, p 80). Local knowledge has to be 'invented' rather than discovered (Bauman, 2000); it emerges through processes of collective interpretation, iteration and induction and is the result of the learning generated by connected conversations and feedback within communities and organisations (MacLean and MacIntosh, 2003; Adams and Hess, 2006, p 5).

Freire's (1972) approach to emancipatory education uses a series of questions to expose the contradictions in social and economic systems, with a view to generating collective action to challenge these.

This process of 'conscientisation' forms the basis for community work practices, which seek major social transformation (Popple, 1995; Purcell, 2005). Freirean methods of conscientisation use 'guided' reflection to examine received wisdom and build up alternative explanations for people's experience that (theoretically) enable them to change their situation (Hope et al, 2000).

Public deliberations which deepen and widen democracy, through consultation meetings, citizens' juries, debates or informal gatherings, are vital to empowerment, but may require facilitation in order to create inclusive spaces for 'new conversational networks'. Community development techniques ensure that indigenous or traditional forms of discussion that reflect ethnic or local differences, are incorporated into formal participatory processes of citizen–centred governance (Guijt and Kaul Shah, 1998; Barnes et al, 2008; Eguren, 2008). Participation, especially in developing countries, can too often take the form of communities being 'invited' to take part in consultation exercises used by "colonial administrators seeking to secure quiescence ... or powerful financial institutions seeking to attain 'legitimacy' for their programmes" (Cornwall, 2008, p 281). Communities affected by proposals have a right to be influential, not merely involved, and this means making empowerment a practical, as well as political, reality; engaging with those who are most alienated or angry, as well as the 'active citizens' who have sufficient time, confidence and skills to become community representatives (Fraser, 2005; Shaw, 2008). Networking, using proactive and explicit targeting of the most disaffected and marginalised, enables these hidden, often dissenting, views to be heard across boundaries, and for new knowledge, drawn on lived experience, to inform the dialogue (Adams and Hess, 2006).

By talking together, comparing ideas, discussing common experiences and perhaps undertaking some kind of joint activity, people usually come to understand and trust one another. This lays the foundation for collective action. "Dialogue becomes a horizontal relationship of mutual trust. Trust is established by dialogue; it cannot exist unless the words of both parties coincide with their actions" (Freire, 1972, p 64). Dialogue is often taken to mean a conversation between *two* parties, but this is a misinterpretation of the word's Greek origins since 'dia' means 'through' (not two), and so a more authentic (and, in this context, appropriate) application is to see dialogue as a means to achieve understanding through words that create a "stream of meaning" (Böhm, 1994, p 7; 1996). Informal networks are essential to processes of social change, especially those which open up access to new ideas or encourage incompatible views to be exposed (Humphries and Martin,

2000). This form of collective reflection encourages experimentation and the creation of new 'paradigms'. Networks allow for a construction of 'reality', which, although subjective, is grounded in experience and able to generate new insights and solutions. Such exchanges can be liberating, leading to radical analyses and transformative action (Ledwith, 1997).

Not only do individuals acquire different ways of thinking about their own lives and the world around them, they are able to learn skills and gain confidence and a sense of their own identity. The feedback and advice provided through personal networks allow people to form judgements about themselves in comparison with others and to keep track of their own reputations. Psychologists have found that people's sense of identity is socially constructed within informal groups and networks (Tajfel, 1981; Abrams and Hogg, 1990). Ethnic identity is not inherited, but rather constructed through narratives and rituals passed down through successive generations or waves of migration (Barth, 1998). It is often articulated and perpetuated by social elites (Brown, 2001), which serve to define boundaries and belonging (Sayyid and Zac, 1998). This sense of community or shared fate is an important ingredient in people's willingness to undertake collective action. Community cohesion is able to transcend ostensible differences in origin and interests, but is also contingent on local circumstances and pressures (Farrar, 2001; Hussein, 2007; Khan, 2007; Phillips, 2007). Networks help to build relationships within and across communities, to span sector boundaries and to develop a consensus that can inform future strategies.

Contact theory suggests that the more positive contact that people experience with 'other' groups, the more likely they are to be tolerant of differences and willing to work together (Hewstone et al, 2007). This model has been used to promote social cohesion in troubled areas of Britain and underpins community-level peace-building strategies in other parts of the world (e.g. O'Brien, 2007). Through careful, conflict-sensitive interventions it has proved possible, over the long term, to forge new, often national, identities that transcend local or tribal divisions (African Peace Forum et al, 2004). West African Peacebuilding Network links various peace-building networks and is seen as a knowledgeable advocate, especially in providing early-warning mechanisms of conflicts brewing below the surface. Similarly, in Macedonia, an organisation called Partners for Economic Development (PRISMA) continued to foster partnerships across different sectors even after war had broken out. By providing a neutral, non-partisan forum in which grievances could be aired and tackled, members of the different ethnic communities were able to rise above the conflict to work together on common issues (Liebler and Ferri, 2004).

A notion of the 'common good' emerges based on a deeper wisdom derived from listening to, interpreting, comparing, reviewing and evaluating views from divergent sources (Robinson, 2004). As Bayley (1997, p 18) asserts:

> the most fundamental tenet of the community development approach is that the worker takes time to develop a real understanding of how things look from the standpoint of those with whom she is working, that is to understand the culture, the assumptions and the priorities of those she is seeking to help.

An important function of social networks is to convey meaning, which is filtered and refined through a series of "nuanced asynchronous and asymmetric exchanges" recurring between mutually interested parties (Stephenson, 2004, p 39). If knowledge is indeed power, then informal and collective learning represents a potentially important route to empowerment, because, as Schön (1990) and others have observed, learning often involves 'unlearning' the older, perhaps more dominant, ways of thinking. Discussion is a very important aspect of 'joined-up' working where organisations with quite different cultures and traditions are expected to collaborate around a set of objectives, often externally set. This takes time. Multi-agency organisations need common aims and priorities if they are to achieve their purposes. Informal networks often provide the spaces for 'behind the scenes' interaction that can ease tensions, enhance understanding and consolidate mutual commitment. The informality of these unrecorded conversations allows people to express their reservations, explore 'wild' suggestions and admit that they might be having problems with the 'bigger picture'.

Many forms of social and adult education acknowledge the importance of people learning from one another and this is viewed as a core process of community integration and citizen empowerment (for example, Woodward, 2005; Mayo and Rooke, 2006). In his study of voluntary and community organisations, Elsdon et al (1995) highlights the learning that takes place within inter-organisational networks, often through chance conversations, involving personal interaction. He stresses the importance of warm, caring, mutually supportive relationships that enable people to overcome barriers to learning and build their self-confidence. For many marginalised communities this is a necessary step along the road to collective action. Networks enable people to identify common concerns for themselves, and to articulate the issues that they want to pursue either through participation in a broad partnership arrangement or through self-organisation and campaigning.

Collective empowerment

Empowerment is achieved through learning *and* collective organising. It has been defined as 'enhancing' people's capacity to influence the decisions that affect their lives and is a central principle of community development. The term is embedded in the rhetoric (if not consistently the practice) of government initiatives across a whole host of policy areas (CLG, 2008). In this context, community development is primarily concerned with enhancing the skills, knowledge, confidence and organisational capacity within communities so that they can engage more effectively with decision-making bodies, such as public authorities and strategic partnerships.

It is increasingly acknowledged that empowerment processes require a redistribution of power, and therefore involve changes in the culture and procedures of mainstream institutions so that these become more transparent, more responsive and less inclined to maintain control. Challenging the power of institutions and oppressive practices is a crucial aspect of community development, as is changing the flow of power through organisations and communities. Collective action is empowering in its own right because it enables people without much influence to assert their interests in decision-making. Networks contribute to empowerment on a psychological level, by enabling people to compare their experiences, learn from each other's successes and develop greater awareness of the wider politics of inequality and oppression. It may be useful to make a distinction between 'perceived' and 'actual' power but, in practice, it is usually impossible to exert one without the other.

As we saw in Chapter Two, radical community development workers have long been aware of the dispersed nature of power and have seen their central task as shifting the balance of power within society by helping people to make connections with others who share their oppression or predicament. Empowerment is not an 'all-or-nothing' strategy involving opposition and conflict. It can be considered as a continuous process of increasing capacity to influence decision-making, of connecting people with power. Relational organising is based on the principle of 'conversation leading to action' and is used extensively by the broad-based organising movement (Warren, 2001; Obama, 2004).

A networking approach to community development seeks to increase influence primarily through processes of connection, negotiation and persuasion. It strives to manoeuvre stakeholders into a position of saying 'Yes' as a group, even if they start as adversaries (Goldstein et al, 2008). Strategies using 'incremental commitment' gradually build relationships through increasing levels of emotional and other forms of investment (Cialdini, 1993). In this model, empowerment occurs by reconfiguring relationships and patterns of influence, rather than 'seizing power' (Hothi et al, 2008).

Organisation development is an important strand of community development and community development workers frequently find themselves assisting in the creation, management and occasionally the demise of formal structures, including partnerships. Their work programmes are dominated by tasks relating to finances, constitutions, administration, legal responsibilities and public relations. What has been less recognised is the role played by community development workers in supporting and managing informal networks that are capable of promoting both autonomy and solidarity. Networks can be used for empowerment by mobilising a 'critical mass' of allies for achieving change, often using collective action strategies.

Communities that have experienced long-term systematic discrimination often need assistance in setting up their own organisations, as well as positive action strategies to challenge existing power blocs (Christian, 1998; CDF, 2008a). If power is distributed across shifting systems of relationships and stakeholders, rather than the political or legal establishment, then strategies for the empowerment of disadvantaged groups require more fluid and decentralised forms of organisation. By acknowledging the diversity of constituent elements, networks channel power to where it can influence decisions or affect the course of events, making things happen and exerting pressure towards (or against) different interests.

Social psychological models of change (Schneiderman, 1988), organising (Hosking and Morley, 1991), collective action (Kelly and Breinlinger, 1996) and protest (Klandermans, 1997) demonstrate that empowerment and participation combine cognitive and emotional processes to discover or define a shared problem and develop a collective solution (see Damasio, 2006). Personal feelings and attitudes affect how people interact and their willingness to work together (Hoggett and Miller, 2000; Hustedde and King, 2002; Hoggett, 2006, 2009). This can generate dilemmas for community development workers who may find their professional accountabilities (in the shape of expectations from line managers and funders) at odds with their personal motivations or politics (Clarke et al, 2006; Hoggett et al, 2008).

Community representatives are similarly driven by a range of emotions, including idealism, loyalty, vengeance and anger (Purdue, 2007). The emotions that flow through community networks are an important dimension of organising and empowerment (Flam and King, 2005). Individuals use their personal networks to raise their esteem, awareness and aspirations. Feelings of compassion, loyalty, admiration, love even, are often the driving force for many community and voluntary activities, but so too are the less positive emotions of pity, resentment, anger and fear, observed in the 'moral panics' that give rise to vigilante groups or campaigns against supposed local threats, for example in relation to suspected paedophiles, asylum seekers and migrant workers (Lewis, 2005; Hudson et al, 2007).

Patterns of power

Within formal and informal arrangements it is impossible to ignore questions of relative power (Mayo and Taylor, 2001). In the early studies of organisation and decision-making, the issue of power was seen as relevant only in conflict situations where there are competing interests. The zero-sum model, as it came to be known, tended to assume that there exists a fixed amount of power and that this is distributed across actors (individuals or organisations) who exercise influence or authority *over* others in order to secure an intended outcome or promote a particular interest (Weber, 1947).

Lukes (1974) extended the debate around power by introducing a pernicious 'third dimension' which infiltrates the hearts and minds of 'ordinary' people to induce attitudes and practices which protect the interests of the elite or governing class. In many respects this is akin to Gramsci's (1971) earlier notion of 'hegemony', whereby 'common sense' and 'internalised oppression' are reproduced through cultural and civic institutions. Both these formulations emphasise the power of indoctrination as opposed to authority exercised through control or coercion. Their approach suggests a model of power that is more diffuse and less attached to particular 'agents' or objective interests. It recognises the possibility of mutual influence and resistance through the development of countervailing ideas and social forces, or, as Gramsci proposed, the construction of an alternative position or 'counter-hegemony'. Post-modernists would call this a dominant discourse, while psychologists refer to mindsets.

Power has elastic, effervescent qualities (Maffesoli, 1996). It can be facilitative and generative: a vital force for achieving co-operation and mutual benefit rather than dominance and exploitation. But networks can be cliquey and elitist, enrolling members through bizarre systems of preferment and ritual, such as experienced by novice freemasons and frat clubs. The 'old boy' (and girl) network, based on public schools and Oxbridge colleges is said to exert a strong and enduring influence on opinion formers within British politics (McCarthy, 2004). A ground-breaking study in Bangladesh using participatory research carried out a rudimentary form of network analysis to reveal a 'net' of powerful men and their followers who were systematically exploiting and abusing landless villagers, intercepting aid intended for the poorest families and subverting democratic and legal processes (BRAC, 1980). This network of the elite had not been visible previously to outside donors and government agents, and could only be dismantled by the combined efforts of villagers, aid workers and civil servants. Chambers describes it as "the lancing of a long-festering abscess" (1983, p 70). A similar exercise might usefully be applied to the partnerships operating in many disadvantaged communities in the UK.

Nevertheless, networks provide the foundation and 'life-blood' for a variety of multi-agency organisations, ranging from formal consortia with specific remits set out in a constitution or memorandum, through open forums, to the most flexible of informal alliances. All of these are important vehicles for developing collective action and are often based more on faith and trust than explicit rules. At a collective level, networks help people to find allies and build organisations to promote their views within and outside the decision-making arena. This can be used to develop internal problem-solving strategies or to assert a particular viewpoint. Networks often underpin techniques for self-organisation among populations which are scattered, isolated or oppressed (Fujimoto, 1992). Terrorists and insurgents organise as networks of cells, and often have widespread links into other networks fighting different causes (Gunaratne, 2005). The resilience of the al Qaeda network derives partly from the absence of central control (contrary to Western propaganda about Osama bin Laden), and its projection of a shared 'vision' and common 'threat' (Riedel, 2008). Political activists will be familiar with the use of caucusing to influence and mobilise others to support a particular position or faction. Community development makes use of similar, but more open, methods of coalition-building to challenge vested interests and empower communities by creating new forms of governance and communication channels, based on 'social networks of trust' (Riley and Wakely, 2005). The bottom-up connections enable a 'capillary approach' that draws influence up from community levels to local partnerships and policy networks (Considine, 2003; Adamson and Bromiley, 2008). Skidmore et al (2006, p 50) assert that "participants in governance will find it much easier to mobilise others and plug into their networks if the formal structures they inhabit are places where real power lies".

Social networks channel power for collective ends by maintaining solidarity and allowing risk to be shared. Wheatley (1992, p 39) regards power as the "capacity generated by relationships" which she sees as energy flowing through organisations, facilitated rather than controlled by those in positions of leadership. Women theorists in particular have asserted the positive aspects of power as a productive and enabling resource (for example, Elworthy, 1996). They have stressed the importance of building facilitative connections in order to initiate and manage organisational change (Kanter, 1983; Helgesen, 1990). As Florence, a rural health trainer in South Africa, recognised:

> I have learned not to under-estimate the strength of each woman, organisation and community.… Every woman is born with that power, it is not created by the [Western Cape] Network, but the Network enables women to use their power. (Womankind Worldwide, 2000, p 6)

Post-modernists have likewise emphasised the dispersed and dynamic nature of power (Foucault, 1977; Bauman, 2000). They focus on the micro-practices governing relations between people, and between people and institutions, arguing that power differentials within systems direct the flow of influence towards and against decisions. Post-modernism regards power as fluid, inherently ambiguous and multi-faceted (Hindess, 1996). It affects the patterns of interaction in everyday life, influencing behaviour and thinking without recourse to explicit force or actual punishment. Power relations are embedded in organisational cultures and personal behaviour to the extent that different dimensions of oppression become internalised in our personal and collective identities. Alternatively, the flow of information and commitment through networks generates synergy and can be seen as empowering, especially for those who have been excluded from or deprived of opportunities to participate in decision-making or collective activity. Deliberate and innovative methods are needed to connect these 'yet to be reached' or 'seldom heard' sections into mainstream opportunities for empowerment.

This articulation of power as flowing through a network of relationships has been further developed by Clegg (1989) in his 'circuits of power' model. A networking approach to empowerment adopts a similar model of power, recognising that it can be positive, contextual and relational. Agency, the capacity to make things happen, is achieved by making connections so that power can flow to where it is most effective. In recent years, community work appears to have adopted, perhaps unwittingly, this post-modern approach to empowerment that reiterates a long-standing emphasis on process and personal empowerment. Although community development workers must avoid abusing the power of their professional role, they will inevitably apply their knowledge and skills to influence the opinions and behaviour of community members, and use their status and connections to change the policies and practices of institutions. As Shuftan (1996, p 260) explains, "empowerment is not an outcome of a single event; it is a continuous process that enables people to understand, upgrade and use their capacity to better control and gain power over their own lives".

At one level, it could be said that it is factors in the social environment that empower (and oppress). Processes of empowerment might include increasing, improving and incorporating useful and positive connections into the routine interactions and habits of people's everyday lives. Networking practices within empowerment strategies can be used to enhance community credibility and influence within decision-making arenas. Empowerment is about self-help *and* collective organising. For the individual, networking is self-empowering because it reduces isolation, provides supportive mentoring and offers opportunities for personal learning and advancement. Almost by definition, empowerment is anti-oppressive and will often be resisted because it involves challenging discrimination, prejudice and marginalisation. This was recognised by the anti-slavery campaigner Frederick Douglass, who declared that "If there is no struggle, there is no progress ... power concedes nothing without a demand. It never did and it never will" (Douglass, 1857).

This has important implications for how community development workers operate to promote and maintain community networks, making sure that the power of leaders and representatives (including themselves) is both earned and accountable. The 'circuits of power' metaphor helps us to see empowerment as altering the flow of power through connected series of events and decisions, often operating through networks of relationships (see Gilchrist and Taylor, 1997). These reconnect people and power and provide an important part of a community's capacity to implement viable and sustainable change strategies. By opening up experiences of oppression, exploitation and injustice to shared scrutiny, community networks encourage mutual responsibility and solidarity based on compassion and interdependence. The complex nature of power – its association with protecting elites as much as with promoting solidarity – presents networking strategies for community development with a dilemma. In Colombo, the role of the Community Development Councils in the slum and shanty areas became distorted by the patronage system linking elected councillors with specific settlements, and made it virtually impossible for new forms of governance to emerge that could develop alternative partnerships within civil society (Riley and Wakely, 2005).

Alliances for social change

Networks are complex and dynamic. Unlike organisations, they cannot be controlled or moulded to a particular purpose. The connections grow and wither away according to their usefulness, rather like routes across a natural landscape (Finnegan, 1989). In this sense, community development workers operate as social engineers, using relationships and inter-organisational links to carve out new channels, construct pathways, clear away the undergrowth, erect bridges and occasionally tunnel into the depths of seemingly impenetrable institutions. Working to alter the flow of influence and information through these networks opens up access to resources and contributes to a redistribution of power. Networks help people to learn from their experience, to articulate personal problems as shared issues and to organise for collective action. Research on social movements reveals that networks are informally maintained and continue to exert influence even when they appear to be dormant (Melucci, 1996). Communities are the 'incubators' of collective activity with social networks acting as 'mobilising devices' (Tarrow, 1994, pp 21, 136). It is useful to cultivate links beyond the immediate community, building alliances with individuals and organisations that have greater access to power and resources.

In the US, Kris Rondeau has developed an alternative model for trade union activity and negotiation that uses this approach, known as relational organising. She describes her methods as 'building a community of workers' and has been remarkably successful in negotiating advantageous deals for union members (Hoerr, 1993; Cobble, 2004). Formal organisations are important but they are not the only means of collective empowerment. The 'new' political movements have consistently stressed their fluid, diverse and organic nature. In contrast to more traditional social movements (such as the trades unions or early tenants' organisations) they might be described as networks of networks in that they are more flexible, avoid central control mechanisms and seem content to operate with high levels of autonomy and low formal accountability. Campaigners 'do their own thing' within a broad set of political goals, with activities loosely but effectively co-ordinated, often via the Internet. The use of information technology has immeasurably changed political organising, enabling actions to be arranged more efficiently, whether at global (Castells, 2001; Edwards and Gaventa, 2001; Mayo, 2005; Tarrow, 2005) or local levels (Hampton, 2003, 2007; Mulgan, 2004), or both at once, a phenomenon that has been termed 'glocalisation' (Wellman, 2002). E-petitions and websites, such as avaaz (www.avaaz.org), are used to mobilise opinion on a worldwide basis, galvanising thousands, possibly millions, of people to express their views on a huge variety of issues.

Social movement theories have recognised the crucial role of informal networks in developing and sustaining involvement in mass political activity (Klandermans, 1997; Tarrow, 2005). There is a growing recognition of the micro-social processes of political and collective action: the interactions, the dialogue and the emotional ties between participants (Ray et al, 2003). The alliances that emerge need to be flexible and robust so that they can accommodate the diversity of experience and values that motivate people, even on an international scale (Bunch with Antrobus et al, 2001; Miller, 2004). This broadness of spirit and the colourful 'rainbow' image of such coalitions provide a model for collective organising that values diversity, promotes solidarity *and* supports challenging interactions.

Coalitions represent temporary, tactical arrangements through which disparate actors combine forces in order to achieve a goal that benefits each of them or fends off an external threat. They are generally semi-formal, ad hoc arrangements whereby separate agencies co-ordinate their activities in order to share resources and operate better in an uncertain environment (Scott, 1992, p 201). As Boissevain (1974) asserted, coalitions tend to emerge from networks of 'friends of friends', including the tangle of loose associations that characterise neighbourhoods or interest communities. A coalition might be built in response to events, forming a pragmatic and informal 'action-set'. Its aims will generally be focused on achieving a limited goal, such as winning a policy decision, organising an event, defending or obtaining a common resource. Once the coalition has achieved its purpose it may either dissolve or transform itself into a more structured organisation that could take on the management of a service, a building or other more permanent project.

Networks may themselves become organisations, through formalising constitutions, or they might spawn new organisations, creating structures for specific purposes while leaving the networking function intact. The transition to more formal structures is neither always universally desired nor even feasible. Difficulties often arise where there is resistance or lack of clarity as to why a network needs to encumber itself with the constitutional trappings and formal accountabilities of a 'proper' organisation. Confusion over function can sometimes lead to networks being set up by external agents rather than emerging organically from participants' interests and interactions. Research into the benefits and limitations of non-governmental networks in the field of international development found that these worked best when donors were prepared to fund the processes of networking, rather than insist that the network followed a normal project cycle. Those networks that evolved endogenously were more effective and more sustainable than those that had been instigated from outside or engineered from above (Liebler and Ferri, 2004).

Developing community action

It is well known within community development that people tend to become involved in community activities or to join a local organisation if they already know someone involved or are persuaded through personal contact with a community development worker. It takes a lot of courage or sheer desperation for someone to come along to an event without a prior introduction or conversation. A poster announcement or leaflet invitation is rarely sufficient, while information provided via websites is usually too remote and impersonal to support sustained participation. Generally, people enter into collective arrangements because they are already linked in some way with others involved. A connection exists which persuades them that the benefits of participation are likely to outweigh the costs. Credit unions and micro-loan schemes operate in this way, though require meticulous administration as well. The element of risk can be countered or mitigated through judicious networking to identify reliable allies and reach a modicum of consensus. Despite the risks of unreciprocated contributions, loss of independence and expenditure of time and effort in meetings or social events, involvement in networks generally helps to reduce isolation and increase credibility. The networking approach to community development helps people to develop useful relationships and find a common cause. In addition to psychological factors, local norms and conventions seem to play an important role in creating the conditions for effective collective action (Chanan, 1992).

Social networks act as communication channels, engender a sense of shared purpose and are used to recruit for community-based organisations (Milofsky, 1987). Networks supply cost-effective means of achieving a 'critical mass' of support, which encourages wider participation. Four key factors appear to influence people's readiness to contribute to a collective initiative:

- the motivation of potential participants;
- the availability of resources;
- ease of communication;
- social processes of interaction.

Marwell and Oliver (1993) suggest that in the initial stages of developing collective activities, organisers use their social ties to contact people who are most likely to participate, ensuring that a threshold for collective action is achieved as speedily as possible. Organisers with many 'weak ties' in their networks are able to target, canvass and recruit potential contributors across many organisations and social groups. These boundary-spanning links are relatively cheap forms of communication, but highly effective in contacting sympathetic allies and mobilising resources. Knowledge about the interdependencies and connections among the network members is vital in making good use of the network as a communications system, otherwise the flow of information might be disrupted by channels that have deteriorated or become dysfunctional because people have fallen out or lost touch with one another.

Effective organising requires a balance between the costs of maintaining networks (time, effort, money or other resources) and the expected gains (Gray, 2003). Each individual makes their own micro-calculations about how they can contribute, but this is influenced by the perceived decisions and behaviour of those around them. Networking is an example of optimising behaviour such that the least amount of effort is expended for the most gain (Zipf, 1965). Marwell and Oliver (1993) emphasise the role of 'entrepreneurs', who may come from outside the community of interest and disproportionately absorb the costs of organising, perhaps for political or moral reasons. These individuals often have useful resources and skills to offer and can act as brokers or catalysts to get things started. They tend to be well connected with other resourceful or influential people.

In this respect, it would appear that extensive and diverse networks are more advantageous than overlapping, close-knit sets of similar people bound by strong ties and shared outlooks. Individuals who are linked, but slightly peripheral, to several distinct networks are more likely to provide the 'bridging mechanisms' that allow for cross-fertilisation of ideas and create the conditions for creative thinking. This is often the role played by community development workers and community leaders, and can prove problematic for those individuals in situations where there are many tensions and differences.

Managing differences

Working within and between diverse communities in ways that simultaneously honour different cultures and challenge inequalities can be a complicated process. The concept of community should be able to encompass and express both variety and unity, but often in reality communal identities underpin a tendency to segregate and promote narrow, rather inward-facing, loyalties resulting in some places in the appearance of what have been termed 'parallel lives' (Cantle, 2001). Inter-faith organisations in Britain have been effective in bringing together people of different religions for joint events and forums that have increased social capital as well as providing important opportunities for sharing ideas and resources (Furbey et al, 2006; James, 2007; Evison, 2008; Dinham et al, 2009).

Networks are generally able to accommodate divergence and dissent, rather than attempting to impose either unity in action or a spurious (and often fragile) consensus. Networks are particularly adept at managing contradiction and are useful organisational tools for promoting genuine understanding and integration, based on what the Commission on Integration and Cohesion called 'meaningful interaction' (CoIC, 2007; CLG, 2009). This is true for organisations as well as individuals. Diversity challenges dogma and orthodoxy by generating alternatives, but it also generates fault lines within society that erode social capital (Briggs, 1997; Putnam, 2007).

Networks offer a means of stabilising 'turbulent' environments (Scott, 1992) and dealing with inter-communal or sectarian tensions.

Box 4.1: Oldham Interfaith Forum

The Forum actively works to bring different groups and communities together by drawing on Lederach's theory of 'critical yeast' (Lederach, 2005), which involves working with chosen small groups. Lederach calls this the 'critical yeast' approach as only a little yeast is needed to cause dough to rise. It involves building networks of relationships – rather like a spider might build a web. The spider finds anchor points that will enable the web to cover the chosen area and then links those points to each other and to the centre. To build the web the spider has to be completely aware of the area in which it operates.

In Oldham, anchor points were chosen from different sections of the political spectrum, different religious backgrounds and positions of social leadership, and they came together for a series of meetings. As well as discussing agreed issues, the meetings also witnessed the telling of individual stories, which were sometimes painful but always engaging.

Adapted from a presentation to the World Conference on the Development of Cities (February 2008) by Rev. Philip T. Sumner and Fazal Rahim (cited in Chauhan, 2009).

Conflicts often arise because people want to use communal space for apparently incompatible purposes. Antagonisms appear, for example, because of differences in age, culture, gender and sexual orientation. Informal networks can be used to foster a "democratic and permissive culture" in communities and organisations, creating "the capacity to contain conflicts without being exploded apart by them" (Jeffers et al, 1996, p 123). Community development workers frequently operate in situations characterised by conflict and resistance, especially when they are helping communities to challenge poverty and discrimination. The 'outsider' can contribute by co-ordinating and facilitating such interactions, acting as a 'weak tie', helping people to communicate directly, and interpreting when things get awkward.

Policy initiatives to promote community cohesion have mainly been concerned with issues around fragmentation and the need to build cross-community contact, rather than addressing deep-rooted racial prejudice and grievances based on real or perceived inequality. Xenophobic attitudes and myths of ghettoisation appear as the 'shadow side' of strongly bonded, but defensive, communities (Clarke et al, 2007; Finney and Simpson, 2009), especially in relation to migrants of any sort (Rogaly and Taylor, 2007). Consequently, strategies for promoting community cohesion tend to assert the need for unity based on the integration of different cultures and experiences within society. At neighbourhood level this requires a great deal of thought and effort (Robinson and Reeve, 2006; Zetter et al, 2006).

Early definitions of community cohesion emphasised the importance of "a common vision and sense of belonging" for all communities, "similar life opportunities", the valuing of diversity and the development of "strong and positive relationships ... between people from different backgrounds" (LGA, 2002, p 6). Often this is related to a desire to forge an overarching national or patriotic identity, such as embodied in the citizenship education and oaths of allegiance introduced in Britain in 2004. This has proved controversial and the current understanding of cohesion has been modified by the Commission on Integration and Cohesion to include a more fluid model, which acknowledges the ebb and flow of migrant workers across national borders, only some of whom choose to settle on a permanent basis. Instead of requiring a shared identity, the Commission recommended that residents acknowledge a 'shared future', based on mutual respect, civility, visible social justice and an "ethics of hospitality" that encourages "strong and positive relations between people from different backgrounds" (CoIC, 2007, p 7). Similarly, the Council of Europe avoids reference to a common identity, preferring a definition of social cohesion based on social bonds, shared responsibility and a minimum agreed level of well-being as the prerequisites for harmonious living.

The networks of refugees and asylum seekers are crucial to ensuring their successful settlement and integration (Temple, 2005), as well as enabling them to access the advice and support they need from mainstream services (Navarro, 2006). Gilchrist (2004) developed a model of cohesion which referred to "a collective ability to manage the shifting array of tensions and disagreements among diverse communities" (p 7). An infrastructure of informal networks based on 'meaningful interaction' and tolerant understanding, underpinned by an equitable distribution of opportunities, material resources and residential stability, helps to create this capacity and should result eventually in mutual respect and co-operative solidarity (Hudson et al, 2007; Somerville, 2009). Recent research by Harris and colleagues indicates that 'bridge-building activities' between different ethnic and religious communities at the grassroots level are often facilitated by remarkable individuals, working through community organisations to organise social, educational, sports and cultural initiatives (Harris and Young, 2009). Community development can both support these individuals and link them with others to establish a more strategic approach.

Box 4.2: City of Sanctuary

City of Sanctuary is a social movement which aims to create a 'culture of hospitality' for asylum seekers and refugees throughout the UK. It consists of a growing network of towns and cities which have committed themselves to providing not only emergency accommodation and sustenance, but friendship, advocacy and opportunities for integration into the wider community. In each of the participating cities, voluntary organisations, faith and community groups and public bodies work together to welcome new arrivals and provide a place of safety while waiting for a decision on their claim.

In Sheffield, the first City of Sanctuary, signs, events and activities have been organised to develop cultural change that goes beyond the refugee sector and reaches into neighbourhoods that would not normally have had direct contact with asylum seekers. As a result, the prejudices fostered by media reports have been countered and networks of support have been set up that have helped individuals and families to integrate more quickly into local communities.

See www.cityofsanctuary.org

Networks can help to anticipate and diffuse tensions before they become full-blown conflicts. Amin (2002, p 11) suggests that in multi-ethnic societies inter-community relations would benefit from "the habit of interaction" in micro-publics where people relate on a day-to-day basis, such as clubs, schools and workplaces. The inevitable 'prosaic negotiations' in these supposedly neutral spaces, if sensitively handled, might serve to tackle ignorance, dogma and prejudice, thus establishing a foundation of understanding and empathy for acknowledging and adjusting to differences (Lownsbrough and Beunderman, 2007). This sometimes involves managing or engineering live, dynamic interactions across informal networks, often through 'banal encounters' in everyday life (Lowndes et al, 2006). The relative informality of networks enables contrasting cultures and perspectives to be explored without them necessarily becoming confrontational, and where there *is* opposition, positive experiences of working together, and of finding consensus in the past, make it more likely that solutions or compromises can be negotiated (Gilchrist, 1998a, 2004).

Cross-cutting area-based forums provide opportunities to build bridging and linking social capital, creating relationships between people from different backgrounds and with different remits. Inequalities in power and access must, however, be addressed if such opportunities are not simply to become occasions for further disempowerment of community members, especially those from already marginalised groups. Community work posts are often located at the margins of organisations and have a special concern with boundaries and barriers (Williams, 2002). Vital and difficult work takes place across interfaces, between partners and between different sections of the community.

Community development values and methods are important in managing the overall web of connections to promote empowerment and support participation (CD Challenge group, 2006). Their work would be considerably eased by the existence of the kind of 'democracy hubs' proposed by the Power Inquiry (2006), resource centres or 'anchor organisations' that would sustain a culture of 'everyday democracy' by providing information and support to encourage communities to contribute at all levels of decision-making (Thake, 2001; Community Alliance, 2007; Skidmore and Bound, 2008). The primary function of the professional community development worker is to establish and nurture the 'bridging capital' to be found among the 'weak ties' and linking capital of community and inter-organisational networks. Community development workers support and facilitate networks that connect people who might otherwise find neither reason nor means to interact. The patterns of power within networks inevitably reflect the social and economic environment, and community development workers have a key responsibility in making sure that the flow of resources and influence through networks is as egalitarian, transparent and democratic as possible.

Conclusions

The evidence presented in this and the previous chapter has indicated just how important networks are in our daily lives and in regulating society as a whole. They seem such a natural part of life that it would be easy to imagine that networks just happen without any particular effort or thought. However, a few minutes' reflection on how we sustain and shape our own networks reveals that time and attention is needed to keep certain links intact, and we probably invest most in those connections that are useful or bring pleasure. Life events, such as births, marriages and deaths, are important occasions for reinforcing family ties and expressing our commitment to friends. Cultural or religious celebrations present opportunities for initiating or at least maintaining friendly relations with colleagues, neighbours and members of our community through the exchange of greetings and gifts, often accompanied by updates on personal news. The activities that are used to do this can be grouped under the generic term of networking, which will be the focus of the next two chapters.

FIVE

The principles and processes of networking

To understand is, as ever, to put choice in place of chance. (Charles Handy, 1988, p 113)

Introduction

Networking involves the creation, maintenance and use of links and relationships between individuals and/or organisations. Networking itself is a neutral tool – it can be used for a variety of purposes – selfish, political, altruistic or simply to get things done. Networking for community development is obviously influenced by key values around equality, empowerment and participation. It is increasingly seen as a popular, albeit mildly manipulative, means of gaining personal and political advancement. Following Dale Carnegie's classic bestseller *How to win friends and influence people* (1937), there are a growing number of guides on how to attract (and presumably retain) useful people into one's personal networks (Too, 1997; Stone, 2001; Bubb and Davidson, 2004). Networking has also become commercialised with websites and agencies helping people to find 'matches' for love, investment funds, travel arrangements or whatever.

This chapter looks at networking as something that most people do in their everyday lives, namely develop and maintain links with a selection of the people they encounter in their work, where they live or in the course of social or leisure activities. Since this book is about community development, it is not primarily concerned with the relationships that constitute our family and friendship networks, although of course there is some overlap (Pahl, 2000). The focus, rather, is on connections with colleagues, neighbours and the people we know through a variety of activities and who we regard as members of our different communities. Some of these may be no more than 'familiar strangers' or nodding acquaintances (Milgram, 1977). Others may be people we chat to while out and about, or at a club, but who we would not necessarily invite to our homes. Others again we may know because of their role in an organisation that is significant in our lives.

Relationships constitute more than mere contacts or connections. They have an emotional content, sustaining people in their jobs and enabling them to undertake specific tasks by providing access to vital resources, knowledge and influence, which might not otherwise be available. To be effective, these relationships must be authentic and reliable. For community development, interpersonal relationships within communities and between organisations need to be established and maintained in ways that contribute to the overall work programme of individual workers or agencies. The networking approach advocated here requires that community development workers have a good understanding of how relationships function and how they can be sustained. Community development workers facilitate these processes by finding connections, creating opportunities for shared activities and encouraging dialogue across apparent boundaries so that even the most disenfranchised community members can be included (Stephenson, 2007).

The evidence used in this and the following chapters was mainly gathered from a case study of the co-ordination of the Bristol Festival Against Racism (Gilchrist, 1994) and a panel study involving 11 community development workers, asking them about their involvement in networks and encouraging them to reflect on their own experience of networking to identify how this contributed to their work and what made them 'good' networkers. The initials after each quote refer to the panellists, all of whom were happy to have their identity revealed in the acknowledgements. (For details of research methodology, see Gilchrist, 2001).

Box 5.1: Bristol Festival Against Racism

In the initial stages of organising the 1994 Bristol Festival Against Racism the co-ordinator used various networks to distribute information about the proposal. Flyers were included in the mailings of several city-wide umbrella bodies, and announcements inserted in the newsletters of others. They were chosen because the organisers already had contacts in these organisations and anticipated that members of these organisations would be favourably disposed towards the idea. In addition, a number of key individuals were 'targeted' to persuade them to endorse the project, knowing that this would encourage others to come on board. Where there were gaps in the network, the co-ordinator made use of personal connections to identify a point of access, for example to the Travellers community.

Every opportunity was found to talk about the Festival and to make sure that the flyers reached the less obvious and less accessible nooks and crannies of Bristol's population. Once the initiative had gained a certain status and momentum, the local media also became interested and publicised the idea to an even wider audience. Thus, from a relatively small, but crucial, set of links, the Festival became a major event, galvanising many people to contribute in some way and to take part in an explicitly anti-racist activity, often within their own community.

Key aspects of networking that are relevant to relationship formation include modes of communication, building trust and managing diversity. The chapter considers how we use connections to:

- give and receive support;
- obtain and share resources;
- influence the behaviour and attitudes of those around us;
- anticipate and deal with conflicts.

What makes a good networker?

A theme that runs throughout this book is the skilled and strategic nature of networking. Like other aspects of community development it involves planning and evaluation. Preliminary research and preparation might be undertaken even before the initial contact, for example, making a conscious decision about whether to attend particular events on the basis of the likely participants. The community development workers on the research panel reported that they scanned the attendance lists to target useful contacts and used their knowledge to decide where to sit or which workshops to attend. They would consider how to present themselves (protocol, dress codes, use of jargon) and generally how to manage that crucial first impression. Clearly this needs sensitive judgements about other people's expectations or about what circumstances dictate as 'appropriate' behaviour.

Non-verbal communication provides important clues about other people's intentions and emotions. For example, an unknown colleague at a conference might be approached because they 'looked interesting', held a certain position or reacted in a particular way that caught the attention, such as laughing at something that had been said or making eye contact. The ensuing interaction fulfils at least three simultaneous functions: to establish rapport, to gain information about the other and to impart information about oneself. The conversation can be fairly informal and often takes place in a social setting, such as during a refreshment break or while travelling. Networking exploits opportunities that are incidental, but a necessary adjunct, to the 'main event'. Such interactions can be used to seek out common connections, and may involve a far-ranging series of conversational leads, including disclosure of personal matters:

> "What I tend to do is try and ask about the person, try and find out a bit about them and ask about their work or find something to talk about which perhaps isn't related to work, find some sort of common point that we could talk about." (TD)

The panellists felt that they generally adopted an informal style, without being or appearing casual. They engaged people in conversations around their likely interests, pitching and moderating their language accordingly, and used humour to put people at ease or when expressing a slightly ambivalent or unorthodox position. There was a strong sense that networking needed to involve convivial experiences, since most such interactions would be voluntary.

Panellists identified interpersonal skills as important and considered themselves as highly proficient in one-to-one interactions (where they referred to counselling-type techniques, such as listening and clarifying), as well as in group situations. Good networking involves accurate interpretations of individual conduct and group dynamics. It sometimes means intervening in situations to shape or open up interactions that are being distorted or blocked for one reason or another. Some of the relationships maintained might not be consciously selected, but develop anyway through reciprocal attention and care. Panellists made sure that they stayed in touch with certain colleagues at a personal level, even where the connection was predominantly work-related. This included phone calls, making time in conversations to share personal news and views, marking significant life events and generally arranging social time together:

> "I would offer help and support, would sort of make some space to have a bit of a personal chat as well as a kind of work chat, so like 'How are you? How's life? How's bla bla bla?' and then 'Oh well then so what's this about?', or at the end of the conversation after we dealt with the business, you sort of say 'Well, how are things going for you then?'" (FB)

Networking requires an ability to operate appropriately in different organisational and cultural settings using the agility and adaptive capacities of a chameleon (Trevillion, 1992, 1999). Good networkers need to be able to interpret and transmit information across boundaries, directing it in appropriate formats to where it might be useful. Flexibility and informality appear to be significant qualities, an important point for people accustomed to working in bureaucratic environments. What seemed to characterise people's aptitude for networking was not so much specific tactics, but the versatility with which people were able to use them to develop their connections with a wide range of people. Good networkers are able to communicate effectively in a variety of modes, using a broad repertoire of communication styles ranging from formal report-writing right through to the subtleties of cross–cultural body language.

The community development worker finds out about community concerns, hears about developments through informal chats and is able to pass this information on to others. People's willingness to engage in conversation is affected by a number of factors, not least whether they like and trust the other person. Networking allows people to shift between roles while maintaining a clear identity and sound ideological base. The panellists were convinced that their ability to form relationships was about being 'straightforward', neither having nor colluding with 'hidden agendas'. They felt that others saw them as honest, trustworthy, reliable and sincere. They found people confided in them readily and seemed to respect their advice. They described themselves as approachable, using words like 'popular', 'charming', 'sociable', 'extrovert' and 'comfortable'.

The community development workers in the Panel Study were able to identify personal qualities that they felt enhanced their networking. These attributes can be clustered according to the table overleaf.

Personality traits seem to have a significant impact on networking ability. This includes a commitment to perceive and value the whole person, showing interest, empathy and attention. Remembering personal details about individuals and their families, and making genuine efforts to understand different points of view, helps to build respect within a relationship. Good networkers make a positive contribution at a psychological as well as a practical level. Being optimistic and reliable helps to maintain morale, while following through on offers and commitments is vital to sustaining relationships. A good networker is oriented towards other individuals, seeks affiliations but values autonomy, is non–deferential and tends to be less tolerant of formal organisational constraints.

Table 5.1: Networking qualities

Affability	Warmth, compassion, empathy, humanity, gregariousness, responsiveness, attentiveness
Integrity	Self-aware, trustworthy, reliable, realistic, honest, open in dealings with others, respecting confidentiality
Audacity	Relishing change and innovation, prepared to challenge authority, take risks and break rules
Adaptability	Tolerant of differences, enjoying cultural diversity, flexible, non-judgemental, open to criticism
Tenacity	Patient, persistent, being comfortable with uncertainty and stress

In community development, effective networkers exhibit many of the attributes that predict transformational leadership: self-esteem, consideration for others and intuitive thinking. They provide leadership and show entrepreneurial flair, but without (apparently) the drive for personal ambition or profit. Networkers need to be able and willing to defy conventions, break bureaucratic rules, operate effectively in unfamiliar (social) territory and establish personal connections swiftly and smoothly. Informal networking necessarily takes place 'off-stage', making contacts and giving encouragement in order to manoeuvre others into the limelight or into positions of influence. It is unusual to claim credit for such interventions and, consequently, the value of this work has often been overlooked.

Establishing contact and forming relationships

Not everyone is capable of managing large social networks, and not everyone wants to. There are costs to offset against the benefits, and some people are more adept at maintaining this balance. Relationships are sustained through opportunity, common interests and social skills. The range and nature of social networks are affected by a number of factors, including class, gender, life roles and ethnicity. Non-family relationships progress through various stages, passing from initial acquaintance through to any number of potential endings. People adopt different strategies to express and consolidate affinity and learn, usually from direct experience, the skills involved in managing social interaction. In extensive studies of relationship formation, Duck (1992) demonstrated the importance of communication in regulating the social processes of adaptation and exchange. The transition from acquaintanceship to friendship involves strategic use of self-disclosure, sharing information about oneself and testing out levels of likeness (Fehr, 1996). The significance of 'everyday chit-chat' lies in the processes of mutual discovery and bonding, through which credibility is established, attitudes are explored and uncertainties about the 'other' are reduced until those involved feel that they know each other and have a certain sense of obligation.

Many theories of relationships are based on examining how these move through different phases while remaining balanced for reciprocity. Different abilities are needed to manage relationships during these different phases. People need to recognise and take advantage of opportunities to form relationships. They need strategies for encouraging likeable or useful people into their personal ambit, based on an understanding of how relationships might evolve. They also need social skills to maintain and repair relationships during periods of conflict or adversity. Good networking requires self-awareness, strategies for self-presentation and skills in establishing rapport in a range of situations.

While networking techniques are usually conscious (identifying useful connections, responding to gaps in the web and so on), the actual processes of building relationships should be emotionally authentic, otherwise the links are perceived as ingratiating and worthless. Non-verbal cues are crucial, especially in the initial stages. Thus using the telephone is preferable to letter writing, probably because more can be discerned about someone from their tone of voice. Face-to-face interaction allows communication of emotional signals through body language, such as smiles, shrugs and posture. Good networkers will pay close attention to the paralinguistic dynamics of meetings and group interactions:

> "Why is it I can go into some situations and the vibes tell me to be cautious? Nobody's really said anything, nobody's done anything to make me think that, but there's just a look, an action ... and you just think be steady in this situation." (LM)

Although they are more time-consuming, face-to-face interactions featured strongly in panellists' descriptions of networking. These seemed to accelerate and enhance the development of personal relationships and commitments. Direct encounters often demand one's full attention and this usually makes the connection more memorable:

> "I'm very aware of that and I think that all those things
> happen at the first meeting. It's almost inevitable that we'll
> have made a relationship and sometimes that's far more
> important than the actual business." (KT)

Non-verbal communication was regarded as important in consolidating
relationships and interpreting responses:

> "You're talking about whether or not people have eye
> contact through conversations, simple things like that or
> whether or not you're making judgements on the basis
> of personal behaviour, whether a person smiles, whether
> a person looks confused, whether a person looks happy,
> or whatever, there are a whole range of judgements there,
> about our personal effectiveness." (CT)

In the course of routine work arrangements, panellists recounted how
they would go out of their way to make occasional face-to-face contact,
even where this was not necessarily the most convenient or 'efficient'
mode of communication. Several expressed a preference for this form
of communication and sometimes made an effort to visit someone in
person, rather than communicate by phone or by post:

> "Last week I decided to consciously hand deliver to
> somebody a piece of paper that I could easily have put in
> the internal mail ... I could have put it in an envelope, and
> I thought, no I'll walk across to that particular office with
> it because I'll be able to say 'Hello' to whoever's in that
> office and just pick up on the gossip and news. That's quite
> a pleasant thing to do, but it also just nurtures in their minds
> the existence of the work that I do." (MW)

Others made a habit of 'popping into' or 'hanging around' places where
there was a high probability of meeting people with whom they needed
to maintain links. One panellist described how she would occasionally
drive home through a particular area in the hope of "catching a wave"
(LM) with residents there, and possibly even stopping for a chat. Others
described how they deliberately structured their work so as to be 'out
and about':

> "I'm not office based, I don't sit behind a desk every day, I
> make phone calls, I'm proactive, I go out of my way to go

and see people regularly, whether it's sitting having a cup of tea in someone's home, being invited to do that, whether it's making a prior appointment to go and do that, or it's because somebody has made a particular point of contact and I've responded by saying 'Yes, I'll meet you'." (CT)

Panellists described how they made themselves 'ubiquitous', 'accessible', 'welcoming' and 'friendly' and were extremely flexible in how they did this. Living locally was an advantage, but other strategies mentioned were 'having lunch in different places', walking between appointments where possible and generally using the same amenities (shops, pubs, transport and so on) as the community members they wanted to network with. This approach creates possibilities of meeting people in ways that were neither intrusive nor overly formal. It is about being in the right place at approximately the right time, and then making good use of whatever encounters happen to occur. This is clearly strategic in that it involves knowledge about local customs and habits and good planning, but also responding serendipitously to opportunities as they arise.

Box 5.2: Two-wheeled neighbourhood networking

"As a neighbourhood community development worker I made a point of delivering letters to local community members by hand, usually cycling around the area to do this and often stopping for a chat if I happened to bump into someone who I knew was involved in some group or activities. When there were events or jobs to publicise, I went round the shops, the health centre, schools and offices of voluntary organisations and local statutory agencies to put up posters and leave copies of our newsletter. Invariably these trips would lead to conversations with people I hadn't encountered before, creating new connections and occasionally recruiting new activists and volunteers for our community organisation. Although this 'outreach' strategy was considerably more labour intensive than simply posting the letters or leaflets, I felt it was worth the time and effort because it got me out of the Community Centre and ensured that my networks were constantly refreshed and extended to include people who might not otherwise have come into the building. Cycling, rather than driving or walking, offered a good compromise between getting around and being able to stop easily." (author)

Making contact sometimes involves being quite audacious, for example 'buttonholing' a comparative stranger from the crowd of potential contacts and then rendering the connection memorable and pleasant, so that the other person also has an incentive to continue with it. Studies of effective management and leadership identify important personal qualities, such as vigilance in processing information about the social environment and sensitivity to the feelings of others. Experience suggests that face-to-face encounters and gatherings are crucial to establish a valid connection between people, probably because they allow a more accurate understanding of what people *really* think and feel. Community development workers need to be sensitive to these aspects of collective behaviour because they often have to make decisions about their own interventions.

Networking requires both analytical and intuitive thinking. It involves an awareness of how people are relating to each other and identifying potential areas of compatibility or friction. This sensitivity is sometimes referred to as intuition and seems to be an important quality for community development. In an early exploration of the community work role, Williams (1973, p 3) advocates the use of an "imaginative sixth sense" when "playing the networks". Many of the panellists felt that their ability to form appropriate links and relationships was based on 'hunches' about what was going on in social situations. It has been suggested that intuitive judgements are one of the characteristics of expert performance, which use learning from previous similar experiences but unfortunately are largely inaccessible to technical analysis (Dreyfus and Dreyfus, 1986). At the heart of professional practice lies an "ineffable knack" that defies measurement and description (Heron, 1996, p 112). The ability to perceive and activate potential connections is one of the 'knacks' of networking. Just as experienced chess players perceive the position of pieces on the board differently from novices (de Groot, 1965), so expert networkers are able to make rapid and sophisticated appraisals of complex and dynamic processes from their observations of informal interactions. These abilities and insights are not developed overnight, but through experience and reflection.

Maintaining and using connections

A crucial but sometimes neglected aspect of networking is the need to maintain mutuality in relationships. This does not necessarily mean that within each and every transaction there has to be an equal balance of give and take, as this is not always possible. Rather it is more about maintaining an overall perception (within the network) that nobody is in charge and that nobody is freeloading. Voluntary relationships tend to be sustained if they are based on fair and equivalent levels of exchange. For individuals, the cost of maintaining the connection has to be more or less balanced by the benefits and there should be a rough reciprocity among those involved. Relationships that lack this balance eventually dissipate or are deliberately terminated.

Although not every contact might prove immediately or obviously useful, nevertheless information about it should be retained. When a link can be established and appears fruitful, it needs to be nurtured. This should not be left to chance. Business cards and leaflets can be exchanged and definite arrangements made to meet again. Alternatively, a way would be devised to consolidate the encounter with some form of contact. This might appear fortuitous, such as noticing and sending a magazine article or hyperlink that would be of interest to the other party:

> "My follow up is to ask them questions and to listen to find out what their interests are, what are their needs, to note them internally and sometimes on paper. I then find that I can follow those up. Whatever people tell you, there's some kind of reverse Sod's Law. If they are interested in matchboxes there'll be an article on matchboxes in your tray or newspaper, in no time at all and so I'm able to follow that up with something concrete." (KT)

Others talked about finding ways of demonstrating a genuine commitment to the other person's well-being or work. Equally they might arrange to be somewhere where they were likely to 'bump into' that person:

> "And if it's something about grassroots level within the community, then ... I would go out of my way to be in a place where that person was if I wanted to continue those links. I mean it may be just something simple like a coffee morning I know they always attend, or [that] they always go round to the shops at a certain time. If I needed to see that person and I wanted to build up the links with them to be the secretary of a particular group or something like that, I would go round it that way, sort of plan my actions but it appears casual." (LM)

Building trust, taking risks

Relationships do not just happen and often involve elements of risk. Learning to trust another person entails being prepared to rely on their judgement and actions. An expectation develops that their behaviour and motivations will be more or less consistent and reciprocal. Gifts and favours express mutual attraction and/or obligation, and provide the vital interchange for voluntary relationships (Fischer, 1982; Werbner, 1990). A balance between the parties involved is usually maintained informally, and not necessarily through material transactions. Conviviality (pleasure, humour, fun) and empathy are valued in themselves, and form the basis for a generalised social relationship whose key components are "trust, reciprocity, altruism, commitment, sacrifice, tolerance, understanding, concern, solidarity and inter-dependence" (Twine, 1994, p 32). Even apparently superficial courtesy represents an acknowledgement that our lives are connected; that our actions have an impact and that the feelings and behaviour of other people are likely to be influenced by what we do or say.

This is illustrated by an initiative in Port Philip, a suburb of Melbourne (Australia), which found that proactively smiling at people on the street increased people's sense of well-being and reduced their fear of crime, as well as increasing the overall levels of smiling amongst strangers, engendering a sense of civil connectedness (Singer, 2007). Similarly, an experiment that gave people a trivial lucky experience (such as finding a coin in a phone box) found that this increased the likelihood that they would assist a stranger in the next few minutes (Isen and Levin, 1972). Generating a good mood appears to predispose more altruistic behaviour and a more communal orientation, even when based on only fleeting encounters.

Relationships are risky in that they involve both hazard (being let down or betrayed) and uncertainty. Relations of trust are important in mediating risk and are a necessary precondition to the exercise of collective power. Trust is developed over time and is renewed rather than eroded through use. It is cultivated in civil society through active, reliable and mutually beneficial co-operation. Between individuals this creates the basis for friendship and neighbourliness. At the community level it translates into shared conventions or social norms that regulate interaction and promote co-operation.

These unwritten mini-social contracts are created and maintained mainly through face-to-face interactions. They allow us to make decisions about whether or not to engage in collective action when it is possible neither to control the outcome, nor even to predict what it might be. Trust was a theme that emerged strongly in both research studies. The Bristol Festival Against Racism was made possible because the key protagonists had built up good reputations within the relevant networks and could be trusted to deliver what they were promising. Stakeholders were willing to contribute to the initiative because they believed their money, energy and effort would be used to good effect. They were prepared to commit organisational resources and their own credibility to what at the time was a fairly risky venture, both politically and in terms of its sustainability. For the panellists, trust had a number of interlocking components. It involved fulfilling commitments and being frank about one's own role and motives:

> "I think the openness is important because the process of networking is carried by people building up trust and relationships between each other. People can suss you out if you say something you don't believe, they know that, and if you say something that you do believe they know that as well. Because they see you in a lot of different circumstances and they see you in different kinds of meetings, they bump into you in the street, they see you at informal meetings, they'll see you making a report to a council committee, and the same message, the same agenda, might be expressed in different tones of voice in the different settings. But it can ring true whether or not you're saying the same thing in those different ways and the different settings to people. It gets back to people.... I think you build up trust with people if you're straight with them about what's possible, what you think, what you disagree with, not promising things that you can't deliver." (MW)

Benefits and limitations

Once established, networks allow people to cut across organisational boundaries and gain access to resources, expertise and advice. This enables problems to be solved quickly and without going through official procedures. Informal and reliable contacts save time and effort because they can be used to request or negotiate support, especially funding, more easily, and to link individuals into relevant groups. Personal contacts also provide access to external professional guidance for specific pieces of work, for example in relation to legislation and grant applications. Reciprocal working relationships develop through regular participation in relevant events and activities; using contacts to build up interdependence by "giving as much as I receive", as one person (KT) put it. This includes offering knowledge and advice, as well as simply sharing information and skills. There were many forms and levels of co-operation referred to in the interviews. People are able to avoid formal procedures by calling in favours:

> "trading in kind rather than having to account for them [which gives] flexibility ... anything that doesn't have to go through the accountants." (GrS)

This seems to be especially necessary for workers in the voluntary and community sector, and may represent a covert redistribution of resources between statutory or intermediary agencies and smaller community groups. It is the personal aspects of relationships that ease the processes of multi-agency working. These allow people to move through and beyond the formal bureaucratic procedures to establish genuine mutuality, rather than 'paper' partnerships. People use their networks to cross organisational boundaries to solve short-term problems and to develop a collective response to common issues. Co-operation need not always imply direct collaboration. It may simply be about making sure that activities augment or complement each other. Networking with other organisations is useful for ascertaining the current 'state of play' and adjusting one's plans accordingly, for example to avoid competition for funding:

> "We contacted other people doing a similar sort of bid; not to pinch what they were doing, but to find out what their experience was and what their particular need was. We wanted to ensure that we weren't all making the same competitive bid which could penalise all of us." (JM)

Helpful connections can be nurtured, avoiding unnecessary (and wasteful) rivalries. Multi-agency partnerships and intermediary bodies are important in providing opportunities for this kind of co-ordination. As we saw in Chapter One, networking is a natural and ancient process that has made humans successful co-operators. Like any aspect of behaviour, it gets better through practice and can be used for personal or collective benefit. Within the context of community development, networking underpins all forms of community activity and should be seen within the framework of values set out in Chapter Two. However, networking can also be a self-promoting, manipulative and superficial way of getting ahead in life through the use (and abuse) of contacts by 'schmoozing' and 'name-dropping' for personal gain. Community development workers need to be alert to these tendencies and adopt strategies to counter them. Networks in themselves do not guarantee improved decision-making or better access to information. Their informal nature and lack of mechanisms for resolving conflict or ensuring a balanced representation means that their activities are frequently unaccountable and exclusive. If left to their own devices, recruitment and communication within networks may become biased towards those 'in the know' or whose 'face fits', while those who might bring a different perspective may be surreptitiously, but systematically, bypassed. Networking usually relies on informal processes and personal perceptions. These are based on local conventions, which in turn reflect the convenience and comfort of those already involved. Networks can reinforce prejudices and elitist practices when they operate predominantly on the basis of cliques, rumour and coincidence. A proactive and strategic approach is needed for community development workers, using what Newman and Geddes (2001) call 'positive networking' to ensure social inclusion within partnerships. It is here that community development, with its core values of equality and participation, can play a role in creating and maintaining accessible and diverse networks.

Relationships as women's work?

Networking demands a complex range of capabilities, covering social, political and administrative skills. In addition it needs an appreciation of the social context and a willingness to intervene actively in order to assist other people to make their own relationships. In many informal networks there often seems to be one individual who keeps in touch with the others, who arranges get-togethers, has up-to-date news and contact details, and generally ensures that everyone stays on more or less good terms. In families this role is often played by women, and there is evidence that women's emotional labour creates and maintains networks within other social settings, such as the workplace or within communities (Innerarity, 2003; Bruegel, 2005).

In the community development literature, networking has been referred to as a 'womanly' way of operating (for example, Dominelli, 1995; Bryant, 1997). Studies have frequently commented on the role played by women in neighbouring and informal networks (Bourke, 1994), running voluntary and community activities (Doucet, 2000; Krishnamurthy et al, 2001), participating in regeneration partnerships (May, 1997), sustaining self-help groups, building inclusive political coalitions (Fearon, 1999) and generally keeping the peace (Kolb, 1992). More controversially, Stackman and Pinder argue in their study (1999) that gender differences appear in men's and women's work-based networks with the latter being more 'expressive' and based on relatively intense emotional ties, while men tend to cultivate fewer, but more instrumental, links with colleagues. This chimes with Ferree's (1992) view that women tend to derive their motivation and identity from the web of attachments in which they are embedded.

Whatever one's position on the importance of gender in the range of skills and experience that underpin networking, it is clear that these abilities can be learned through observation and experience. Everyone can become more skilled and strategic in their networking. While women may not be *necessarily* or *instinctively* better networkers, it can nevertheless be argued that this work of building, maintaining and mending relationships should be valued more. As we shall see in Chapter Eight, networking abilities are acquired in complex ways: from role models, practice situations and, possibly, formal training courses. Simply being more aware of techniques, traits and tendencies that support effective networking will encourage people to adopt this approach more explicitly in their community development work.

Conclusions

This chapter has indicated the key elements and tactics for successful and sustainable networking. It has emphasised the importance of interpersonal relationships and face-to-face interaction, arguing that the work involved in networking should be properly appreciated as contributing to the development of community capacity and effective partnerships. The next chapter examines the specific contribution that community development workers can make to these processes through assisting people to make connections that might otherwise prove difficult or fragile.

SIX

Networking for community development

You have to go by instinct and you have to be brave.
(From Anderson, 1995, *How to make an American quilt*)

Introduction

Interpersonal relationships within communities and between organisations need to be given greater significance to ensure that they are developed and maintained in ways that contribute to outcomes such as empowerment, cohesion and capacity building. Networking clearly involves both 'common' courtesy and good communication. It is about maintaining a web of relationships that can support a useful and empowering flow of information and influence. In particular, this chapter will examine how community development workers facilitate the networking of others, whether colleagues, partners, policy makers or members of the communities they work with. It looks at what community development workers actually do to establish and maintain connections that are useful to themselves and others, what aptitudes are required and what strategies are deployed in a networking approach to community development and how these might be improved. There will be particular emphasis on the creation and use of links that span organisational and community boundaries in order to promote partnership working, release social capital and foster community cohesion. The idea of meta-networking is introduced, looking at the role of community development workers in 'networking the networks' and in devising opportunities for people to meet and work together.

Community development often feels somewhat nebulous, creating capacity and cohesion from unpromising beginnings. Good networking practice requires planning and proficiency; and can therefore fairly be described as work. It supports collective organising and sustains mutual co-operation, especially during periods of dispute and demoralisation. Many of the difficulties and frustrations faced by community development workers derive from their position on the edges of organisations. They are 'everywhere and nowhere': marginalised, misunderstood and yet in constant demand as mediators between different agencies or groups. They 'network the networks', forming boundary-spanning links across which information and resources flow to where they can best be used. This role is rarely acknowledged, yet it is crucial to community development practice. Good community development workers act not as gatekeepers, but as signposts and springboards, helping people through the barriers and navigating 'safe' routes over unfamiliar or difficult terrain.

Networking as practice

The use of 'network' as a verb has quickly become a widely popularised term to describe all sorts of social encounters. It has inevitably produced its own parody in the question: 'Is it networking, or not working?' In recent years there has been a sea change in the use of the term and networking has been increasingly recognised as a vital aspect of community development work (see Taylor et al, 2000; Wilson and Wilde, 2001; Henderson and Thomas, 2002; Gilchrist with Rauf, 2005). In recent years, job adverts and person specifications have frequently included 'networking skills' as a requirement, and posts have been created specifically to develop, co-ordinate and manage networks, indicating the value attached to this way of working, especially within the voluntary sector.

Box 6.1: Canada – Sharing Strengths

A group of child and youth health practitioners in Nova Scotia worked together with 11 separate communities in the province using a community development approach to build capacity to support communities to participate in health planning and to devise a number of practical initiatives to measure community capacity, promote youth resilience and establish an inter-sectoral working group.

Despite its lack of core funding, the Sharing Strengths project was able to establish good relations with communities, as well as with professionals in the health system. There was a particular emphasis on research: gathering data and evidence, including input from communities, to use in planning and evaluation. Regional and local events were organised to bring together those concerned with child and youth health from the Community Health Boards, local health service providers and communities themselves. This encouraged mutual learning based on different perspectives and experiences, rather than imposing a particular medical orthodoxy. An asset-based approach to community development was used, which valued the strengths and solutions to be found even within the most disadvantaged communities.

As a result of this networking, communication and co-operation improved between decision-makers in regional government departments, enhancing joint work on child and youth health and ensuring better co-ordination of initiatives.

Contacts: Cari Patterson (cari@horizonscda.ca) and Doug Crossman (dcrossman@ssdha.nshealth.ca)

In the Panel Study described in the previous chapter, interviews with the community development workers revealed the amazing vitality and richness of networking, with comments such as "absolutely central", "the start of everything", "the life and breath", the "sap" of community development, and "pretty vital to all of it". Networking was seen as a core process of community development, and also a key purpose:

> "Community development happens through networking ...
> the process of community development work is a process
> of developing relationships with people and encouraging
> people to build relationships with each other which are
> for the purpose of getting things done, but which will
> also have the benefit of educating people about the way
> in which they can best live together and to how they can
> best relate to sources of resources and power.... So the way
> you do community development work is through this kind
> of multi-directional process of relationship building which
> is networking.... It's essential. You couldn't do it without
> networking." (MW)

The community development workers in this study deliberately allocated time and effort to develop and maintain their networks:

> "I consciously in my own mental work plan, say that I must
> spend a certain proportion of my time networking and
> proactively setting up networks of different sorts." (GrS)

They were often tactical about who they formed links with, careful in their approaches to different people and conscientious in monitoring and maintaining connections. People acted with design and deliberation:

> "I'm strategic ... in the sense of almost making a list and saying 'Who do I need to pay attention to next?'; 'What network do I need to invest some of my time and energy into next?'" (MW)

Community development workers in the Panel Study took risks and were extremely proactive in making contact with others. But they were also pragmatic and opportunistic in their use of happenstance encounters and conversations. Networking was both serendipitous and strategic in the sense that the workers deliberately created or sought out occasions where they were likely to make useful connections. Panel members were skilful in their networking and versatile in applying different techniques in different situations. Responses to my interview questions often began with the phrase, "it depends ..." followed by a sophisticated appraisal of the context and purpose of interactions, including explanations of why one approach would be more appropriate and effective than another. Nevertheless, there was considerable agreement that effective networking involved certain core organisational skills, loosely clustered around communication, interpersonal relations and knowledge management.

Participation and leadership

Community and inter-agency networks can and should be vehicles for empowerment, affording greater access to decision-makers and facilitating the emergence of community leadership (Sullivan et al, 2006). It has been argued that the role of the leader in the 21st century is not to organise directly, but rather to inspire and connect people so that they gravitate towards exciting projects that solve problems through collaboration, rather than competition (Gratton, 2008). Perhaps this is a good model for the networking community leader or community development worker. Community development aims to empower disadvantaged people through collective self-organisation. Identifying allies and building coalitions around a common vision involves working across a range of different experiences and perspectives to find (or construct) a working consensus. This requires imagination and diplomacy. It is rarely a straightforward matter of aggregating the separate parts:

"It's really difficult but ... often those people with completely opposite values can actually develop a relationship because there might be some other common issue that they share and eventually the fact that they're a different colour or different sexuality doesn't matter.... They may have an interest in a piece of land that they didn't want to see destroyed and they work together on that." (TD)

Assisting people to 'self-organise' on the basis of a shared interest or oppression can be regarded as a legitimate form of consciousness-raising and empowerment. Networking is used to identify and to recruit individuals likely to be useful to collective ventures. 'Rising stars' are nurtured, volunteers are invited to take on more responsibilities and community members are cajoled into new roles as management committee members. This is particularly necessary in the early phases of developing a project or setting up a new organisation:

"We set up discussion meetings to which we invited people who we thought would be interested in the idea. Before and after those meetings we chatted people up ... and sold the idea to them, sometimes through letters, sometimes meeting people over coffee." (MW)

At community level, informal conversations support a constant process of matching interests, needs and enthusiasms. One-to-one work with individuals might be followed up with suggestions that they join a particular group:

"If I think it would be really good for them to be involved in that, I'd say to them, 'Oh you should know about this, this is the person to contact to invite you to the next meeting', and then I ring the person who I suggested they contact and say 'Oh I met so and so the other day and I've suggested they phone you, I think they would be really good to invite along to this next meeting'." (FB)

The 'grapevine' offers an efficient and far-reaching means of gathering participants for community activities. Social networks appear to be more effective than posters, leaflets and newsletters in mobilising people for collective action because of personal motivation and a sense of shared risk. However, it is important to use public forms of communication as well to ensure that information is openly available to everyone you might want to attract.

Networking can be used to lobby decision-makers around specific concerns and as a means of building people's capacity to influence decisions that affect them. Panellists admitted to using personal connections with policy makers to promote particular points of view, but they also saw their role as enabling other people to develop their own links with powerful bodies:

> "It's processes which empower people to be more able to voice their own views, to shape their own lives, their own organisations. That's the driving principle. So when you're networking ... the particular outcomes that I'm aiming for are things that I think will strengthen the ability of the local community to represent itself and to get resources for itself and to develop a relationship with big power agencies like the local state." (MW)

Community networks are a means of developing a collective, but not necessarily unanimous, voice through which different views and interests can be channelled. A more formal kind of networking is to create community forums that can be used as part of public consultation processes, although constant work is needed to make sure that these remain genuinely representative, transparent and accessible. Strategies for enhancing community engagement should include support for networks that create space for dialogue and dissent, not just for selecting and supporting community representatives. Genuine empowerment must be developed through support for communities to become better connected by strengthening and tapping into the informal networks that are the forerunners of civil society organisations, especially for new communities arriving as asylum seekers or economic migrants (Beirens et al, 2007; Theodore and Martin, 2007). Arts activities offer reassuring and inspiring ways for people to relate to each other and share their stories.

This poses particular challenges in areas of super-diversity or population fluidity where community development support can additionally be used to set up links between incoming communities and those in the public, private and third sectors who have power, resources and technical expertise (Blake et al, 2008).

Box 6.2: Sweet Freedom – singing asylum seekers

Asylum seekers fleeing intimidation and torture in many countries found refuge at a centre in Brisbane, Australia. While trying to establish new lives and livelihoods for themselves in their new homeland, songs became a way of expressing solidarity, nostalgia and hope. Workshops facilitated by friendly musicians helped the early ideas to take shape in lyrics and tunes, and eventually 12 songs were composed and produced as an album, 'Scattered people'.

The asylum seekers from South America, South East Asia, and northern Africa all had in common a deep commitment to countering oppressive regimes and standing up for human rights. Language barriers and cultural differences were inevitable difficulties but by focusing together on the creative process, the asylum seekers were able to convey their experience and promote their cause through developing a collective voice resonating across international networks of allies and friends.

Thanks to Brian Procopis, www.sweetfreedom.net

Meta-networking

In community development, good networking is about developing and managing a diverse array of contacts and relationships. Workers make judgements about how best to initiate and support useful links between themselves and others, and, more importantly, use these to help people make and maintain connections with each other. This latter function I have termed 'meta-networking' to indicate that it is about the work involved in supporting and transforming *other people's* networks. It represents an essential contribution to the development of the 'well-connected community' (Gilchrist, 1999, 2000). The concept of 'meta-networking' will be explored further in the concluding chapter, but for now the key components of effective meta-networking can be identified as:

- mapping the social and organisational landscape;
- initiating and maintaining interpersonal connections through referrals and introductions;
- creating spaces and opportunities for interaction and conversation;
- managing and monitoring relevant networks;

- anticipating and dealing with tensions within and between networks;
- encouraging and supporting participation in networks where there are obstacles or resistance;
- assisting in the development of structures and procedures that will ensure that networks are inclusive and sustainable.

Meta-networking is especially important if the social environment seems alien and fragmented or if people lack the confidence or the skills to initiate contact for themselves. This might be due to cultural differences, impairments, prejudices, power imbalances or perceived conflicts of interest. Community development workers can facilitate these processes by finding connections, challenging preconceptions, creating opportunities for shared activities and encouraging dialogue across apparent boundaries (Gilchrist, 2004). Many communities already have such people, the 'moving spirits' (Gibson, 1996) that people in villages and neighbourhoods look to for information and encouragement. These 'linkers' are vital assets within communities. They are often women and often operating below the public radar so can be overlooked by outside agencies (Fraser et al, 2003, pp 53–4). Community development workers need to identify and work with these individuals, rather than relying just on leaders who may be self-appointed or represent only one set of interests within a community.

Because meta-networking is about assisting the networking of others, it requires a working knowledge of shifting power dynamics and allegiances. Given current social inequalities, meta-networking also includes the use of positive action measures to overcome practical obstacles or oppressive attitudes (Gilchrist, 2007). The worker's own networks provide an 'intangible resource' that can be used to build 'bridges to participation' (Rees, 1991) and this means they must take care to ensure that these are as inclusive and diverse as possible.

Box 6.3: Local Links

The Local Links programme in West Yorkshire was developed by the UK organisation Common Purpose to encourage and enhance networking between key players within relatively small local areas, such as an urban district or small town. Selected individuals, each playing prominent roles in their communities or local services, were invited to a series of discussion meetings, where the group got to know one another, learnt more about local public affairs and had an opportunity to debate a variety of current issues. The project enabled people to share information and to build relationships across different sectors and between different sections of the community. A variety of methods were used to support the active participation of group members, including photography, walkabouts, story-telling, mapping, semi-structured dialogue and joint working on specific projects.

The programme was carefully designed to be inclusive and to build connections that would open up new opportunities for co-operation and overcome divisions, for example between young people and the older generation. Attention was also paid to 'reaching out' to those most difficult to engage in civic activities, as well as redressing power imbalances between 'the establishment' and those who wanted to challenge things a bit more. After a few months of meeting together on a regular and supported basis, participants reported that they were more knowledgeable, more confident about expressing themselves in public and had a better understanding of some of the more contentious local issues.

See Hay (2008).

One community development worker felt that it would be difficult to initiate effective collaboration

> "if there isn't the infrastructure of networking, if you don't know who is around and could usefully be involved in partnerships. Again I suppose it's the information and knowledge in the first place, then the personal contact." (GrS)

One of the major benefits of knowing how networks operate and having a mental map of the relations and attitudes of individual members, is the ability to channel information through certain people in order to influence decisions and enhance the likelihood of particular outcomes. In developing multi-agency working, it helps to know who in an organisation is likely to respond favourably to an invitation so that sympathetic individuals can be targeted within a larger bureaucracy in the hope that they would either contribute themselves or find a suitable alternative from among their own contacts:

> "I've got to try and get all the people there who I think should be, so then I would be quite strategic, suggesting specific people who would be useful to invite from specific

organisations.... Because if you just send a blank letter up
to the agency, the chance of anybody picking it up is kind
of minimal really." (FB)

Networking involves forethought, sensitivity and a thorough knowledge
of the context, including knowing how to engage someone's attention.
This is made more difficult in environments of short-term contracts,
caused by project funding, restructuring and low pay because people are
forced to change jobs frequently and often cannot continue working
with a community for long enough to properly build up their local
networks. Community development workers are often points of entry
to other networks or more formal systems. A personal link makes it
easier for people to access the specialist help they need:

> "I think referrals to be effective need more than information
> ... but there is no guarantee they'll follow it up. It's much
> better if you can say, 'Well I'll phone my mate Fred and say
> that you're here and while I'm on the phone you can make
> an appointment to go and see him', or whatever, and in
> some cases with particular sorts of people it's actually better
> to go along with them." (GrS)

Importance of informality

In community development, as in life itself, the formal and the
informal are inextricably and symbiotically enmeshed (Misztal, 2000).
Networks operate through informal interactions and this is key to their
effectiveness. Formal events can be useful for networking, not primarily
because of the items on the agenda, but in order to obtain contacts
and advice. The discussions 'around the edge' of the meetings are often
more productive than the main business and are a way of exploring
how people stand on different issues. Equally, meetings are occasions
for fostering links in the professional network and maintaining one's
profile. Even in these formal situations, humour and informal remarks
are used to reveal paradoxes, ambiguities or potential resistance.
Network gatherings are usually characterised by an informality that
allows people to talk directly across organisational and status boundaries
on a seemingly more equal basis. The absence of formal structures and
procedures allows people to be candid in their comments. This was
identified as a major advantage of one network's meetings:

"People have also said that they have been able to say what they would not [otherwise] be able to say ... because they're not seen as representing their organisation really, so they can say things about their own department that they wouldn't say in a formal situation perhaps." (PH)

The development of more personal relationships provides the durability and flexibility of many community-based organisations:

"I think it's at the informal level that you build up trust and real relationships ... It's not just people, ideas and resources ... the informal networking is absolutely crucial, not only because you need it in a practical sense but, I think, because it actually reflects community." (KT)

The Festival Against Racism illustrated how informality made it possible for participants and contributors to become involved on their own terms. This is important for community development, which relies on the voluntary engagement of community members. Informality encourages spontaneity and commitment while paradoxically creating a sense of security. People use their informal networks to check things out, and then are able to make a more informed decision. The situation feels less risky, reducing the sense of trepidation, and is experienced as empowering. One organiser described it thus:

"If the approach is informal, the person being approached can measure their involvement, whereas if it's some kind of formal invitation you either make a commitment or you don't, whereas if it's informal you can bargain around how much commitment there is. It doesn't feel difficult in an informal setting." (LC)

In organising the Festival Against Racism a lack of bureaucracy released people's initiative and imagination:

"People were not being regimented into any kind of structure I suppose ... I think that therefore people were able to be a lot more creative.... They could feel free and I think people tend to be a lot more responsive that way.... [They] didn't feel pressured. They felt trusted to come up with the right thing." (RS)

Informal methods of organising require less explicit commitment and provide easy escape routes. Such encounters allow people to explain, to elaborate and to explore what might have happened at a formal level. Informal interactions are used to clarify ambiguous or contrary interpretations of events:

> "People stay behind and talk to you and check out:'How do you think that went?','What went on?','Who said what?', 'How do you think ... ?'. I'm checking out, reviewing and evaluating what's going on, making sure I've been to the same meeting as everybody else. Checking out what's happening." (GaS)

Conversations held at intersections and exits, where people have easy routes and excuses to depart, can often be the most interesting, probably because people feel they can take risks with what they reveal. They may take place at the corners of streets or at the end of shared journeys, when the pending 'escape' encourages the sharing of confidences and heretical ideas. I have called these 'threshold' or 'crossroad' conversations because that is where they often take place in a physical sense, but because they can also lead to shifts in people's thinking, activities and relationships. A good networker will make use of these opportunities as they can be rich in significance and trust.

Seemingly casual comments or encounters are often neither observed nor recorded, evading surveillance by the authorities. Consequently, these exchanges appear to be more sincere, revealing what others really think as opposed to the official 'line'. Subversive or downright bizarre views can be voiced, usually resulting in further contentious or creative discussion. Informal conversations are where news is exchanged about personnel changes, the results of funding applications or a chance to 'float' projects that are still only sketches on the mental drawing board. News of proposed policy changes travels through the 'grapevine', which allows them sometimes to be 'reformed' even before they are formulated.

Networking as information processing

Community development workers are important channels or relays in this communication lattice because they are in touch with many different groups. This is especially valuable around complex areas of knowledge or contentious issues, where a range of perspectives brings additional intelligence, insights and a broader understanding. Panellists were conscientious in using networks to convey information to where it could be useful, thinking about

> "how to use what knowledge I've got and pass it back, because I really do believe this thing about information is power and that's part of networking." (SM)

They noticed and passed on items of news, not always immediately but saving it for the right opportunity or person. Receiving and storing information is an important area of competence, notably asking questions and really listening to the answers so as to notice (and remember) potential connections:

> "Sometimes it's just storing that little bit of information away in my brain, and it might not be apparently of use to me at that time, but I am aware that sometime in the future it might be of use to me or someone else." (FB)

This aspect of networking practice ranges from simply transmitting information, through to convening and servicing network-type organisations. Community development workers are a resource that others use to obtain information. One community development worker referred to their role as a conduit through which information flowed, as well as acting as a databank for other groups and the media. They become a kind of human encyclopaedia of local knowledge, "a walk-in file index" as one person (FB) described herself, but one which functions actively as a key node in a vast communication system. Good administration is a neglected aspect of effective networking; using notebooks, filing systems, card index boxes, diaries and address books to keep records and contact details. Computer programs such as Microsoft's Outlook or Access database can be helpful but are only useful storage systems if the information held in them is accurate and retrievable.

Obviously there are limits to the amount of information one person can be responsible for, so talking to colleagues and membership of various umbrella organisations are vital for staying up to date with the latest issues and news. Making time to read the relevant minutes, newsletters and periodicals is also important, although being on dozens of mailing lists can result in information overload, particularly in these days of computer-mediated communication when every other e-mail seems to offer yet another set of facts, opinions, requests and invitations to be assimilated or declined. Information can sometimes seem too much of a good thing.

Widening horizons

Informal networks are a source of inspiration and challenge, supporting a continuous flow of information and opinions. They enable people to gain an overview of situations and debates, gather useful insights, establish the 'bigger picture' and identify disparities. Networking is a way of monitoring reputations and appraising the links between groups. This is helpful at an individual level and contributes to the construction of a communal model of the world that can be used to determine collective strategies for change. Networking enables community development workers to intervene directly in political or social processes, and to advise others on how these can be influenced:

> "You've kind of got a sense of where people fit on the map of networks and you have a sense of where you fit ... you gradually build it up and you hear different and contradictory things from different people and you form your own judgements. So it's a gradual process of becoming part of that landscape of relationships, networks and power dynamics." (MW)

For community members, networking extends horizons and broadens perspectives, enabling people to gain an overview of the (policy) context and develop a broader understanding of issues. Networking enables people to stay in touch with changes in the organisational field, as well as the dynamics of community politics. It is especially useful for obtaining unofficial views to compare with the public pronouncements.

Exchange visits between similar organisations encourage the transfer of ideas and learning from one community to another, so that they do not need to 'start from scratch' in setting up a project. This means that groups are

> "not inventing the wheel all the time. Somebody has done something, they can learn from that, they can learn from other people's mistakes so they don't make the same mistakes, they can go one step further." (PH)

Groups discover that local difficulties may be part of a broader problem that neighbouring communities are also facing:

"I try and keep in mind that we've got to learn from other people's experience, locally and wider. Keeping ideas coming; and of course that's key and crucial to networking anyway. It's one of the purposes of getting as broad a spectrum of experience together as possible so that you can compare, contrast and learn." (KT)

This is recognised in the increasing popularity of learning exchanges or 'communities of practice' set up to support the implementation and review of policy initiatives. There are regional forums for practitioners and policy officers involved in cohesion work and a national network for community development workers engaged in the Department of Health's Delivering Race Equality in Mental Health programme. These operate through e-groups as well as meeting periodically face-to-face. Participants report that they are useful, though they are yet to be systematically evaluated.

Negotiating diversity

Although difference brings complications and challenges, it provides dynamic opportunities for comparison and debate. It promotes greater levels of satisfaction for those involved and has benefits for collective problem-solving. A major role for the community development worker involves convening and servicing groups which bring together individuals across organisational and identity boundaries to develop 'critical alliances' (Ledwith and Asgill, 2000). Such coalitions recognise and respect differences but nonetheless are able to find sufficient temporary alignment to tackle a common grievance or achieve a shared goal. As well as identifying areas of common interest between groups and between individuals, networking ensures that community members have access to a range of views, skills and knowledge. This may involve some ingenuity and a certain amount of risk in bringing together experiences that could be mutually challenging.

Building bridges across perceived community or organisational boundaries is a first step in generating a dialogue, which might eventually break down barriers of fear, prejudice and antipathy. Networking creates occasions and spaces where people can learn from one another to develop greater tolerance and understanding (Bailey and Jones, 2006; Chauhan, 2009). Judicious assessments may be needed about when and how to bring people together in situations that match their level of comprehension and commitment, and when to withdraw so that people can manage their own interactions. A major aspect of community development practice involves supporting communication and co-operation across psychological edges and organisational boundaries. This may include direct introductions at pre-arranged meetings or visits. It might involve accompanying people to events and assisting them to make contact with those who might be useful to them by

> "trying to break the ice between people ... making connections between people and convince them that talking to a particular person is a good idea.... I'll encourage people to come to a meeting perhaps because I know that somebody else is going to be at that meeting that they could make use of so it's generally not just a 'spur of the moment' thing." (PH)

Networking inevitably reflects personal interests and prevailing dynamics so networks easily become exclusive and cliquey. Community development workers should use anti-oppressive practice to reduce practical barriers and political biases, and to support the contributions of people who are less confident or articulate. One panellist described how she would accompany people from the community on their first attendance at a formal gathering:

> "That does happen more in the Asian community ... or young people maybe. They would ask to come along with me ... just to give them a bit of confidence really. I mean when I'm there, I don't hold hands with somebody all day. I mean I would deliberately not do that. I would find an excuse to move out the way, and give the people their own space." (LM)

Networking is not simply about cross-validation and corroboration. Panellists actively sought out views that would challenge their own interpretations by meeting with people in other organisations or from different backgrounds. If connections with like-minded people are important elements in the network, so also are those that bring difference and dissent. As John Stuart Mill remarked over a century and a half ago, "It is hardly possible to over-rate the value of bringing human beings together with people dissimilar to themselves ... it is one of the primary sources of progress" (1848, p 581). It is precisely these links that require more effort, more diplomacy and more imagination. This is where the *work* of networking takes place: setting up and maintaining the links between different (and sometimes antagonistic) sections of society. Marginalised sections of the community may need additional or alternative strategies in order to connect them into existing networks, and this may mean challenging or circumnavigating dominant interests and cultures. One panellist explained, for example:

> "the homeless, the poor, the elderly, black ethnic minorities, women, children, elderly people, people with disabilities and mental health, new people to an area, for instance. So you're trying to take all of those on board. Sometimes it is noting in a network that I'm in that they're *not* there. Sometimes it is so that the network can get them in but sometimes it is just reminding ourselves that we need to also do something else. We need to go out and talk to these people, as well as the valuable work we've done in the network because it's not always possible to get them into a network." (KT)

Drawing in new perspectives seems to be particularly crucial in this respect. Community development workers used connections outside the immediate arena of their work to inject fresh, sometimes challenging, ideas. One community youth worker on the Panel justified her decision to become involved in other projects beyond the remit of her job thus:

> "There is no doubt that [this experience] benefited the community of young people because they then got input that they would never have got if I'd stayed as a peripheral suburban youth worker, not networked into inner-city projects and current political thinking and stuff like that.... If networking brings something new then it has to be a good thing, even if it's a different perspective and ... that is a product of having bothered to go out of your usual circle." (SM)

Another panellist contrasted the outlooks of two clubs for older people, only one of which was prepared to make links beyond their immediate membership. Its members

> "are prepared to listen to others, to learn from others, to contribute themselves, so it's a two-way thing which makes this communication important.... This need to want to listen to others, to improve not just the thing you're involved in

but your knowledge of things generally and have a wider look. Is networking really just a wider look on things?" (LM)

As a result of their links with other bodies, such groups become more adaptable and improve their chances of survival in an unpredictable funding climate, especially where there is increasingly an expectation that organisations will work in partnerships and mergers are actively encouraged (Harrow and Bogdanova, 2006). Good meta-networking involves a capacity to communicate across a range of different cultures and perspectives:

"The fact that I've got a multi-disciplinary background helps me in a practical sense of being able to anticipate but I think more important is the theory that not everybody understands the same thing from the same set of words or concepts and having that in mind is really helpful when it comes to mediating. It leaves me open. I don't make a judgement." (KT)

Mediating conflict

Getting people to work together who have different cultures, interests and social status is fraught with difficulties and tensions. Networks can be used to manage that plurality in very positive ways by building personal links and mediating between factions to overcome dogma and intransigence. It helps to demonstrate interest in other people and curiosity about different lives and cultures. Good networking values diversity and deliberately seeks out experiences that will educate and challenge. Networking is used to mediate, translate and interpret between people and agencies that are not in direct or clear communication with one another. Community development workers are frequently invited to act as intermediaries between opposing parties, using their role to find common ground. If their relationships are robust and authentic, then disagreements may be dealt with amicably and effectively. Conflict can be anticipated and averted or handled informally. Disputes often erupt in communal facilities where people want to use the same space for different purposes. Tensions run high and this seems to be particularly the case when young people are involved. One panellist described how she was able to contain the antisocial behaviour of local young people by relating to them personally. It was a "huge advantage because I know them [the teenagers] by their names ... especially if they're the kids that also can cause quite a lot of trouble....The fact that they're not anonymous actually makes an enormous amount of difference, and also working with the detached youth workers makes a lot of difference.... [The kids] know that their behaviour is what we do not like, it is not them." (FB)

Informal discussions are often useful in addressing controversies before they become confrontational or require that one party retreats from their chosen position:

"If there is another point of view which they have not taken account of....You have to talk to people about that as well. So in that networking ... it's the place where differences of agendas, differences of opinion ... get had out." (MW)

In order to co-operate, organisations must acknowledge competing interests or divergent ideologies. There may be differentials in power and perceived ownership that the community development workers have to be aware of and seek to minimise.

Diversity also creates the possibility of innovative combinations and adaptations:

"Collective, collaborative action [is] a means to solve problems, to make changes. It's just being open to finding the new. This is what's exciting about having a mixed community. It sets problems when new people come in and there's a mix but one of the good things is that you might come up with new solutions because of that." (KT)

Where disputes exist or are anticipated, it is vital to create a 'safe space' for discussing contentious issues and for members to have the opportunity to get to know one another personally. The experience of cross-community working in Northern Ireland and other situations torn by sectarian or ethnic divisions demonstrates the value of trust and informal relationships in peace-building and conflict resolution (Harbor et al, 1996; Kuzwe, 1998; Veale, 2000). Tensions are inevitable within and between communities, but they can generate an important impetus for learning and transformation:

"I really genuinely believe that conflict is a really healthy thing ... for two reasons. I abide by that statement that says 'From conflict breeds consciousness', but also because in my experience if you constantly live your life with people of the same values and shared vision then you never tighten up your arguments." (SM)

In community development it is often necessary to challenge existing practices and assumptions. Networkers can use their informal connections to 'grasp the nettle', asking awkward questions or giving constructive criticism. Personal networks are an effective, but occasionally risky, way of circumventing bureaucratic procedures, and undermining the rigidity of corporate culture.

Networking the networks

As well as maintaining their own links and relationships, panellists described an additional role of 'networking the networks':

"I think my networks work ... they are actually very diverse. There is some overlap with them but there isn't a very core tight-knit group. I'm sort of very conscious I'm the hub of lots of networks." (GrS)

Community development workers deliberately and strategically maintain their involvement in a number of networks, adjusting the level of their participation to ensure that the range of connections reflects current and potential work priorities:

"Networking the networks has become very much my job, initially by default – it had to be done like that ... linking past, present and future, these things are always very important to me but implicit rather than explicit.... I think I'm always bringing a broad overview." (KT)

Community development workers often play a vital role in setting up and co-ordinating umbrella bodies that bring together people and projects operating across a variety of settings and issues. Several panellists were active in convening and chairing such forums. They performed a 'behind the scenes' function: servicing meetings, maintaining membership lists, sending out mailings and providing a point of contact. Multi-agency networks facilitate exchange and discussion across organisational or geographic boundaries. Forums and federations and, to some extent, local associations (such as neighbourhood or parish councils) aim to represent different sections of a community and to articulate a particular perspective possibly to another co-ordinating body, such as a cross-sectoral partnership.

In Britain, it has been found that community development workers play crucial roles in supporting interface connections between communities and local government offices and politicians, thereby enhancing democracy and civic participation (Bowles, 2008). This aspect of community development, strengthening the links between communities and external resources, is an essential component for both empowerment and engagement (Kubisch et al, 2002; CDF, 2008b). Informal networks create opportunities for people to link up with others who may have different interests and various identities and yet share some kind of common values or purpose (Brah, 2007). Their ability to function effectively is determined by the quantity and quality of both internal and external connections.

Conclusions

Much of the literature on community, organisations and networking highlights the importance of one-to-one personal relationships, developed at the micro-level of interpersonal skills or at the macro-level of structure and agency. Less has been written about the meso-level of collective activity: establishing and managing effective networks that can be used for a variety of purposes, including collective problem-solving, resource mobilisation, organisation development and social change. Traditionally community development has emphasised the role of the professional in establishing groups and organisations with specific aims and activities. The idea of meta-networking as a core function shifts the focus of practice away from formal arrangements to encompass more informal processes. It is another way of looking at the well-rehearsed arguments about the balance between 'goal' and 'process'. Meta-networking creates and maintains linkages within complex and dynamic situations that enable new organisational arrangements to emerge, through processes of adaptation and evolution, in response to changing circumstances. These ideas of emergence and complexity will become important themes in the next chapter, which sets out a model of community development as helping communities to operate as complex systems of interactions poised at the 'edge of chaos'. The final chapters explore the implications of this for policy and practice.

SEVEN

Complexity and the well-connected community

One must have chaos inside oneself in order to give birth to a dancing star. (Nietzsche, 1878, p 9)

Networking can be used to develop the 'well-connected community' but why are networks such a ubiquitous aspect of community life? We have seen that networks are especially effective modes of organisation in managing changing and complex situations. They are based on relationships, not simply connections, which are sustained through interactions and reciprocal exchanges between individuals. The personal, emotional dimensions are important. The evidence from practice suggests that networking is a holistic process, involving a strategic interweaving of knowledge, skills and values. It is a vital aspect of community development, as well as supporting multi-agency partnerships and alliances that span organisational boundaries.

This chapter uses complexity theory to present a model of interactive networks creating the conditions for the evolution of new and adaptive forms of organisation that make up a dynamic voluntary and community sector. Chapter Eight explores key issues and dilemmas associated with a networking approach to community development, and highlights some implications for policy and practice. Chapter Nine draws the book to a conclusion by setting out a model of the 'well-connected community', and making recommendations for ensuring that networking practice is both effective and ethical.

Networks serve an important function in society, as we saw in Chapter One, and patterns of interaction and connection are strongly related to what is generally understood by the term 'community'. This has important implications for community development as an intervention for managing social complexity and strengthening the web of interpersonal connections. The idea of 'community' continues to reflect core values associated with a socially just and sustainable civil society, namely respect, equality, mutuality, diversity and, more recently, cohesion (Harris, 2006). Why does the desire for 'community' persist and remain so prevalent across all societies? How does networking contribute to the development and survival of a well-functioning 'community', equipped with the capacity for organising collective responses to shared problems?

Chaos in the community

Networks offer useful ways of organising within turbulent environments, managing apparent 'chaos' in ways that enhance creativity and promote innovative forms of co-operation. As we saw in Chapter Three, organisational studies suggest that network forms of organisation are very effective at coping with high levels of uncertainty and ambiguity. Globalisation and the spread of Internet usage has ensured that we live in a world that is more diverse and yet more connected than ever before, in which role boundaries are blurred and personal identities have broken free from traditional social and geographical categories (Mitchell, 2003; Mulgan, 2004; Parekh, 2007). Communities can be seen as complex social environments characterised by interpersonal connections that comprise fluid networks and small-scale, self-help groups and voluntary organisations. Ideas from complexity theory may help us to understand some of the more puzzling features of our social and organisational world (see, for example, Wheatley, 1992; Jaworski, 1996; Byrne, 1998; Mitleton-Kelly, 2003).

Most community development workers would admit that many aspects of their work are unplanned or unpredictable. Happenstance encounters represent familiar but unexpected opportunities for sharing ideas and information that may lead to a change of direction or a completely new initiative:

> "Often it's the accidental meeting in the street where something completely new comes up that wouldn't have come up in a planned way.... It's just that chance." (KT)

It is normal for there to be an element of serendipity in community development so community development workers need the flexibility and confidence to respond opportunistically to events occurring outside of their intentions or control. Developments often flow spontaneously from chance happenings:

> "There's a strength in being organised out of informal chaos, I suppose." (CT)

An experienced community development worker will relish these kinds of situations, excited by the synergy while providing some continuity and stability for those around:

> "People see me as that person who's always there ... as someone who holds everything together throughout masses of chaos ... you are seen as a kind of rock ... that people keep hanging onto." (TD)

For years community development has argued against predetermined targets and performance criteria, asserting that intervention strategies must be non-directive and nurture organic development rather than deliver an external agenda. This is the difference between the top-down imposition of rigid action plans with preset outputs versus a bottom-up approach that works *with* the grain of the community, helping them to define and achieve their own solutions using processes that simultaneously empower and educate. Networking prepares the ground for community-led projects to emerge that match perceived needs and actual circumstances. The linkages between people and organisations are a vital part of a community's capacity to act collectively and engage with public decision-making bodies. A well-functioning community is vibrant with many different groups and activities that are connected through a complicated matrix of organisational links and personal relationships. When this state of connectivity is reached, anything can happen, and frequently does, because a variety of experiences and interests are 'interjacent' within relatively safe environments (see Thomas, 1976). Small occurrences trigger much bigger events in ways that can be neither predicted nor controlled:

> "I do find that you're building up [a web] in terms of your networking. It is about outreach, it is about exploration ... but I get to a point where there's suddenly a critical mass of outcomes. I think 'Yes, this is making a difference'." (KT)

This unfurling of ideas and energy is a familiar, but misunderstood, feature of community development practice that is exciting, generative and mildly subversive. Change does not take place in a linear fashion, which can be systematically predicted and measured using scales or predetermined outputs (Byrne, 2005). Rather, incremental developments in capacity or awareness can be largely invisible until a sudden leap in activity or consciousness occurs, resulting in a major shift in levels or direction of community activity. This phase transition might reflect the propensity among a set of people for community participation, and would reflect the susceptibility of individuals to be active citizens as well as the local traditions or conditions for civic engagement, such as a sense of collective efficacy or community empowerment. This will be shaped by the policy environment and by specific practices, including community development interventions.

Gladwell (2000) refers to a 'tipping point', when trickles of apparently unrelated events become a torrent of co-ordinated behaviour. He highlights the role played by 'connectors', people who appear to 'know everyone', and act as key nodes in a vast and complex network. Popular websites, such as YouTube, are subject to sudden and intense flurries of interest in particular videos, which spread like a virus through the Internet as people direct their contacts to them. The networking approach to community development locates this connecting function at the heart of practice, with the community development worker facilitating many of the more fragile filaments that make up the complex web of community and inter-organisational life. In effect, the community development worker is shaping and facilitating a mainly informal ecosystem of people and organisations who interact to influence each other's behaviour. As a consequence, collective priorities, preferences, policies and practices emerge that reflect a multiplicity of individual actions and attitudes.

Key elements of complexity theory

With this in mind, it is worth looking at theories about complex systems because there are some interesting parallels with how communities operate, and how voluntary and community sector organisations evolve over time. Complexity arises as the "result of a rich interaction of simple elements that only respond to the limited information each of them are presented with" (Cilliers, 1998, p 5). Complex systems are open: they are affected by changes in the wider environment and they also have an impact on what happens around them. The basic tenets of complexity theory were derived concurrently across different scientific fields: quantum physics, artificial intelligence, embryology, sociobiology and meteorology (Lewin, 1993). More advanced theory has developed through the study of non-linear systems in which apparently insignificant events have far-reaching, even catastrophic, consequences (Gleick, 1987; Mitleton-Kelly, 2003). The most familiar example of this is known as the 'butterfly' effect, whereby the flap of a delicate wing is said to precipitate a hurricane on the other side of the world.

Complexity theory assumes that connections between elements are subject to relatively simple rules of interaction (known as Boolean logic) and that, in the absence of central control mechanisms, local clusters exhibit only limited awareness of the total system. Each unit responds to signals received from its immediate neighbours, and eventually the entire system settles into a state of dynamic equilibrium, featuring familiar, but unique, configurations known as 'strange attractors'. The system has evolved, apparently spontaneously and without external interventions, from an initially random set of interacting elements towards stable patterns of self-organisation (Jantsch, 1980; Strogatz, 2004). The *actual* configurations that emerge cannot be predicted in advance, but they invariably adopt forms that are characteristic of the system, its components and operating environment. A fundamental feature of complex systems is that of overarching properties that *emerge* as a result of localised interactions. Such a 'property' appears to function as some kind of integrating mechanism by which 'chaos' is averted. Thus the co-ordinated flight of a flock of starlings is the result of simple rules of interaction governing the relative positions of a multitude of individual birds, enabling them to migrate safely across continents.

The history of a complex system is significant because what happens in the present is influenced by adjustments to previous interactions. Complex systems have a capacity to process and store information from a variety of sources and are thus able to 'learn' from the past and to adapt to changing conditions. This seems to be an important feature of complex systems. The neurophysiological structure of the human brain is a prime example of a highly evolved parallel information processing system consisting of interactive neural networks that respond to and synthesise particularly salient inputs and memories to 'produce' our perceptions and behaviour (Bechtel and Abrahamsen, 1991). It has been suggested that consciousness and personal identity are the emergent properties of a complex system of neural activity that integrates our individual experiences within the highly plastic, self-organising, but functionally specialist, structures of the brain (Dennett, 1991; Rose, 1998; Greenfield, 2008).

It is not too far-fetched to envisage 'community' as the collective equivalent, an "intricate network of mutual nudges" (Ball, 2004, p 135) generating social identity and intelligence through its ability to receive, compare and disseminate human knowledge and emotions. Perhaps this is what constitutes social capital, the shared resource that can be accessed by all who are connected. In a complex social system the collective behaviour of the community is not directly deducible from the characteristics of individuals but evolves according to successive interactions between nodes in the networks (Ball, 2004; Johnson, 2007).

Complexity theory encompasses chaos theory and is concerned with understanding how 'order' appears 'immanent' (enfolded) within apparent chaos. It is observed that a complex system will, over time, adjust its arrangement of connections until it achieves a state of dynamic but stable equilibrium. Complex systems comprise a multitude of units (nodes), interacting in ways that are mutually influential, yet relatively 'local'. A state of chaos is said to exist where a large number of elements influence each other's behaviour to produce dynamic and *unpredictable* patterns of activity. Contrary to popular belief, a system in chaos is not operating at random. The configurations implicated (known as fractals in complexity theory) are familiar, and by no means arbitrary. In nature, snowflakes are perhaps the most easily understood example. As the Japanese scientist, Ukishiro Nakaya (1954), demonstrated in the 1930s, every snowflake is unique but recognisable in its basic morphology. The exact shape is determined by an 'interplay of chance and regularity': the laws of crystallisation for water molecules and the conditions at which the moment of freezing (the transition state) takes place, notably temperature and humidity.

The natural sciences provide ideas from physics and biology to examine different aspects of crowd or 'swarm' strategies in particular the emergent behaviours and collective intelligence that characterise these 'superorganisms' (Wheeler, 1928; Johnson, 2001). These models of 'social physics' explore the 'entanglement' of individuals, their 'spin' (psychological biases) and the 'tilt' of prevailing conditions which result in the emergence of self-organising phenomena such as the residential separation of slightly different populations, social 'crazes', the 'invisible hand' of markets and people's choices about what social venues to frequent (Johnson, 2001; Ball, 2004; Johnson, 2007). Feedback and preferences are seen to be of critical importance (both about past events and current propensities to act in certain ways), alongside levels of connectivity. It is these factors which seem to influence how sets of people behave (and think) so that order appears out of apparent disorder and seemingly individual decisions. These 'vivisystems' are characterised by the absence of imposed central control; the (relative) autonomy of the sub-units; the high connectivity between the sub-units; and the non-linear (web-like) influence that the sub-units have on their immediate neighbours (Rheingold, 2002).

Every community is unique and operates according to different conditions but it is not too far-fetched to see communities as sharing similar characteristics, with people as the 'sub-units', collectively displaying remarkable levels of coherence despite the apparent lack of organisation. Clutter and chaos in communities (as in personal life) can actually be quite productive and creative (see Abrahamson and Freedman, 2007). Bureaucracies find it difficult to deal with the inherent messiness of communities and networks (Alter and Hage, 1993) but these are vital in enabling connections and groups to evolve without hindrance. Tendencies for cultural conformity and self-organisation appear in groups, organisations, coalitions and cliques through mutual observation and expectations. Collectivities of all kinds align or expire in response to changes in the social, economic and political environment.

Chance interactions between people against a background of 'social noise' (or 'jostlings' in the social physics jargon) are crucial in determining the actual form (and membership) of these social configurations (Ball, 2004). Their basic shape (or fractal) will be familiar to most community development workers: the intermediary body, the community council, the pressure group, the self-help group, the village forum and the informal clusters of neighbours and friends who come together to help each other or to pursue a mutual interest. It could be argued that community development involves 'tweaking' the conditions, the connections and, sometimes, the capacity of communities to make it more likely that certain groupings will emerge and be sustained for as long as they are useful. A group is not merely a scaled up version of individual activity. One of the hallmarks of an open, complex adaptive system is its unpredictability (Rheingold, 2002). It is not, however, possible to specify in detail what will happen in a given community, only to forecast likely trends (Byrne, 2005; Burton et al, 2006). Attempts to monitor the effectiveness of community development using prescribed targets and timescales is therefore inappropriate, although indicators which track changes in capacity, connectivity and cohesion are probably valid (Phillips, 2005).

A system's complexity increases according to the number of elements in the system, their diversity and the levels of interconnectivity. Complex systems can be imagined as ranged along a spectrum of activity from 'stagnant' (where nothing significant happens and there are no noticeable changes) to 'chaotic' (where small incidents produce upheavals across the system) (see Table 7.1).

Computer models of cell automata have been used to simulate the behaviour of complex systems. Kauffman (1995) identifies three broad bands of operation for these systems: 'frozen', 'melting' and 'chaotic'. Complexity theory suggests that systems with low levels of connectivity and highly similar elements freeze. Populations that have

Table 7.1: Spectrum of complex social systems

→→→→→→→→→ Increasing levels of connectivity →→→→→→→→→			
	Static	'Edge of chaos'	Chaos
Nature of interactions	Frozen, stagnant	Vibrant, creative, adaptive	Unpredictable, volatile
Level of connections	Sparse, few boundary-spanning links	Rich and diverse, plenty of 'weak ties'	Saturated, high-density networks
Community characteristics	Isolated from wider society and external influences; fragmented or homogeneous	Cohesive, social structures and informal networks are inclusive	Volatile, mobile or transient population, few linkages between clusters and sectors
Typical examples	Closed, long-standing community such as a monastery; rigid structures and strong centralised control	Multi-ethnic neighbourhood with fairly stable population, mixed tenure housing; range of self-help community groups and umbrella organisations	Unpopular peripheral estate, housing dominated by single social landlord, transient population; absence of formal structures and community activities

these levels of fragmentation or homogeneity (either by choice or circumstance) are unable to innovate or adapt to change. At the other end of the continuum, systems in which the behaviour of elements is influenced by a multitude of highly diverse connections are too volatile and cannot achieve stability. We see this in neighbourhoods that have excessive levels of buy-to-let properties, especially when populated by students or migrant workers who are temporary residents only and tend not to connect with locals (Robinson and Reeve, 2006). The ability to collectively organise in welfare camps for refugees and internally displaced people is similarly limited by this transience, except in situations where whole communities have been relocated or are forced to remain over an extended period.

The optimal state for a system operating in an uncertain, turbulent world is in the 'melting zone' on the 'edge of chaos'. This latter term was coined by the mathematician Norman Packard (1988) to describe an intermediate zone of 'untidy creativity', between rigidity and chaos, where the system is best able to function, adjusting constantly to slight perturbations but without cataclysmic disruption. A complex system at the 'edge of chaos' maintains itself in a state of dynamic equilibrium through processes of self-organisation, known as autopoiesis (Maturana and Varela, 1987; Mingers, 1995). The emergence and experience of 'community' achieves this for human societies, through the integrating functions of informal networks. Thus the development of 'community' as a desirable emergent property of complex social systems can be seen as the primary purpose of the networking model of community development.

Communities at the 'edge of chaos'

The idea of 'community' as an antidote to 'chaos' was first proposed in a paper published more than half a century ago by the National Council of Social Service (White, 1950). In Greek mythology, the gods Chaos and Gaia were regarded as inseparable and complementary partners, acting in tandem to maintain the world as a self-sustaining system (see Lovelock, 1979). Using this framework, it is possible to reconceptualise the purpose of community development work as helping to achieve optimal levels of connectivity. This includes enhancing people's capacity to network individually and through their collective organisations. Traditionally in community development the emphasis has been on establishing and managing specific forms of association as goals in their own right. The 'edge of chaos' model of community suggests that the purpose of such activities is primarily to create opportunities for interaction.

In human societies, groups and organisations crystallise and evolve in an environment of complex and dynamic personal interaction. Studies of local voluntary activity, social movements and the community sector identify a degree of order and co-ordination within community settings, demonstrated at organisational level through mutual affiliation and liaison, and between individuals through friendship networks and overlapping membership (Curtis and Zurcher, 1973; Chanan, 1992; Tarrow, 2005). These mechanisms maintain a social system at the 'edge of chaos' and need to be properly understood if they are to be nurtured for collective benefit. As the biologist O. Wilson observed, "by itself, emergence can be no explanation at all if you don't have any insight into the mechanics of the system" (cited in Ball, 2004, p 155).

The social mechanisms school of sociology attempts to get beyond a superficial narrative, to identify not only what is happening, but how the various factors interact in causal ways (e.g. Hedstrom, 2005; Tindall, 2007). Passy (2003) identifies three mechanisms that encourage participation in social movements, which she terms socialisation, structural connection and decision-shaping. These refer to the linkages and interactions between people which serve to draw individuals into activism (or not). In this context collective efficacy is a plausible candidate for the mechanism that translates social capital into community-led change (Ohmer and Beck, 2006). Whatever the basis for the connections between individuals, it is evident that personal networks are crucial to the development and maintenance of collective action strategies. People's sense of 'community', their social identity, derives from the unpredictable dynamics of mutual influence and interaction. This reflects real experience and emotions, encompassing the negative aspects of human relationships, as well as rose-tinted notions of belonging, trust and loyalty.

Community is the 'emergent property' of a complex social system operating at the 'edge of chaos', ensuring co-operation and cohesion without imposing formal or centralised control. In this respect, 'community' is not simply equivalent to a 'social system', but is rather the outcome of continuous interactions within networks. 'Community' represents both the context and the process through which collective problem-solving emerges, in much the same way as life forms evolved from the 'primordial soup' of previous aeons (Kauffman, 1995). The sociologist George Herbert Mead recognised this phenomenon many years previously, observing that

> when things get together, there arises something that was not there before, and that character is something that cannot be stated in terms of the elements which go to make up the combination. (1938, p 641)

This prescient form of systems thinking recognises that different properties appear at successive levels of analysis and are the product of 'organised complexity' (Capra, 1996, 2004). Complex networks are the pattern of all living systems, in which evolution uses chance and necessity to assemble new entities and to sustain diverse and resilient eco-populations. Those combinations that best 'fit' the current environment are those that survive. The precise format and membership of these cliques, clusters and coalitions are influenced (but not determined) by factors in the environment, such as public interest, political expediency, funding regimes and the existence of similar organisations competing for the same resources (Phelps et al, 2007). A familiar range of collective entities can be discerned in the groups, forums, federations, clubs and societies that populate civil society, and the voluntary and community sector in particular. These reflect prevailing cultural expectations, local conventions and often perpetuate existing differentials of power and privilege. These are the 'strange attractors' of complex mature systems that have evolved at the 'edge of chaos'.

Creating opportunities for networking

Networking is an active and ongoing process that flourishes more readily in some circumstances than others. Traditional community work activities, such as festivals, local campaigns or support for self-help groups, do not seem to be primarily concerned with building relationships. Nevertheless they provide vital opportunities for informal networking and should be organised in ways that do not unintentionally exclude some people or perpetuate inequalities. Networking must therefore be based on anti-oppressive practices that address issues around access, cultural appropriateness and the assumptions and feelings that constitute internalised oppression. Networking can be conceived at one level as a method of opening up and shaping communal spaces and places in order to facilitate integration and cohabitation while promoting equality and diversity (Nash and Christie, 2003).

Changing the structures and cultures of an event or organisation can radically alter patterns of interaction. This could mean anything from the arrangement of chairs to form a circle at meetings to the use of ice-breakers and exercises to encourage participation (see, for example, Bradley, 2004). There are an increasing number of organisations that host networking events, such as Business Network International, which have the explicit aim of facilitating connections as efficiently as possible, including the use of 'speed networking' to encourage people to move on after just a brief encounter that may or may not be followed up. This approach allows no time to get beyond superficial impressions, let alone to build trust; nor do they address or even acknowledge power differentials. Community development workers' professional commitment to empowerment makes it necessary to intervene in situations so that people are more able and more likely to interact with one another in ways which promote respect, trust and mutuality.

Attempts to involve people from disadvantaged groups should be genuine and practical, not tokenistic, and may require prior work to build confidence by supporting smaller, self-organised groups until they feel able to participate equally in wider activities and partnerships. Funding for what are sometimes referred to as 'single-identity groups' is often necessary so that these communities can develop the confidence and capacity needed to be influential and integrated into mainstream services and decision-making (CDF, 2008a). It is likely also to require tackling oppressive attitudes and behaviours among people who assume (often unconsciously) privileged territorial 'rights' based on previous custom and practice. This can generate resentment, even outright conflict, and must be handled carefully (Gilchrist, 2007). Above all, networking should protect people's autonomy and accommodate their diversity.

Meta-networking strategies commonly involve food and entertainment. These might be regular opportunities to meet and mingle in a convivial atmosphere, such as a community centre cafe. Preparing and sharing food together is an enactment of 'communion' which exemplifies the origin of the word 'community' but, as Nelson et al (2000, p 361) observe, it is also a "gendered burden" mainly undertaken by women. Cultural and sporting activities (even competitive ones) are another means of forging closer links, perhaps because of their semi-structured and yet informal nature. Team-building exercises often use these activities to create situations for improving trust and co-operation among disparate groups. It has been suggested that many communal games were developed in order to express and diffuse tensions within a safe arena where roles are clearly defined and power differentials limited (Milofsky, 1988b).

Spaces and places for networking

Community spaces, groups and activities provide integrating mechanisms that are neither bureaucratic, intimidating nor remote. They are useful for introducing awareness and advice into the grass-roots ecology of attitudes and behaviours, for example for health promotion (Wharf Higgins et al, 2008). Ecologists emphasise the importance of 'biodiversity' in preserving a sustainable global environment. The same can apply to society as Capra recognises in his model of the 'web of life':

> in ecosystems, the complexity of the network is a consequence
> of its biodiversity, and thus a diverse ecological community

is a resilient community. In human communities, ethnic and cultural diversity plays the same role. Diversity means different relationships, many different approaches to the same problem. A diverse community is a resilient community, capable of adapting to changing situations. However, diversity is a strategic advantage only if there is a truly vibrant community, sustained by a web of relationships. If the community is fragmented into isolated groups and individuals, diversity can easily become a source of prejudice and friction. (1996, p 295)

Some commentators have argued that modern trends are leading to a deconstruction of society with individuals increasingly separated into different communities or networks of affiliation, for example in relation to faith and ethnicity (Day, 2006). Socio–diversity guarantees a continually enriched society, with all its contradictory values and experiences. For diversity to flourish, communities need neutral communal spaces, which are neither private nor public, where the integrative processes of community and civil society can be continually renewed (Warburton, 1998).

These 'third places' are accessible and accommodating to different people, and feel like a 'home away from home' where there are neither guests nor hosts, simply regular users who share the space and engage with one another as and when they choose (Oldenburg, 1991). The importance of public places for community interaction is increasingly recognised by urban planners (Barton, 2000; Lownsbrough and Beunderman, 2007; Worpole and Knox, 2007) but is equally important in rural settlements. In participatory appraisals in Sri Lanka, communities of poor and internally displaced people consistently prioritised facilities, such as playgrounds, youth clubs and communal halls, in their list of needs, alongside water supplies, decent housing, roads and livelihoods (Rural Development Foundation, 2006).

Communal spaces provide arenas for social interaction that are not governed by overly formal etiquette but where safety, open access, cultural diversity and civic responsibility can be assured. These places can be shaped in incremental ways, creating a pride of place and sense of belonging for local people that enable them to connect with each other and to where they live (Walljasper, 2007). Factors such as traffic flow through local streets can have a major impact on the level and quality of community interaction (Appleyard, 1981) and have often been the target of community campaigns. The creation of traffic-free 'home zones' should be a consideration in planning designs for sustainable neighbourhoods (www.homezones.org).

Familiarity and mutual recognition affect how users of public space relate to one another. It helps to build a sense of belonging if local interests and cultures are acknowledged, perhaps even celebrated (Worpole and Knox, 2007). Such spaces can be designed and decorated (using community art such as murals or sculptures) to encourage processes of interaction that promote diversity and equality, rather than simply reflecting the dominant presence (see, for example, Lownsbrough and Beunderman, 2007). Issues of perceived safety and accessibility are especially important for older people and those with reduced mobility (Connolly, 2003; Help the Aged, 2008).

How can local spaces become genuinely 'communal' places that people use for specific purposes but where they will also encounter *on an equal basis* people with different needs or lifestyles? To some extent, community development workers have always been involved in creating and maintaining 'third places' where people can meet for a variety of purposes or simply to hang out with friends (Marriott, 1997, p 9). Youth clubs provide a similar space for young people (Robertson, 2005). Community development workers can help people to share such facilities, dealing with the inevitable clashes while encouraging conversation, integration and understanding. As many people living in mixed neighbourhoods will testify, co-residence does not guarantee either interaction or mutual obligation (Forrest and Kearns, 2001; Madanipour, 2003; Power, 2007; Cantle, 2008). Community development workers can play a role in facilitating communication and co-operation where it does not occur 'naturally', building bridges between different sections of the population while trying to create (and sometimes defend) spaces for marginalised groups to empower themselves and affirm their own identity (Gilchrist, 2003; James, 2007; Chauhan, 2009).

Communal spaces are where people meet regularly, exchange pleasantries and eventually begin to form low-intensity, but potentially helpful, relationships (Dines et al, 2006; Holland et al, 2007). This may explain the enduring dominance of the geographical dimension to definitions of community. It reflects the importance of 'place' as a site for unplanned, informal interaction, but the tendency to romanticise the village or neighbourhood as the pre-eminent (if not only) basis for 'community' should be avoided. Perhaps we need to reinvent a (post)modern equivalent of the Italian *passagiata*, a regular promenade of citizens that encourages face-to-face interchange in an environment that has open access and few rules of engagement. Can markets or out-of-town shopping malls act as the 21st-century equivalent or are they too anonymous?

Seen from this perspective, community festivals, village fairs, open days and similar events are vital activities in the local calendar because they encourage people from different organisations and groups to work together, strengthening the trust and ties between them, and re-igniting community spirit (Derrett, 2003; Mellor and Stephenson, 2005). Just as significantly, such events themselves provide opportunities for 'ordinary' residents to participate in something that does not require a deep commitment, but brings them into contact with neighbours and other members of the community in a friendly, semi-structured and non-threatening environment. Street parties in urban areas create temporary 'third places' for people who are neighbours, but often unknown to each other, to come together on home ground and with minimal formal planning.

Such occasions have been used effectively to develop social capital and community cohesion (Gittings and Harris, 2008). Community development workers play a key role in helping community activists to organise (and publicise) these events, and, crucially, in ensuring that they are accessible and inclusive for all residents and potential visitors. It is particularly important that people from different cultural backgrounds feel welcome, and that the access requirements of disabled people are met. Considerable hidden work is needed to ensure that such 'open' events are genuinely comfortable and relevant to all sections of the community.

Developing the well-connected community

The overall function of such interventions (whether by paid professionals, volunteers, social entrepreneurs or active citizens) is the development of a complex social system operating at the 'edge of chaos'. I have termed this model the 'well-connected community'. Ideally this is based on flexible, self-reliant networks that contain, or have links to, a 'sufficient diversity' of skills, knowledge, interests and resources for the formation of any number of possible groups and collective initiatives. The task of the community development worker is to enable people to establish these connections and maintain the web. As Zeldin notes in championing the role of intermediaries, "respect cannot be achieved by the same methods as power. It requires not chiefs, but mediators, arbitrators, encouragers and counsellors ... whose ambition is limited to helping individuals to appreciate each other and to work together even when they are not in complete agreement" (1994, p 144). What people choose to do with these connections will be affected partly by individual motives, partly by local circumstances and partly by the wider social and political environment.

The acknowledgement of 'chance' and emotion within the process does not diminish the influence of policy makers or the skilled input of community development workers. Instead it highlights the difficulties of accurate forecasting and the need for flexibility around evaluation. However, this creates challenges for implementation and evaluation because holistic, joined-up interventions in the form of whole-community (or area-based) programmes are inherently "complicated, complex and unpredictable" due to the number of participating agencies, including community members, and the constantly changing context (Burton et al, 2006, p 302). Attempts to quantify the costs and benefits of participation have discovered both practical difficulties and professional resistance due in part to the intangible nature of community-level contributions and outcomes (Andersson et al, 2007). Nevertheless, two recent toolkits for evaluating community involvement have been developed that emphasise the role of networks as conduits for information and hooks to participations (Fairfax et al, 2002; Skinner and Church, 2007). Community development cannot be realised through business plans or the achievement of specific performance criteria. Rather it is about helping a given population (social system) move towards the 'edge of chaos' as a way of managing uncertainty and developing shared infrastructure. This involves the establishment of dynamic and diverse networks to create patterns of interaction that are neither utterly confusing, nor frozen rigid.

A well-connected community is immensely capable of responding to changes in the external environment. It is certainly not isolated from the outside world. Links that cross system boundaries offer a further advantage in allowing for the import of new ideas and comparisons between different experiences. 'Weak ties' provide the communication channels within communities, spanning boundaries and bridging schisms. They are often embodied in individuals, variously termed 'switches' (Castells, 1996), 'social hubs' (Gladwell, 2000), 'linkers' (Fraser et al, 2003), 'weavers' (Traynor, 2008), 'critical nodes' (Dale and Sparkes, 2008) or 'community catalysts' (Creasy et al, 2008). These are able to mobilise bridging and linking capital across separate groups or organisations by acting as connectors in their role as messengers, negotiators and dialoguers (Dale and Sparkes, 2008, p 151). The 'well-connected community' has strong internal relationships, but also benefits from useful links with people and organisations beyond its immediate borders. These give it a resilience so that it is able to recover from damage, to resist threats and to adapt to change (Innes and Jones, 2006).

The principles of empowerment and equality can easily be incorporated into a complexity-based model of community development. Discrimination, prejudice and social exclusion are not just 'morally wrong'; they can be seen as dysfunctional in that they disrupt the free flow of information across the system and restrict the development of potentially advantageous collaborative arrangements. Equality issues must be addressed in order to dismantle barriers to communication and to promote diversity within the networks. Anti-oppressive practice promotes the *integrity, diversity and authenticity* of the whole system, guaranteeing individual rights as well as eliminating illegitimate social biases (Gill and Jack, 2007). This involves tackling institutional discrimination as well as attitude change, and the embracing of political, practical and psychological levels of transformation.

Conclusions

Networking and 'meta-networking' are fundamental methods of community development, and underpin the core policy themes of cohesion, empowerment and inclusion. Professional practice assists individuals in making strategic and opportune connections that create and maintain collective forms of organisation. In systems such as human society, 'community' reflects both the objective experience and the imagined 'spirit' of complex interactions, from which emerge the familiar 'strange attractors' of self-help groups and citizens' organisations. A sense of community expresses that dimension of our lives that is about tolerating difference, promoting equality and acknowledging mutuality. The model of the 'well-connected community' does not attempt to reinvent a nostalgic version of traditional villages or urban neighbourhoods. Instead, it proposes a vision of a complex, but integrated and dynamic, network of diverse connections such as depicted in the sociological revisitings of Young and Willmott's (1957) East End London (Mumford and Power, 2003; Dench et al, 2006). The purpose of community development is simply to support and shape formal and informal networking in order to facilitate the emergence of effective and sustainable forms of collective action. As society becomes increasingly complex, the maintenance of interlocking flexible networks around a variety of interests and identities will constitute our best strategy for building mature, resilient and empowered communities.

EIGHT

Issues and implications

Chaos or community? Where do we go from here?
(Martin Luther King, 1968)

It is now generally accepted that networking is essential to the community development process and that without it other functions that are more formally recognised as the purpose of community work become difficult or impossible to carry out. The National Occupational Standards for community development practice in the UK identify networking as a key role (FCDL, 2009), reiterating the assertion in the Standing Conference for Community Development Strategic Framework, which states that:

> Networking is important because it provides access to information, support, resources and influence. It enables co-operation between practitioners, researchers and policy makers in different sectors through the development of trust and understanding.... Community development workers facilitate networking by putting people in touch with one another, by creating opportunities for people to meet, and by providing safe spaces for interaction and learning. (SCCD, 2001, p 20)

Community development workers frequently hold pivotal positions or play a key role in setting up and servicing network-type organisations, such as area- or issue-based multi-agency forums. They provide 'maintenance' and 'leadership' functions, sometimes chairing meetings, organising mailings, monitoring and generally encouraging participation. In short, they establish situations in which networking flourishes, and work hard to ensure that these are inclusive, productive and equitable by paying attention to issues around access, reciprocity, diversity and power. This 'breadth of spirit' is demonstrated through compassion, tolerance and patience. Networkers show respect, not condescension, and are willing to learn from others.

Being seen as human, even slightly vulnerable, helps to build genuine links with others. So does generosity in sharing resources, time, skills and knowledge. People in the 'helping' professions need to remember that for networking to be effective and sustainable, it is as important to *receive* as well as to *give* in order to maintain reciprocity with colleagues and 'clients'. It is therefore helpful to create opportunities for service users to be the givers, the contributors, rather than always the recipients of services or charity (Gilchrist, 2006b). Strengthening the personal networks of disabled people with learning difficulties or mental health issues is an important aspect of community-based interventions and can be appraised effectively using a standards framework, recently published by In Control (Kennedy et al, 2008).

Box 8.1: Case study of Small Sparks

Small Sparks is an initiative first created by Carolyn Carlson in Seattle. In the UK it has been developed by the In Control charity which works with disabled adults and young people. It provides small grants (of around £250) to individuals (for them to match with their own voluntary labour or other resources) so that they can carry out a project of benefit to their community. This could be an event, a service or some kind of regular activity. In the past these have included: setting up a gardening network, a nightclub, a sports festival, a sponsored cycle ride, skittles and a stall displaying materials on 'easy steps to banking'.

In the earliest days in Seattle, Mark, a young man with learning disabilities, used his grant to acquire a trolley cart to run a community magazine swop, known as Walking the Wagon. This involved visiting neighbours to collect their old magazines (mostly about their hobbies), which were then exchanged for the discarded magazines of others. This local service enabled the young man to meet members of his community on an equal footing, to find out about their interests and to facilitate connections between them. He was using his assets (his time, enthusiasm and the trolley) to actively engage in community building, instead of being regarded as someone who could not quite fit in.

An important aspect of the Small Sparks initiative is to start from a 'whole-community approach', value the relationships that develop and provide initial support to the individuals. Social services departments have found it a useful way of encouraging social inclusion and integration, which could be extended to anyone experiencing stigma and marginalisation.

Thanks to Carl Poll, www.in-control.org.uk

Informal networking complements formal liaison mechanisms by creating the conditions that support effective co-ordination across boundaries. The *connections themselves* appear to provide a foundation for collective and individual empowerment. Sound working relationships are vital for joint action and collaboration. They create a collective power-base that enables individuals and groups in communities to influence the decisions of more powerful bodies. This emphasis on networking raises a number of questions concerning the position and function of the community development worker, which have implications for policy and practice.

Managing roles and accountability

Networking has been portrayed as an activity in which people engage as 'themselves', and the importance of 'authentic' relationships has been constantly emphasised. But, like any other occupation, community development workers need to maintain their accountability and standards vis-à-vis colleagues, employers and community members. As we have seen, trust and informality are important aspects of networking, and good practice must also consider issues around power, role boundaries and impact. Sustainable networks have to be based on genuine commitment and mutual interests. Community development workers use 'themselves' but should not lose sight of their responsibilities as agents representing their employers or as accountable to different sections of the community. In his examination of personal networks, Heald (1983, p 213) suggests that the "art of networking is to do it naturally and with pleasure", but for the professional community development worker personal preferences cannot wholly determine the nature or content of useful connections. Good community development requires the maintenance of real and reciprocal relationships.

Networking is effective for community development because it is *personal*, involving more than superficial connections devoid of emotional content. Networking is *not* about exploiting contacts in a manipulative or selfish way, but about establishing levels of trust, goodwill and mutual respect that run deeper than a sporadic and perfunctory exchange of information, business cards or favours. Personal relationships make it easier to make requests and suggestions, especially when these are inconvenient, complicated or hazardous:

"The personal touches are so important. If the personal stuff and the foundations are right, then I think the work will come out of it, because people will have such faith in you." (TD)

This is particularly important when working with disadvantaged and oppressed people, who may feel more vulnerable and more suspicious of professional interventions. It is vital not to let people down or to deceive them. Being 'oneself' is crucial, while also taking care to negotiate and maintain roles – an essential but delicate balancing act. Adequate supervision and training would improve this, helping workers to be more conscious of role boundaries and better able to assert or, at least, manage these. The growth of multi-agency and multi-layered partnerships has accentuated this issue, making it ever more important that community development workers are able to work across organisational boundaries while maintaining both professional identity and accountability. Networking carried out in one's professional capacity usually needs to stop short of friendship and personal intimacy. This applies to colleagues as well as community members so as to minimise difficulties around confidentiality or misplaced loyalty that could distort decision-making:

> "I try to make sure that I don't take advantage of somebody, because it's easy to mislead people into thinking you're developing what could be a friendship with them, when really what in fact you're doing is developing a working relationship.... I find this especially so in the mental health field, or people who are unemployed or just vulnerable for whatever reason." (TD)

Constantly 'being oneself' means that it is difficult to change or lower one's standards without being seen as hypocritical. The chameleon-like nature of networking also creates strain, in that "you can't be all things to all people all of the time" (PH).

Notions of 'good practice' include operating as transparently as possible, maintaining accountability and ensuring that relationships are balanced and non-dependent:

> "Networking needs to take place at all levels [so that it is] mutual, it's supportive, it's not exclusive [and] must involve all sections of the community with different levels of experience. It needs to occur purposefully and explicitly." (CT)

This can create an additional burden for community development workers in that this work is hidden from public view and can be taken for granted by others. It is not always appreciated that someone's capacity to provide relevant information and contacts has probably taken a great deal of time and attention in acquiring (and storing) that knowledge in the first place. Practitioners need to work hard at cultivating the less convenient or more uncomfortable links in their networks. This involves making efforts to stay in touch, to send apologies and to show a continuing interest in different projects and communities. Networking can be stressful and tiring, creating invisible or un–negotiated accountability webs that are often confusing and onerous.

This aspect of networking is often overlooked, and is the most probable cause of 'burnout' so often encountered in this type of work (Maslach, 1982). 'Burnout' is very common in community development and appears to be the consequence of a mismatch between expectations of what can be given and what can actually be achieved by the worker (Fernet et al, 2004; Briner et al, 2008). It is characterised by emotional exhaustion and a reduced sense of personal accomplishment, possibly because the demands on 'well–connected' community development workers can come from anywhere in their extensive networks, and because networking seems so much to involve using one's own character and beliefs to build and maintain relationships (see Eksted and Fagerberg, 2005). This can amount to a kind of 'prostitution of the personality', trying to be endlessly helpful, kind and caring to any and every member of the community. It may be helpful for workers if they can find mentors within their networks who can keep them focused and professional.

This issue of boundaries and 'burnout' is particularly relevant to discussions about whether community development work is best undertaken by people who are themselves community members or by outsiders. In many contexts it is difficult to demarcate 'work' from 'life', and some people prefer not to do this anyway, for example those working from overtly faith or political perspectives. In most employment situations a deliberate shift to informality can be used to indicate when roles are being blurred, by changes in the style of communication, relaxing of dress codes and using alternative settings or timings. Within most professions and bureaucracies, work conventions are recognised and generally adhered to, and so this switch from formal to informal is obvious. But community development workers have no 'uniform', often work 'unsociable' hours, occupy no fixed 'workplace', may themselves be members of the community and would normally converse in everyday language. Experienced community development workers develop tactics to distinguish between their professional roles and personal lives. At an interpersonal level it is probably alright to slacken role boundaries but not to ignore them altogether. The informality of settings and encounters is a crucial aspect of networking that makes it different from formal liaison and inter-agency collaboration.

Occasionally it may be expedient to dissolve the boundaries between paid and unpaid time, between activist and professional roles, and it is common for people in community development to be 'wearing several hats' at once. This multiplicity of ties and roles can be useful in terms of gaining access to different networks and building credibility but it also creates confusion around mutual expectations, confidentiality and professional accountability, especially when your friends and colleagues may also have formal responsibilities as your employers and managers, as is often the case in the voluntary sector:

> "Networking the networks is very much part of my job but networks have aims, have policies and so if I'm in a network I take very much on board what their aims and objectives are, what their policies are and I try and work within those." (KT)

Paid community development workers need to be clear about their role as members or representatives of organisations, especially within interdisciplinary teams or multi-agency partnership bodies. Nevertheless, participation in a network allows one to enjoy a degree of autonomy to make suggestions and take stances that might not be possible within a more rigid organisational framework.

Networking provides informal mechanisms of accountability. It allows people to monitor their own performance and credibility, while simultaneously providing a means of informal reporting. Managers should help community development workers to clarify their roles and to review on a regular basis the effectiveness of their networking by asking people to examine how their relationships with people in the community are developing and being maintained. Otherwise the almost infinite complexity of informal networking can be somewhat bewildering for the workers *and* those they work with (Gilchrist, 2003).

Addressing power differentials

Networking is easier and more enjoyable where there are common interests and mutual affinity. People tend to associate with people who are like themselves, and this dimension of networking militates against inclusion and equality of opportunity. Understandably people will seek company and stimulation where they feel appreciated or comfortable, and this also applies to 'off-duty' community development workers. Personal preferences should not be underestimated as a source of inequality in networks and this can have an unacceptable impact on community participation and joint working. The effect of envy, anxiety, resentment and fear on personal and professional networks is rarely considered, but these negative emotions obviously affect the availability of ideas and resources within the community and voluntary sector. Personal affiliations and antipathies are endemic in community networks and this creates a quandary for people who are committed to principles of equal opportunity and democracy.

Major issues arise around power and dependency in relation to networking activities. All too often strategic and decision-making networks simply reflect and preserve current privileges, perpetuating inequalities and social exclusion (Russell, 2005). An important role for the community development worker is to expose and challenge semi-covert 'wheeling and dealing' by cliques operating in the corridors (or more usually pubs) of power. Good practice involves transparency, integrity and inclusion – working towards the wider benefit of the 'target' community or area. Community development's commitment to empowerment means that effective networking must span institutional boundaries and counter discrimination within organisations and communities.

Dominance by professionals can present a problem, especially in situations where the pace of change is prescribed by external factors, such as funding programmes or performance criteria. The Joseph Rowntree Foundation's neighbourhoods programme demonstrated how 'light touch' support for communities can help them to engage more effectively with local partners to pursue common agendas (Taylor et al, 2007). Community development also operates within political systems where workers can be persuasive either because of their position in the networks or because of their professional status. Practitioners must acknowledge their own influence while working to reduce power differentials.

Balancing ethics and efficiency

For a profession that asserts that participation should be open and equal, it might seem strange, even heretical, to promote networking as a core method of community development. Networking itself is a neutral tool and can have 'good' or 'bad' consequences, depending on circumstance and motivation. It needs to receive better recognition within community development practice and be underpinned by the values and commitments set out in Chapter Two. The term 'networking' has been used disparagingly to refer to tokenistic interactions that are short term, superficial, expedient and often elitist. Networking has become 'fashionable', sometimes carried out solely for selfish reasons or to meet the requirements of partnership working. 'Bad' networking takes many forms. It might involve poor communication between individuals or a failure to understand how information will spread through a network. Networking can be both ineffective and unethical if it does not involve a balanced gain for all participants, and if it is not based on a level of genuine commitment. This is a superficial and unsustainable form of community development. 'Bad' networking pays insufficient attention to gaps and inequalities, preferring to maintain only connections that are comfortable or convenient. Priorities and positive action to ensure equal opportunity within networks must be considered in order to minimise unwitting or deliberate biases.

While it is feasible to keep information on a huge range of contacts, it is not possible to keep alive an unlimited number of links or relationships since these usually wither away unless actively maintained and must be constantly reviewed to take account of changing priorities and circumstances. Strategic judgements must be made about how to prune or nurture different bits of the network to avoid missing opportunities by over-attentiveness to the 'wrong' people. The most deprived people, such as the rural poor, often inhabit the social peripheries of society, so that their experiences are overlooked due to biases of convenience, culture, cost and climate (Chambers, 1983). Deliberate efforts need to be made to reach out to those on the margins of communities, who are usually the most deprived and disconnected from opportunities and assets. The use of information technologies to network can exacerbate this tendency, since the most vulnerable and excluded people have limited access to the Internet.

Opportunities for unplanned networking need to be protected within busy work programmes. Long-term strategies of nurturing potentially useful relationships are more difficult to justify and yet they are just as necessary because these informal, sometimes serendipitous, connections provide vital channels for information, resources and energy to flow through the circuits of civil society, linking community groups, local government politicians and officers, funding bodies and the array of voluntary organisations. However, there are clearly limits to the amount of time community development workers can spend simply tending relationships. Managers and funders expect outcomes and often need these delivered across a range of issues and within a given timescale.

Job constraints necessitate a division of labour and it is useful to keep strategic links with a variety of networks in order to stay in touch with areas of policy where direct involvement is limited or precluded. In some situations, the worker's identity (as perceived by others) may be a block to forming relationships, especially if differences in status or culture are involved. The characteristics and capabilities of the community development worker may be a factor in negotiating access to certain communities or self-organising groups, such as specific ethnic populations.

There is no reason why alternative means of staying abreast of developments in these groups cannot be found in order to gain up-to-date information and expertise around relevant issues, such as newsletters, websites, television programmes or attendance at events as a supporter. Preparation is helpful because the more that is known and understood about the other people (their role, their interests, their background, the context in which they operate), the easier it is to find connections and to avoid causing offence or embarrassment. In many ways the competent networker will use the skills and quality of a good host at a large party: making people welcome, drawing them into conversation and introducing them to others who they might find compatible or stimulating. Good networking should be neither too blatant nor overly focused. It is about facilitating, not controlling, interaction, helping people to make useful contacts and supporting the processes of relationship formation. Brokering and interpreting are important aspects of this.

Time for reciprocity

There needs to be greater acknowledgement by managers and funders that effective networking involves reciprocity – you have to *give* in order to *get*. Informal gifts and favours are an investment for an unpredictable future return (see Gray, 2003). Helping out another organisation with a temporary problem, taking a turn to do the minutes of a meeting, offering advice or a sympathetic ear to a colleague, 'lending' the use of a meeting room or computer facilities – all detract from one's own work in the short term, but lay a longer-term foundation for relationships of mutual support, respect and trust. The benefits of this work for the individual or the organisation rarely register in balance sheets or records of achievement, and yet are valuable contributions to community development.

The costs of networking are often invisible or absorbed by a few individuals. They need to be recognised and shared more fairly, with attention paid to gender and role issues. This is important not only on grounds of equity, but also to ensure that power (administrative and emotional) does not accumulate to a small, unrepresentative clique. Time is needed to establish credibility and to develop a mental map of the various community and social networks. This may stretch over several years, often through a number of successive or overlapping jobs. Good networkers are recognised as a stable feature of the social and professional environment, operating as a 'rock' during times of upheaval, a 'fulcrum' to provide leverage, a 'fountain' of useful information and the 'key link' between separate networks.

Networking takes time, but time to network has become an increasingly scarce commodity for practitioners faced with the imperatives of targets and deadlines:

> "Giving time is a very valuable thing. But you've got to be strong to do it. To hold out against all the pressures not to do that and try and keep an eye on the overall plan, but when it's really appropriate being able to make a critical judgement, [that] this person needs the time." (KT)

Short-term funding for projects being 'parachuted' into areas from national agencies and increasing emphasis on performance criteria can result in less efficient inter-agency working, strained relationships, frustration and a growing sense of isolation. Networking has been insufficiently supported or recognised by employers, and often relies on the dedication of individuals either by default or because they have a particular talent or inclination. Greater recognition of this role would justify the flexibility and looser accountability of generic community development posts in local development agencies or intermediary bodies. It would also mean that community development resources could be more strategically deployed in larger areas, rather than being focused on projects, groups and neighbourhoods (Longstaff, 2008). Networking rarely has tangible or attributable 'outputs' and, consequently, funders and managers often do not appreciate its value:

"It's quite difficult to justify the fact that networking is an efficient way of achieving something, because a lot of people don't think it is; a lot of people think it's just chatting and wasting time." (TD)

There has been a lack of investment in long-term community development that would allow workers to build up and maintain their contacts in an area. As a result, spontaneity and flexibility has been 'squeezed out' of many community development activities. This clearly has an impact on community development workers' capacity to respond sensitively and strategically to needs and aspirations arising from community members, either collectively or as individuals:

"What you're trying to do is to build up the ability of local people, the organisations that they create to shape their lives as much as possible ... the process is in some ways more important than the outcomes. It's never one thing or another. A process is pointless if it isn't generating outcomes but in a way it's more important to get the process right." (MW)

Community development workers should be encouraged to experiment, to take risks and invest time in building up relationships within the community and with colleagues in organisations that they are likely to be working with. Giving time is an expression of commitment and respect. This should be acknowledged as 'work' invested in building social capital, even if it does not appear to have immediate or tangible outcomes.

Monitoring and evaluation

Nevertheless, some thought should be given to assessing the overall impact of networking on the development of community benefits, as well as wider social outcomes. Networking interactions are often informal and happenstance. The connections set up are so delicate that they are sometimes not even recognised as such and are barely noted. Attempts to monitor and evaluate are clumsy by comparison, especially where they detect only predetermined performance criteria or quantifiable measures. It is important to review which sets of linkages may need strengthening or repairing, and which might be allowed to lapse or lie fallow for a while. The mental map needs constantly updating in the light of changes to organisations, policies or personnel.

The essence of 'good' networking lies in balanced and recurrent interaction, rather than transitory and purely instrumental contact. Most forms of evaluation fail to acknowledge the 'serendipity' factor in community work, namely that many perfectly useful and decent outcomes are not planned – nor even sometimes imagined. They appear instead from a happenstance synchronicity to be found in everyday interactions (Cohen and Stewart, 1994). Fortunately, the complexity of context and interventions is being increasingly acknowledged in the examination of communities as open, adaptive systems in which a number of initiatives (and their interactions) influence what happens in often unpredictable ways (Barnes et al, 2003; Byrne, 2005; Burton et al, 2006).

The theory of change set out in the well-connected community model for the *intervention* of community development is that 'community' as a broad *outcome* is developed through the *process* of networking using *mechanisms* of interaction, relationship-building, co-operation and exchange (see Rogers et al, 2000; Sullivan and Stewart, 2006). The challenge of monitoring and evaluating the effectiveness of networks is addressed, for example, in Skinner and Wilson's (2002) guide to assessing community strengths, but more evidence is needed on whether there is an optimal level of connectivity (equivalent to the 'edge of chaos') to be achieved by nurturing community networks. Some versions of 'social capital' emphasise the importance of networks over norms of trust, and this approach has generated useful methods of measurement, as well as some methodological challenges (Roberts and Roche, 2001; Boeck and McCulloch, 2001; Coffé and Geys, 2007). Possibilities emerge from the concept of 'network capital' propounded by the Toronto school of network analysis (Wellman, 2000, 2006). The New Economics Foundation has developed an approach to evaluating renewal programmes, which identifies the 'liveability' benefits to communities of growing trust and new, diverse connections formed through participation in local projects (Lingayah, 2001; Kennedy et al, 2008).

Derricourt and Dale (1994, pp 84–5) proposed a 'matrix' form of evaluation that could be used to track changing agendas and alliances in an "unpredictable arena" of shifting loyalties and identities. Unfortunately, rigid procedures can discourage innovation and risk-taking. It is rarely possible to predict the exact consequences of community development, and in any case the requirement to do so stifles the initiative and synergy that networking generates. In the past, community development work has been reluctant to demonstrate (and claim) its effectiveness in tackling problems and achieving results.

As a profession, there has been an overemphasis on 'process' rather than product and it is right that this apparent lack of accountability has been challenged (CD Challenge group, 2006). It should be possible to develop evaluation frameworks that capture the hidden benefits of networking. The 'ABCD' approach first developed in Northern Ireland provides a realistic and credible model for evaluating community development interventions, identifying informal networks as an important feature of community life:

> As well as tangible assets, communities are in one sense a sum of interpersonal and inter-group relationships. In a well-functioning community these will be well established ... and a crucial part of how the community actually works. (Barr and Hashagen, 2000, p 56)

The benefits of networking should be viewed over the long term, but networking without eventual outcomes can also be criticised. At some stage there have to be results in terms of things actually happening – new projects, enhanced services, proposals agreed, funding secured and so on. The less visible improvements should also be recognised, such as increased co-operation among agencies, better representation on forums or consultative bodies and more subtle changes in relationships and attitudes:

> "The things that I try to get done can't get done unless people invested personal commitments, so they're proof of whether networks have come alive, or whether things have been done well.... In the course of achieving the different practical results you do kind of note whether there are shifts in the tone of relationships between yourself and other people." (MW)

Community development workers know their networking to be effective when they are in demand. Other people hear of their work and they are invited to contribute to joint initiatives, their suggestions are taken up and implemented, they are used by others as an information resource and as a point of access into other networks:

> "People say directly to you things like 'you've got an amazing network' ... or, more to the point (the real test of it), they send other people, particularly new people, new workers coming into the borough. I get a constant stream

of them coming to me ... you do feel a sense of being appreciated. That's the main thing that indicates that I'm there as a resource person." (GrS)

Acquisition of networking capability

As we saw in Chapter Five, networking requires high levels of intuition. Some people feel that it involves skills that cannot be taught through formal training, but must be learnt through experience. In this respect the community development worker can be seen as a significant role model for community activists. Studies of professional competence emphasise the intuitive aspects of professional practice that are evident in an ability to deal with complex and dynamic problems in "situations of uncertainty, instability, uniqueness and value conflict" (Schön, 1990, p 49). But how are these acquired?

> "Maybe it stems right the way back as to how you were brought up in the first place ... in the sense that you accept people for what they are, you're no better or worse than anybody else, that we're all there to help each other ... maybe there's that in the background that comes over to other people." (LM)

Training in feeling and expressing empathy has been suggested as a way of enhancing attention and sensitivity to other people's feelings. Similarly, being immersed in collective activities is a chance to learn skills in organising, communication and social interaction. In the Panel Study, community development workers referred to adults, especially female relatives, as important role models. Kinship or community networks were described that provided a stable background in which trust, diversity and a sense of community were key components. Most of the Panel thought that their capacity to network was based on a subconscious 'inclination' or predisposition, rather than requiring specific knowledge and skills. And yet there was also a suggestion that networking was a 'trick of the trade', a knack which *could* be acquired through experience, observation, practice and even training.

Workshops can make people more aware of the strategic nature of effective networking, and more willing to develop skills in establishing, maintaining and using their networks proactively. Early childhood shapes our 'personalities' through a process of socialisation – observation, action and selective reinforcement. We acquire those attitudes and abilities that are rewarded, and we seek out or create situations where we can exhibit behaviours that gain approval and tangible benefits. However, by understanding these influences and identifying traits that seem to support good networking, it is possible to adopt practices that make it easier to develop links with others and to be clearer about how to present one's 'self' in different arenas (see Goffman, 1959). Anyone who is willing to put in time and effort, as well as to listen to feedback from others, can improve their networking skills.

Women may have some advantage here due to upbringing and social status. There is evidence that women, compared to men, may think in more fluid and lateral ways, making more effective use of intuition and inductive logic (Belenky, 1986). Gilligan (1982) suggests that this is particularly relevant to understanding gender differences in the skills and strategies that are used to manage social situations. She argues that girls learn patience, awareness of others' needs and relationship skills through childhood games that emphasise co-operation and role-playing. As a result women have "developed the foundations of extremely valuable psychological qualities" (Miller, 1976, p 27), including enhanced abilities in non-verbal communication and emotional perception. In addition, adults tend to praise girls for being kind and thoughtful, while boys are rewarded for behaviour that is brave and independent.

These differences become internalised as 'feminine' and 'masculine' characteristics and are translated in later life into gendered roles, styles of working and moral frameworks. These tendencies are not genetically determined and it would be invidious to over-generalise but evidence, including the findings from the Panel Study, supports the observation that men are more achievement-oriented, more instrumentalist, while women tend to see themselves as responsible for managing relationships through the expression of care and attention towards others. The suspicion that women are more diligent and proficient networkers raises issues about how the outcomes of this work are acknowledged (and rewarded), because evaluation schemes often emphasise measurable performance targets and overlook the underlying processes that have contributed to their achievement. Skill and effort underpin effective networking, and it should be celebrated as valuable, but hitherto neglected 'women's work' developing 'community' and building social capital (Blaxter et al, 2003).

Trouble-shooting

Networks provide extremely effective modes of organising and communicating in situations that are complex and uncertain, but they can also be muddled, biased and fragile. A lack of clarity over remits and responsibilities can cause problems when there is much work to be done or competition for scarce resources. This can lead to the kind of rivalry, mistrust and recriminations that beset those voluntary organisations that are overly reliant on trust and assumed common values. In developing countries, non-governmental organisations (NGOs) are reluctant to network because there is so much pressure to secure funding from foreign aid agencies for the next project, which sometimes is the only way of ensuring the survival of the organisation.

This is unfortunate because the benefits of networking for NGOs are well documented, notably the increased capacity that comes from working with others to build alliances and share knowledge. In their examination of a series of case studies from international development in Mexico, Bolivia, Nicaragua, West Africa and Canada, Liebler and Ferri (2004) observed that country-wide networks operate better (and more sustainably) if they develop organically rather than being engineered through the interventions of external donors; when they are 'coalitions of the willing'. Several characteristics, or generative capacities, are associated with the survival of networks: the prior existence of good relations between the members, a strategic fit between form and function, a commitment to joint learning and internal democracy and a style of leadership that operated *between* members rather than from above, resulting in a sense of shared ownership, not centralised control (Sotarauta, 2003; Skidmore, 2004).

Networks often have no organisational mechanisms for resolving disagreements among the contributors and this can be problematic when everyone is under pressure and nobody is willing to take a lead. Networks are sometimes expected to perform functions for which they are ill-suited, such as delivering services or managing staff and resources. A culture of flexible and informal decision-making is excellent for reaching people 'on the edge' and encouraging them to organise events or participate in community activities. Loose structures and informal methods of organising facilitate the flow of ideas and enable relatively disparate initiatives to emerge. Networks allow 'wild' ideas and tentative expressions of interest to crystallise into something more tangible.

But for this to have a wider impact it needs co-ordinating, moulding into a collective demand or aspiration. Faith and favours are fine up to a point but they are not sufficient when organisational demands exceed resources, or when there are competing external pressures and internal disputes. Networks support organisation, but more formal procedures are needed for decision-making and unified, rather than parallel, action. This is not always recognised and tensions emerge within networks when it appears that conventions or expectations are being violated, even though these are rarely made explicit.

Community development workers need to be aware of when networks might need to make this transition and be prepared to offer advice about how to establish more appropriate structures and procedures. This shift from informal network to formal organisation needs to be carefully handled and fully acknowledged by all concerned. Often it is not, and this can lead to confusion and disagreement over how to move forward. Ideally, the new organisation should be set up to manage formal functions while leaving the networking capacity intact, but in reality this is not always possible.

Box 8.2: Sarvodaya – Sri Lanka

The Sarvodaya movement was set up in 1958 and has grown to be the largest non-governmental organisation in Sri Lanka, with one third of all villages affiliated to the programme in some way. Its name means 'wakening' and community development principles are used to work with a network of villages to promote rural development at the grass-roots level. The work takes a holistic approach based on extensive community participation to ensure that basic standards of nutrition, sanitation, housing, education and health are achieved.

The concept of *shramadana* underpins the approach: the voluntary sharing of time, effort, talents and thinking for mutual benefit. The emphasis is very much on collective learning and working, using analysis and discussion to identify village concerns and priorities so that these can be addressed through setting up youth and community groups to carry out the necessary work. Villages are encouraged to co-operate with one another by using a local network of one 'pioneer' village supporting the development of ten others in the surrounding area, for example in the construction of a library.

Sarvodaya are particularly keen to build relationships between the generations and between different ethnic groups, especially during times of civil conflict, and to create opportunities for dialogue, such as village seminars and regional events.

See www.sarvodaya.org

It would be useful to enhance our understanding of the evolutionary processes of informal groups and networks, perhaps looking at the optimal relationships between size, form and purpose. Morgan (1989, p 162) suggests that networks are manageable only up to the limits of personal engagement and surveillance, and I have accumulated ample anecdotal and empirical evidence that networks function optimally with around 35–40 participating members. This observation may reflect a trade-off between the costs of maintaining this number of links, and the benefits of their diverse contributions to voluntary collective action. Computer simulations of networked systems also indicate that excessive connectivity can be a problem, reducing the adaptability of the whole system (Mulgan, 1997, p 186). This has implications for computer-mediated networking and suggests that, within community development, direct networking between individuals has to be tempered by some degree of formal structure, to avoid information overload and the danger of tipping a system into chaos.

The impact of technology

Laslett (1956) was among the first to identify the importance of face-to-face communication in the creation of social groups capable of making collective decisions and building tolerance between strangers. In-person contact is a major component of networking because it allows non-verbal communication to function: managing first impressions, exerting subtle forms of influence, interpreting responses and regulating the pace and level of interaction, especially in the initial phase of relationship building. It has been estimated that non-verbal communication conveys at least two thirds of the message, particularly when this is emotionally ambiguous or highly charged (Dunbar, 1996). Studies of human interactions emphasise the importance of paralinguistics (such as facial expression, posture, tone of voice) in regulating relationships. This recognition has influenced the design of buildings, office layout and organisational structures but tends to be overlooked by the current enthusiasm for computer-mediated communication, possibly to the long-term detriment of 'real' community connections that thrive on the face-to-face interactions and serendipitous encounters (Foth, 2006, 2008).

Increasingly, information and communication technology (ICT) has made it easier and immeasurably cheaper to connect and collaborate using social software (Foth, 2008). Community informatics comprising e-mail lists, intranet facilities, notice boards, chat circles and blogs are usually available, including at community level, to assist the exchange of information and ideas. The distinction between face-to-face interaction and computer-mediated communication is becoming increasingly blurred and often depends on what is sought from the connection

(Davies, 2003; Foth and Hearn, 2007; Ryberg and Larsen, 2008). Wellman (2006) refers to the rise of 'networked individualism' through which people maintain links with a variety of online communities, using these to promote themselves and meet their social needs.

Developments in mobile and computer-based technologies have added a new (and somewhat contentious) dimension to the debate on community (Gordon, 1999; Chayko, 2002), raising issues around personal authenticity and accountability. Concerns have also been raised about the disturbing effects that concentrated attention within the two-dimensional sphere of electronic media (rather than real-world interactions) may be having on young people's ability and willingness to develop flesh and blood identities (Greenfield, 2008). Differentials in access and confidence, the so-called 'digital divide', pose major problems to societies increasingly oriented towards the Internet and e-citizenship (Loader and Keeble, 2004).

However, experience in developing countries indicates that even the most marginalised rural communities can be empowered using Internet-based networks (Rahman, 2006). Technology certainly appears to facilitate information flow and connection across the 'digital society', but can community informatics replicate (or even replace) the emotional basis of face-to-face interaction that constitutes genuine 'community' (Harris, 2003)? There are many examples of communities using online facilities to connect and organise off-line (real-world) activities. This trend is likely to continue as more households acquire broadband.

Box 8.3: ResidentsHQ

During the early stages of a new residential development at the Royal Arsenal in Woolwich, London, households were provided with access to a purpose-built social-networking-based residents' website. Within the first month of its introduction, neighbours who up till then had failed to make contact with one another made use of the website, provided by a company called ResidentsHQ, to identify shared enthusiasms and establish connections. These were then used to initiate a variety of networks, including a running club, a toddlers group, salsa classes, and to organise social gatherings, such as a party in the park. Residents also shared tips and information on local services, traders and amenities. Discussion topics emerged on areas of mutual concern and interest, and the site was used by some people to sell or give away unwanted items. It is also used by the Managing Agent and Residents' Committee for their communications with residents (posting minutes, announcements, surveys and feedback).

> The technology provided an easy way of 'breaking the ice' without having to actually knock on neighbouring doors. It created a virtual forum for many of the exchanges and interactions that used to take place in face-to-face settings such as in the local shops or on the street. As word spread on how useful ResidentsHQ was becoming, more and more neighbours signed up. More than half the residents had joined in the first six months and, of these, approximately 20 per cent use the site on a daily basis to interact with their neighbours. Communication and a sense of 'community' is developing fast, accelerating cohesion and co-operation within this new estate.
>
> Acknowledgements to Asesh Sarkar, www.ResidentsHQ.com

There is a plausible argument that social software services provided through the Internet (e-mailing, teleworking, surfing, shopping, virtual chatrooms and the like) actually improve communication, releasing time for community interactions within the neighbourhood and civil society (Watt et al, 2002). Websites such as Upmystreet enable people to find out what activities, amenities and services are available and recommended nearby without the need to engage directly with the neighbours. Migrant and diaspora communities use the Internet to exchange personal news as well as cultural ideas (Hiller and Franz, 2004).

The advent of Web 2.0 software has immeasurably changed the way many people interact with friends, colleagues and virtual strangers. The ease with which user-generated material (photos, messages, games, videos and so on) can be uploaded, viewed and edited online has led to a massive explosion in the use of social networking sites such as Facebook or MySpace as forums for people to stay in touch with friends and family, to set up virtual communities and campaigns, to recruit and induct new employers, to search for expertise and for self-promotion (Dutton and Helsper, 2007).

More altruistic sites, such as LinkedIn and Horsesmouth, enable people to seek and offer advice and support around an array of topics, matching experience and expertise to where these are needed or requested. The use of IMS (instant messaging service) and 'Twitter' applications to supply a continuous news stream about people's plans and preoccupations is the 21st-century equivalent of gossip, providing a constant update on the comings and goings within a community or the wider world. Many blogs have become an alternative channel for dissemination of news and debate, when the official media are blocked or biased against certain views. Transactions take place through eBay and PayPal, between traders and customers who need never meet and may live on opposite sides of the globe.

Knowledge production and exchange has been democratised through problem-solving chatrooms that are open to anyone with an e-mail account. Wikipedia, an online encyclopaedia, allows all-comers to contribute and to change entries. It is claimed that the involvement of thousands of participants in these cyber-forums ensures that they maintain their legitimacy as trusted sources of information through feedback, corrections, reviews and reliability ratings. This 'wisdom of the crowd' is similar to the way that face-to-face communities operate but on a much larger and more impersonal scale (Surowiecki, 2004; Johnson, 2007). Models of m(obile)-learning have been put forward to enable individuals to 'swarm' towards shared learning opportunities or sources of expertise, using common wireless access to locate these and share knowledge with one another (Nalder and Dallas, 2006). Whole new virtual worlds have been created such as Second Life, consisting of simulated societies that exist only in cyberspace and yet are populated with avatars representing the alter egos of actual people.

The boundaries between reality and life on the web are being gradually blurred as corporations establish a presence in these Internet realms, and communities organise to have an impact in the real world. Mobile technologies have been used to gather 'smart mobs' for mass demonstrations and also to connect individuals with compatible potential 'mates' in the real-world vicinity (Rheingold, 2002). The Internet can also facilitate the emergence of community and corporate 'hot spots' (Gratton, 2008) or 'col-laboratories' (Taylor, 2004) which bring together highly motivated and diverse teams of people to focus their energy and expertise on solving problems or delivering a project. Co-operation rather than competition is encouraged through virtual feedback and video-conferencing, allowing rapid flow of information and innovatory ideas to flare. The impact of cyber-society and virtual networks on our lives is only beginning to be assessed empirically, although studies of the use of computers to co-ordinate social and community activities are producing some encouraging findings (Wellman and Haythornthwaite, 2002; Hampton, 2003; Wellman, 2006; Webb and Animashaun, 2007).

Conclusions

This chapter has explored some of the challenges associated with a networking approach to community development. As practitioners, people working with communities need to be aware of the complexities and ambiguities in the community development role, and be prepared to manage their personal and professional networks in ways that promote co-operation, participation and empowerment. Issues around power, equality and diversity need to be constantly addressed in order that communities themselves develop the connections, capacity and confidence to maintain, extend and use networks to manage internal tensions and to have influence over decisions that affect their circumstances and choices. Being 'well-connected' can only be an advantage in today's complex but unequal society.

NINE

Developing the
well-connected community

Only connect! That was the whole sum of her sermon.
(E.M. Forster, 1910, p 188)

Community development as meta-networking

The complexity model of community development suggests that an important outcome of the community development worker's interventions is being overlooked – namely the extent to which community networks are strengthened and diversified. As indicated earlier, crucial aspects of community development can be reconceptualised as 'meta-networking': the maintenance and co-ordination of interpersonal and inter-organisational relationships within complex systems of interaction (Gilchrist, 1999). Community development workers perform an undervalued function in facilitating interdisciplinary and cross-sectoral partnerships, with a particular role in identifying and supporting community members to work with others around shared issues and goals (e.g. Oladipo Fiki et al, 2007).

The community development worker frequently performs the boundary-spanning function, the person who is able to operate within different settings and constituencies acting as broker or interpreter, especially in situations of misunderstanding or conflict (see Taylor et al, 2007). The community development worker has a crucial role in 'networking the networks'. They spin and mend strands across the web: putting people in touch with one another, helping them to communicate effectively and generally supporting the more problematic or tenuous links – the ones blocked by organisational barriers, misunderstandings or prejudice. When performed well, this is a strategic function involving a myriad of micro-decisions about where to be, who to speak with, what to say, what connections to make, what information to convey and so on. Sometimes, the community development worker may simply operate as a 'go-between', keeping the pathway open as a route for future co-operation.

The community development worker often acts as an important node in community and cross-sectoral networks: a source of information that others can use to make connections or to obtain resources. Networking is of intrinsic benefit to community development practice and to communities. The Panel Study identified specific strategies and outcomes that were achieved through networking. A model of 'good networking practice' is proposed that draws together the experiences of the practitioners Panel and the Festival Against Racism. This includes recommendations for community development work as an occupation in terms of core principles, role management, training and support structures. It may be helpful to summarise the key recommendations (see Table 9.1) before going on to explain why they are important.

Networking enhances the quality of community development and service delivery generally. The morale and knowledge of individual staff is improved because practitioners benefit from critical discussion with colleagues by developing a sharper, more reflective, analysis of their work. These networks operate as a kind of informal 'community of practice' (Wenger et al, 2002), where there is some kind of occupational connection, "an aggregate of people who come together around mutual engagement in some common endeavour" that is defined as meaningful to the participants (Eckert and McConnell-Ginet, 1998, p 490).

These facilitated networks allow participants to explore contentious issues, upgrade their professional skills and knowledge and reflect critically on their own practice. Informal comparisons and discussions encourage people to keep their ideas fresh, to stay informed, to review their work, to maintain key values and principles and to challenge poor standards and complacency. This is how 'promising practice' can be examined and consolidated so that theories may develop as to why some approaches seem to work better than others. Networks are a source of friendly support that recognise and reinforce commitment to the job, without which many community development practitioners would become isolated and discouraged.

Networking with other community development workers or like-minded people creates opportunities for informal support, coaching, advice and mentoring. In the absence of formal supervision arrangements and in-service training, this form of peer education enables community development workers (who are often in lone or peripheral posts), to cope with stress and to manage what are often quite complicated work programmes. Networks provide a useful 'sounding board' at moments of crisis and an occasional shoulder to cry on. Feedback from informal mentors and trusted allies is an important source of constructive criticism, enabling people to examine the validity of their own ideas and to consider

Table 9.1: Summary of key recommendations

Recommendation	Explanation
1. Networking should be explicitly acknowledged as a core activity within community development practice.	Its inclusion in national occupational standards should inform job descriptions, person specifications, work programmes and funding applications.
2. Networking should be better monitored and managed through work reports, which identify informal interaction with key or new contacts as well as formal inter-organisational liaison.	An index of effective networking practice could include criteria for performance appraisal. This could incorporate short-term impact measures, as well as longer-term outcomes.
3. The meta-networking aspect of generic community work should be incorporated into employment conditions through long-term contracts with secure funding.	Supervision and training should be available to community development workers (and others) to improve their networking abilities, and to recognise the difficulties and dilemmas inherent in networking approaches.
4. The less tangible aspects of human interaction derived from intuition and informal networking should be recognised and valued as important ways of working with people to develop collective action and multi-agency initiatives.	Greater flexibility in work programmes allows for experimentation and unexpected developments that emerge as a result of networking activities.
5. The importance of networking as a foundation for partnership arrangements needs to be recognised in the timescales for developing bids, delivery plans and formal management structures.	Partners need time together to develop a shared vision, to build trust, to deal with disagreements and to address power differentials. Team-building exercises may help, as will informal social activities.
6. A code of good practice in networking may need to be established setting out ethical standards.	This should cover issues around role boundaries, reciprocity, accountability, confidentiality, equal opportunities and covert influence.
7. Opportunities for informal networking should be included (and sometimes facilitated) within formal events, such as conferences, training courses or inter-agency meetings.	A balance is needed between structured time at events, and time when participants can make contact and informally follow-up discussions with one another.
8. The function of intermediary bodies in helping community and voluntary organisations to develop co-operative and 'learningful' connections across identity and geographic boundaries should be strengthened.	Umbrella bodies, such as Councils for Voluntary Service or specialist forums, provide vital opportunities for information exchange and debate across the whole sector and need support to make sure their facilities are accessible to all sections of the sector.
9. Techniques of network analysis should provide a baseline 'snapshot' of how communities are operating.	This could provide a good opportunity for participatory appraisal research involving community members in identifying changes to networks.
10. Evaluation of community development programmes should include outcomes that relate to improved relationships and connections within communities, and between communities and organisations in other sectors.	Longitudinal network-mapping exercises should indicate how the linkages between groups and organisations within communities change as a result of community development interventions and show in graphic form any isolated clusters and gaps in communication.

alternative perspectives, correcting and adjusting their plans accordingly. Informal networking creates safe and supportive environments where practitioners can talk things through with like-minded colleagues.

Just as other forms of identity are forged through relationships with others, so occupational identity is reconfigured and preserved through our interactions and observations of colleagues, creating a form of 'connected identity' (Oliver, 2007). Fellow practitioners appear to exhibit a similar set of values and techniques, which are discovered and reinforced through networking, as well as being set out in occupational standards (Lifelong Learning UK, forthcoming, 2009). Learning in these communities of practice helps to build a strong collective identity, but can also lead to collusion and complacency if discussions are confined only to 'like-minded' people. This can be especially unproductive during times of transition or organisational restructuring when a 'democratic discourse' is crucial for 'an open flow of ideas' and critical reflection (Oliver, 2006). Nevertheless, as we saw in Chapter One, the social support provided by peer relationships can be crucial to survival, job satisfaction and success, helping people to cope in environments that are unfamiliar, precarious or threatening.

Box 9.1: Oxfam – gender justice peer learning

The Oxfam International Youth Partnerships (OIYP) work with young people in developing countries to support the sharing of skills, knowledge and experiences among 'action partners' to enable them to work for change and social justice in their communities. A peer-led learning network on gender issues has compiled and promoted a collection of stories and resources used in face-to-face and on-line discussions. The experiences included in these materials reflect the global diversity of cultures and issues facing practitioners, providing a rich source of ideas and insights.

Differences within the more than 300 members of the Gender Learning Group, spanning over 90 countries, sometimes create difficulties in finding common ground or identifying tools and techniques that participants could use in their own situations. But overall, the network was successful in raising the profile of gender equality and building the capacity of young people to champion these issues. Further work is being undertaken to improve accessibility by producing online and off-line resources and encouraging wider involvement from 'action partners'.

Thanks to Anna Powell, Training and Development Coordinator, Oxfam International Youth Partnerships, Oxfam Australia.

Professional community development involves proficient, sometimes expert, networking, requiring intelligence and ingenuity. It requires thoughtful self-presentation, preparation and exploration of the 'lay of the land'. Effective networking is skilled, strategic and sustainable. It can be improved through reflection, practice and experience. Networking involves two layers of competence. The first refers to the maintenance of relationships between the worker and others. The second aspect, here termed 'meta-networking', is about supporting and shaping the connections that weave across communities and link them into the wider world. Meta-networking involves the usual skills and processes of networking, such as making contact, finding connections, crossing boundaries, building relationships and interpersonal communication. It also requires an ability to facilitate the resultant network of relationships as a resource that others can make use of. This is difficult because the links themselves are multi-faceted and delicate, while the web as a whole comprises a complex system of intricate connections.

It is possible to increase people's capacity to network by improving skills, knowledge and motivation. Training courses and conferences now include sessions for networking that aim to make people more aware of how they can use and develop their networks. Bubb and Davidson (2004) identify eight networking competences, which are a mixture of skills and traits: openness, organisational ability, strategic ability, communications, social skills, personal branding, supporting and tenacity. Twelvetrees (2008), in the latest edition of his classic text *Community work*, sets out six rules for networking, in which he recommends opportunism, integrity, empathy, active listening, reciprocity and scepticism as key qualities for effective grassroots practice.

Practical manuals on networking are available and several guides or training packs have been produced to improve people's strategic and technical capabilities (for example, Lyford, 2001; WCAN, 2002; SCCD, 2003). The ability to develop and maintain relationships with a *range* of people, and to communicate in a *variety* of modes, is given insufficient recognition as a necessary competence and this could easily be improved by encouraging community development trainees to gain experience in a wider range of practice situations than is currently the norm. Motivation is an important factor and most good networkers seem to possess a genuine curiosity in other people and other cultures.

An Internet search for material on 'community networks' invariably generates copious references to information and communication technology (ICT). This privileging of technological networking over human interaction is a worrying but salutary reminder that knowledge management is an essential function of networking. Knowledge management is about enabling people collectively to share and apply knowledge so that they can achieve their respective goals and objectives. To be effective, the successful networker needs to be able to acquire, assimilate and access information, preferably in a form that will benefit those who might need it most. This requires good administrative and organisational skills, notably some kind of system for storing and retrieving information. This might be an excellent memory, but it may also be wise to use notes, a computer database or all three.

Box 9.2: CharityTracker

CharityTracker (www.charitytracker.net) is a website that enables community and faith-based organisations to compare information about what each other is doing at grassroots levels to support individuals and groups. It was devised to support work with a sudden influx of families seeking refuge in Northeast Alabama from the devastation wrought by Hurricane Katrina along the Gulf Coast of the United States. Community networks that include local churches, non-profit charities, and government agencies are successfully growing in 165 cities in the United States.

Having an ICT network has improved online communication that in turn has resulted in better co-ordination of off-line interventions, which has evolved into face-to-face collaboration across sectors and community development. CharityTracker is currently being further developed as an ICT tool for pragmatic use in building city-wide partnerships and alliances. Community bulletin boards have been included as a new feature, which residents can access to find out about opportunities for volunteering and community activities.

Thanks to Mike Simon of Simon Solutions, www.simonsolutions.com

Knowledge management is not simply about the dissemination of information. Community development workers analyse, interpret, evaluate and synthesise ideas from an extraordinary range of sources. This deluge of information includes official statistics, gossip, rumour, policy statements, ideological dogma, legal documents, political demands, cries for help, dreams, aspirations, half-remembered impressions and formal reports. The effective networker is able, somehow, to make sense of this kaleidoscope of inconsistent and incomplete versions of the world, assemble some kind of coherent assessment and then present this for others to consider. This requires complex cognitive processes by which patterns and congruencies are identified amid apparently contradictory opinions, facts and beliefs. Community development workers use their networks to develop insights and intuition. They should be able to fairly and accurately present opposing views and make sensible forecasts of future developments based on their knowledge of past and current events. The good networker must therefore develop and exercise a political analysis of situations, taking into account power dynamics and personal interests, alongside their own ideologies and role status.

Adaptable communication skills are needed so that the community development worker can understand and interpret messages and impressions across cultural and institutional boundaries. People from different organisations and communities think in different ways and may use language differently, including non-verbal forms of communication. It is therefore important to understand how body language carries different significance in different settings and cultures, and to behave accordingly. Good networkers need to be alert to potential misunderstandings and anticipate friction among people from different backgrounds, whether this is about working with people from different sectors or from different parts of the world. It is useful to have an understanding of the diverse conventions and traditions in complex social or organisational environments.

An important component of networking capacity is an overview of the environment in which one is operating, including an up-to-date 'map' of the organisational landscape (and the relationships that weave across it). Network-mapping exercises enable people to be more aware of existing links among organisations, and more explicit about how they use (or could use) connections with other individuals or agencies. By identifying actual and potential forms of co-operation, it is suggested that people can become more proactive, and consequently more effective, in their networking. In the English East Midlands, the government has used a new technique of virtual network analysis (VNA) to illuminate the exchanges and blockages for partnership working in the region. This has led to improvements in knowledge transfer and co-operation between different agencies with overlapping aims (Stephenson, 2004).

Organisational diagrams are helpful in conflict situations because they encourage participants to interrogate (and adjust) network relationships rather than antagonise each other. Similarly power mapping has been used in developing countries and in the UK to trace and, where possible, 'unscramble' divergent interests (Estrella and Gaventa, 1998; Mayo and Taylor, 2001). Understanding how the people one is working with are connected (or not) and how this affects the organisation of collective activities is crucial to all successful community development strategies. Computer simulations, network analysis and visualisation programs are being developed to promote, manage and evaluate organisational change, but have not yet been systematically applied to community development (Huisman and van Duijn, 2005).

Intermediary bodies and partnership working

Since networking clearly takes time, effort and attention, this work needs to be recognised and adequately funded. Core funding for long-term community development posts would be helpful, allowing workers to understand and engage with community dynamics, build meaningful relationships and respond to issues identified by community members themselves. Community participation and collective empowerment emerge from a complex infrastructure of informal networks and self-organising groups developed through a long experience of collective organising (McInroy, 2004). It is this layer of interaction and confidence that is neglected by, and yet essential to, successful community-led regeneration programmes and neighbourhood management (Taylor, 2007). It needs to be supported both by generic community work posts and by adequately funded, but independent, umbrella bodies. It may seem obvious that the existence of 'community' is a prerequisite for community involvement, and yet few policy officers or regeneration managers realise that key elements of community capacity – networks, interaction, common purpose, collective identity and organisational infrastructure – ideally need to be in place *before* there can be effective and equal partnership.

Many governments across the world have been strongly influenced by communitarian thinking and a commitment to subsidiarity. This return to ideas of community participation in decision-making is to be welcomed, especially where it is based on collective empowerment rather than notions of individualist 'user' or consumer rights. The World Bank regards 'empowered communities' as an important outcome for its investments (Narayan, 2002; Alcock, 2005). It acknowledges that its formal procedures and systems have often not been conducive to long-term processes of empowerment and building social capital (Kumar, 2005). The World Bank uses a definition of empowerment that talks of "tackling the differences in capabilities that deny actors the capacity to make transforming choices" (Alsop et al, 2005, p 15) and has adopted a framework combining agency and structure using four elements:

access to information; inclusion/participation; accountability; and local organisational capacity (Narayan, 2002, p 18).

Further emphasis on partnership and 'joined-up' working has been accompanied by a growing understanding that this requires capacity building and social mobilisation in order to make and maintain the requisite connections (Medd, 2001). While there is still a tendency to assume that the deficit lies with local communities rather than the officers and institutions of the private and statutory partners, there is evidence that shared capacity-building programmes (where all partners train together) are most effective in promoting learning and trust (Scott et al, 2002). Without commitment and clarity around the *practice* of partnerships and devolution (the need to develop a common understanding *with* communities), there is a danger that independent community initiatives will be subsumed into a rather top-down approach that delivers to governments' and donors' agendas rather than pursuing community priorities (Burgess et al, 2001; Bartley, 2003; Rai et al, 2007). The training of frontline workers in community development techniques and values has the potential to make a real difference to strategies for community empowerment (CLG, 2008).

Community initiatives and processes are organic, needing space and support to grow. Voluntary sector 'umbrella' bodies provide both the trellises and the nutrients for this growth, but have been under threat from local authority funding cuts and from the appearance of agencies with a more specialist function, for example, supporting volunteering, delivering services or encouraging social enterprise. Intermediary bodies often act as social relays and brokers, enabling smaller organisations to network with one another and connecting informal networks into more formal partnerships (Taylor, 1997). Many intermediary bodies perform a co-ordinating function: convening meetings, producing mailings, running training workshops, providing specific advice and facilitating consultation exercises. Local forums, federations and network bodies provide a similar service, sometimes with paid administrative support, but more often reliant on the dedication of a few hard-pressed individuals who are able (just about) to undertake these tasks on top of other work commitments.

Studies of multi-agency partnership working (Adamson and Bromiley, 2008) invariably find relationships and informal networks to have a major (and not always positive) impact on the quality of decision-making and co-operation. Partnerships tend to involve prominent and 'well-connected' key players: community leaders, voluntary sector professionals or local authority officers who are able to influence decisions through their contacts with politicians and funders. Access to such networks is rarely either transparent or equitable, and can be a major source of resentment and cynicism. Community development can help to open up such policy networks to community participation and wider scrutiny.

Community involvement in government initiatives depends on a foundation of community sector activity that is low profile, but somehow enduring over time (Chanan, 2003). Supporting this layer of active citizenship, self-help and collective action is a core function of community development, which should be better supported whether by paid professionals or unpaid volunteer activists (CD Challenge group, 2006; Packham, 2008; Richardson, 2008). Sometimes participation requires a more proactive approach to overcome shyness, unfamiliarity or prejudices, encouraging people to get to know one another rather than simply pass on the streets.

Funding policies need to secure existing good practice at community level, including money for positive action measures, such as crèches, the provision of interpreters and personal assistance for disabled people. The tendency for government and grant-giving bodies to prefer new or innovative projects has distorted community work practice and undermined the basis for creative thinking and genuine community participation. Nonetheless, there appears to be an increased willingness among politicians and policy makers to trust agencies and professions that are not under their immediate control, and to acknowledge that risk, discretion and occasional failure are inevitable corollaries of strategies that urge community enterprise and innovation. If these approaches are to be successful, community development needs space and opportunity for informal and serendipitous activities to operate alongside more formal task-related projects.

A new paradigm for sustainability

The terms 'sustainability' and 'well-being' reflect two linked policy agendas. On the one hand, sustainable development refers to the integration of social, economic and environmental objectives within a single strategy or programme. It is about improving the quality of life by making sure that gains in one area of policy do not jeopardise the achievement of other goals. This includes strategies for protecting the planet and reducing climate change (Church, 2008).

Sustainability is also concerned with ensuring the continuing effectiveness of development initiatives through changes to mainstream services. If funding is for projects, then it is vital that the methods used to plan, implement and evaluate these encourage the formation of relations and linkages between stakeholders and communities that can sustain a lasting mutual commitment. Informal networks create a foundation for effective collective action and the empowerment of disadvantaged communities. The networking approach to community development argues that a core function of practice is to help individuals and organisations to establish and make use of connections that reach across boundaries. Networking, therefore, is not an incidental or peripheral activity. It must become more strategic, more skilful, better managed and more realistically funded.

Well-functioning communities need both 'weak' and 'strong' ties. Higher-level networks, such as federations or forums that link together smaller community-based organisations, are useful in 'scaling up' the efforts and achievements of the smaller groups, enabling them to have more impact and to build alliances for future campaigns (Donelson, 2004; Opare, 2007). This is particularly important for oppressed and minority groups where resources are limited and yet there is an urgent need to influence policy. It is vital to provide channels for marginalised and dissenting voices to be heard and create cross-cutting forums that encourage discussion, democratic decision-making and collective problem-solving.

The boundary-spanning aspects of informal networks are crucial in creating a climate for learning and innovation because they encourage knowledge transfer for problem-solving (Hargreaves, 2004). 'Weak' ties contribute to social cohesion by providing links between sections of the networks that might otherwise remain isolated and mutually antagonistic (Granovetter, 1978; Gilchrist, 2004). 'Strong' ties, characterising intimate kin and friendship clusters, where members are connected through many overlapping links, provide an informal infrastructure of multiple communication channels. This internal redundancy gives communities their resilience. If one relationship fails or becomes overloaded, there are several other possible information routes or sources of support (Ball, 2004, p 476).

Community development is fundamentally concerned with long-term well-being and social justice. Networks are vital to maintaining the first and achieving the second. Butcher (1993, p 17) sees the 'end product' of community practice as a "neighbourhood alive with activity and cross-cut with networks of relationships, providing a locus for informal support and mutual aid", to which might be added 'and for collective organising'. In many respects, the model of the 'well-connected community' presented in this book was pre-empted long ago by Flecknoe and McLellan who recognised in their introduction to neighbourhood work that:

> The community development process sets out to create
> the context within which meaningful relationships can
> be formed and through which people have the spaces
> to grow and change, and fulfil their potential.... A high
> quality of relationships is the foundation for all community
> development work. Unless people are able to trust in
> others and share a part of their lives, collective activity
> is impossible.... 'Community' is that web of personal
> relationships, group networks, traditions and patterns
> of behaviour that develop against the backdrop of the
> physical neighbourhood and its socio-economic situation.
> Community development aims to enrich that web and
> make its threads stronger. (1994, pp 7–8)

As we saw in Chapter Seven, complexity theory provides an explanation
of *why* networks form the basis for an optimally functioning social
system. These can be characterised by mildly 'chaotic' interactions
leading to the evolution of collective forms of organising that adapt or
die according to changes in the social environment. The model of the
'well-connected community' sees 'community' as neither a place, nor
an agent, of change, nor even a 'fuzzy set' of characters. 'Community'
is conceptualised as an experience or capacity that emerges as a result
of the interactions within a complex open system of overlapping
networks. The development of 'community' is an aspiration, a principle
and an outcome. Managing the 'web' of interpersonal and inter-
organisational linkages is a vital function for community development
that acknowledges the diversity, the difficulties and the dynamism of
communities, all important features of complex systems.

While it is true that a proportion of the work is conducted through
one-to-one conversations, assistance and support, networking for
community development is not primarily about helping people to
form connections that will be beneficial to them personally. Rather it
is about strategies for overcoming psychological and other barriers so as
to facilitate their participation in broader activities and decision-making.
Work with individuals is a necessary, but not sufficient, contribution
to the establishment and maintenance of groups, organisations and
coalitions. Thomas (1995, p 15) refers to this as the 'lost meaning'
of community development, the work that "strengthens the social
resources and processes in a community by developing those *contacts,
relationships, networks, agreements and activities* outside the household"
(emphasis in original). The paradigm set out in this book seeks to

restore the value of this work by locating networking at the heart of community development.

Collective action and partnership working rely on and are enhanced by largely unacknowledged networking. Much of this takes place informally through face-to-face conversation and mutual co-operation. Networking requires knowledge of local customs, organisational structures and cultural institutions, as well as a commitment to building trust and respect across community and sectoral boundaries, especially those relating to ethnicity, class and other dimensions of difference in society. Networking offers an effective tool for honouring diversity and promoting equality to achieve empowerment and cohesion.

Conclusions

The model of the 'well-connected community' and the idea of 'meta-networking' are presented here as a core purpose of community development practice. This is fundamentally about nurturing informal social, political and professional networks using interpersonal links and organisational liaison. Well-connected communities attain a level of self-organised criticality, in which individuals become aligned through clusters of interaction (networks, groups and organisations) and achieve the critical mass of 'received wisdom' and shared motivation necessary for collective action (see Ball, 2004). Some kind of intervention is necessary to create 'order from chaos' in a complex system. In some circumstances, the commitment and connections supplied by community development workers are crucial in helping the 'well-connected community' to adapt to changing conditions in its organisational and political environment. The community development worker as meta-networker must be both strategic and opportunistic. They need to maintain a balance between the formal and informal aspects of community life, operating within a complex accountability matrix in a context that is shaped by political, cultural and psychological processes. They are both catalysts and connectors (Gilchrist, 1998b).

The networking approach to community development opens up access and communication routes across the social landscape, by making use of personal habits, local conventions and institutional power in order to improve the quality of life for communities and create mechanisms for collective empowerment. Complexity theory suggests that a community poised at the 'edge of chaos' is able to survive in 'turbulent times' because it evolves forms of collective organisation that fit the environmental conditions. If, as I am suggesting, meta-networking is a key professional function, then we need to find ways of evaluating community development in terms of improvements to interpersonal and inter-organisational links within wider networks. This involves looking at the intricacy and effectiveness of the individual relationships as well as levels of diversity and 'connectedness' across the whole web, including interactions with the 'outside' world.

Community indicators used in participatory appraisals that measure the feel-good factors of community life offer further possibilities (Theis and Grady, 1991; Walker et al, 2000; Chanan, 2004), as do the relational audits suggested by the Relationship Foundation (Baker, 1996). Morrissey (2000) reports on an action research study to evaluate citizen participation and learning that included as progress indicators: 'development of new networks', 'levels of trust', 'alliances among organisations', 'organisations with networks formed', and (for individuals) 'expanded network of relationships' and 'learning the importance of networking'. In particular, it will be important to develop ways of assessing the robustness of networks and measuring the 'interconnectivity' between individuals and organisations (Skinner and Wilson, 2002, pp 152–4). More work is needed to establish the link between networking practice and community development outcomes, perhaps by harnessing the growing interest in measuring social capital (Boeck and McCulloch, 2001; McDonnell, 2002). This would be ideally suited to an action research approach using participatory enquiry methods (e.g. Burns, 2007).

The 'well-connected community' model reconciles individual interests with the common good through the development of locally appropriate problem-solving strategies. Complexity theory encourages us to see informal and inter-organisational networks as an extended communal 'brain', processing information intelligently to construct a resilient body of knowledge, and generating a collective consciousness at the same time (Rose, 1998). As Wilson observes, "the brain is a machine assembled not to understand itself, but to survive.... The brain's true meaning is hidden in its microscopic detail. Its fluffy mass is an intricately wired system" (1998, p 106). By analogy the capacity of a community to respond creatively to change and ambiguity is to be found in its web of connections and relationships, rather than in either the heads of individuals or the formal structures of voluntary bodies. A well-connected community is able to solve problems through reasoning, experimentation and strategic engagement with external bodies, not just trial and error. The well-connected community will demonstrate insight and imagination, responding to local or external perturbations and accommodating internal diversity. It will develop 'collective efficacy' by learning from experience and developing strategies for dealing with unusual situations and eventualities (Morgan, 1989; Capra, 1996; Sampson, 2004).

The starting point for this book was a recognition that 'things' happen as a result of informal interactions even though these often failed to register in formal auditing, monitoring and evaluation procedures. Social relations and networks represent intangible resources in people's lives that can either be nurtured or allowed to wither through neglect. Networking ensures that connections and trust are generated and maintained within communities. Community development workers have a particular responsibility for the 'weak ties' that span socio-psychological boundaries, thus keeping open the channels of communication within and between diverse communities, promoting integration and building 'alliance across difference' (Mayo, 2000). In a world characterised by uncertainty and diversity, the networking approach enables people to make links, to share resources and to learn from each other without the costs and constraints of formal organisational structures. Empowerment is a collective process, achieved through compassion, communication and connections. This book is a contribution to the discussion on how community development uses networking to develop 'community' and to promote 'strength through diversity'.

Suggested further reading

Banks, S., Butcher, H., Henderson, P. and Robertson, J. (2007) *Critical community practice*, Bristol: The Policy Press.

Bartley, T. (2003) *Holding up the sky*, London: Community Links.

Castells, M. (2000) *The rise of the network society*, Oxford: Blackwell.

Chambers, R. (1983) *Rural development – putting the last first*, Harlow: Pearson Education.

Cilliers, P. (1998) *Complexity and post-modernism*, London: Routledge.

Craig, G. and Mayo, M. (eds) (1995) *Community and empowerment*, London: Zed Books.

Crow, G. and Allan, G. (1994) *Community life*, Hemel Hempstead: Harvester Wheatsheaf.

Day, G. (2006) *Community and everyday life*, Abingdon: Routledge.

Eade, D. (1997) *Capacity building: An approach to people-centred development*, Oxford: Oxfam.

Ebers, M. (2001) *The formation of inter-organisational networks*, Oxford: Oxford University Press.

Field, J. (2003) *Social capital*, London: Routledge.

Fraser, E., Thirkell, A. and McKay, A. (2003) *Tapping into existing social capital – rich networks, poor connections*, London: Department for International Development.

Gilchrist, A. with Rauf, T. (2005) *Community development and networking* (2nd edn), London: Community Development Foundation.

Halpern, D. (2005) *Social capital*, Cambridge: Polity Press.

Harris, K. (2006) *Respect in the neighbourhood: Why neighbourliness matters*, Lyme Regis: Russell House Publishing.

Henderson, P. and Thomas, D. (2002) *Skills in neighbourhood work* (3rd edn), London: Allen and Unwin.

Hoggett, P. (ed) (1997) *Contested communities: Experiences, struggles, policies*, Bristol: The Policy Press.

Johnson, N. (2007) *Two's company, three is complexity*, Oxford: Oneworld.

Kretzmann, J.P. and McKnight, J. (1993) *Building communities from the inside out: A path toward finding and mobilizing a community's assets*, Evanston, IL: Institute for Policy Research, Northwestern University.

Ledwith, M. (2006) *Community development*, Bristol: The Policy Press.

McCarthy, H., Miller, P. and Skidmore, P. (eds) (2004) *Network logic: Who governs in a network society?* London: Demos.

Nash, V. (ed) (2002) *Reclaiming community*, London: IPPR.

Nohria, N. and Eccles, R.G. (eds) (1992) *Networks and organisations: Structure, form and action*, Boston, MA: Harvard Business School Press.

Pitchford, M. (2008) *Making spaces for community development*, London: Community Development Foundation.

Taylor, M. (2003) *Public policy in the community*, Basingstoke: Palgrave Macmillan.

Twelvetrees, A. (2008) *Community work* (4th edn), Basingstoke: Palgrave Macmillan.

References

6, Perri (2002) 'Governing friends and acquaintances: public policy and social networks', in V. Nash (ed) *Reclaiming community*, London: IPPR.

Aberdeen City Council (2008) *Real lives, real needs, real people – working together for change*, Aberdeen: Aberdeen Community Regeneration Network.

Abrahamson, E. and Freedman, D. (2007) *A perfect mess: The hidden benefits of disorder*, London: Little, Brown & Company.

Abrams, D. (2006) 'The psychology of neighbourliness', in D. Pilch (ed) *Neighbourliness*, London: Smith Institute.

Abrams, D. and Hogg, M.A. (1990) *Social identity theory*, Hemel Hempstead: Harvester Wheatsheaf.

ACW (Association of Community Workers) (1975) *Knowledge and skills for community work*, London: ACW.

ACW (1978) *Conditions of employment for those working in the community: Guidance for workers and employers*, London: ACW.

Adams, D. and Hess, M. (2006) 'New research instruments for government: measuring community engagement', in C. Duke, L. Doyal and B. Wilson (eds) *Making knowledge work: Sustaining learning communities and regions*, Leicester: NIACE.

Adamson, D. and Bromiley, R. (2008) *Community empowerment in practice: Lessons from Communities First*, York: Joseph Rowntree Foundation.

African Peace Forum, Centre for Conflict Studies, Consortium of Humanitarian Agencies, Forum on Early Warning and Response, International Alert and Safer World (2004) *Conflict-sensitive approaches to development, humanitarian assistance and peace-building: A resource pack*.

Agranoff, R. and McGuire, M. (2001) 'Big questions in public network management research', *Journal of Public Administration Research and Theory*, vol 3, pp 295–326.

Åkerstrøm Andersen, N. (2008) *Partnerships: Machines of possibility*, Bristol: The Policy Press.

Alcock, P. (2005) 'Maximum Feasible Understanding – Lessons from Previous Wars on Poverty', *Social Policy and Society*, vol 4, pp 321–9.

Alexander, C. (2000) *The Asian gang: Ethnicity, identity, masculinity*, Oxford: Berg.

Alexander, C. (2007) 'Imagining cohesive identities', in M. Wetherell, M. Lafleche and R. Berkeley (eds) *Identity, ethnic diversity and community cohesion*, London: Sage Publications.

Alinsky, S. (1969) *Reveille for radicals*, New York, NY: Vintage Books.

Alinsky, S. (1972) *Rules for radicals*, New York, NY: Vintage Books.

Allport, G. (1958) *The nature of prejudice*, New York, NY: Doubleday.

Allport, G.W. and Postman, L. (1947) *The psychology of rumour*, New York, NY: Henry Holt and Co.

Alsop, R., Bertelson, M.F. and Holland, J. (2005) *Empowerment in practice – from analysis to implementation*, Washington, DC: World Bank.

Alter, C. and Hage, J. (1993) *Organizations working together: Coordination in interorganizational networks*, Newbury Park, CA: Sage Publications.

AMA (Association of Metropolitan Authorities) (1993) *Local authorities and community development: A strategic opportunity for the 1990s*, London: AMA.

Amin, A. (2002) *Ethnicity and the multi-cultural city: Living with diversity*, Swindon: Economic and Social Research Council.

Anastacio, J., Gidley, B., Hart, L., Keith, M., Mayo, M. and Korwarzik, V. (2000) *Reflecting realities: Participants' perspectives on integrated communities and sustainable development*, Bristol/York: The Policy Press/Joseph Rowntree Foundation.

Anderson, J. (1995) *How to make an American quilt screenplay*, Los Angeles, CA: Universal City Studios.

Andersson, E., Warburton, D. and Wilson, R. (2007) 'The true costs of public participation', in T. Brannan, P. John and G. Stoker (eds) *Re-energising citizenship: Strategies for civil renewal*, Basingstoke: Palgrave Macmillan.

Andrew, F.A. and Lukajo, N.M. (2005) 'Golden opportunities – myth and reality? Horn of Africa female migrants, refugees and asylum seekers in The Netherlands', *Community Development Journal*, vol 40, pp 224–31.

Anwar, M. (1985) *Pakistanis in Britain: A sociological study*, London: New Century.

Appleyard, D. (1981) *Liveable streets*, Berkeley, CA: University of California Press.

Archer, T. (2009) *A future for community development*, Working paper, London: Community Development Foundation.

Argyle, M. (1996) *The social psychology of leisure*, Harmondsworth: Penguin.

Ariyaratne, A.T. (1995) *Tolerance as a positive characteristic for personal and structural change*, New Delhi, India: UNESCO and the Department of Culture.

Arneil, B. (2006) *Diverse communities – the problem with social capital*, Cambridge: Cambridge University Press.

Ashman, D. (2003) *Towards more effective collaboration in NGO networks for social development: Lessons learned from the NGO Networks for Health project and a framework for planning, monitoring and evaluation*, unpublished report for NGO Networks for Health.

Back, L. (1996) *New ethnicities and urban culture*, London: UCL Press.

Bailey, G. and Jones, K. (2006) *Our kids, our community*, London: Community Development Foundation.

Baker, N. (ed) (1996) *Building a relational society: New priorities for public policy*, Aldershot: Arena.

Baker, W. (1994) *Networking smart: How to build relationships for personal and organisational success*, New York, NY: McGraw-Hill.

Baldock, P. (1977) 'Why community action? The historical origins of the radical trend in British community work', *Community Development Journal*, vol 12, pp 68–74.

Ball, P. (2004) *Critical mass: How one thing leads to another*, London: Arrow Books.

Bandura, A. (2001) 'Social cognitive theory: an agentic perspective', *Annual Review of Psychology*, vol 52, pp 1–26.

Banks, S., Butcher, H., Henderson, P. and Robertson, J. (eds) (2003) *Managing community practice: Principles, policies and programmes*, Bristol: The Policy Press.

Banks, S., Butcher, H., Henderson, P. and Robertson, J. (2007) *Critical community practice*, Bristol: The Policy Press.

Banks, S. and Orton, A. (2007) 'The grit in the oyster: community development workers in a modernising authority', *Community Development Journal*, vol 42, pp 97–113.

Barnes, M., Matka, E. and Sullivan, H. (2003) 'Evidence, understanding and complexity', *Evaluation*, vol 9, pp 265–84.

Barnes, M., Newman, J. and Sullivan, H. (2004) 'Power, participation, and political renewal: theoretical perspectives on public participation under New Labour in Britain', *Social Politics: International Studies in Gender, State & Society*, vol 11, pp 267–79.

Barnes, M., Newman, J. and Sullivan, H. (2007) *Power, participation and political renewal: Case studies in public participation*, Bristol: The Policy Press.

Barnes, M., Skelcher, C., Beirens, H., Dalziel, R., Jeffares, S. and Wilson, L. (2008) *Designing citizen-centred governance*, York: Joseph Rowntree Foundation.

Barnett, S.A. (1888) 'Charity up to date', in S. Barnett (ed) *Practicable socialism*, London: Longmans Green and Co.

Barr, A. and Hashagen, S. (2000) *ABCD handbook: A framework for evaluating community development*, London: Community Development Foundation.

Barr, A., Stenhouse, C. and Henderson, P. (2001) *Caring communities: A challenge for social inclusion*, York: Joseph Rowntree Foundation.

Barth, F. (1998) *Ethnic groups and boundaries – the social organisation of cultural difference*, Long Grove: Waveland Press.

Bartley, T. (2003) *Holding up the sky: Love, power and learning in the development of a community*, London: Community Links.

Barton, H. (2000) 'The design of neighbourhoods', in H. Barton (ed) *Sustainable communities: The potential for eco-neighbourhoods*, London: Earthscan.

Batten, T.R. (1957) *Communities and their development*, Oxford: Oxford University Press.

Batten, T.R. and Batten, M. (1967) *The non-directive approach in group and community work*, London: Oxford University Press.

Bauman, Z. (2000) *Liquid modernity*, Cambridge: Polity Press.

Bauman, Z. (2001) *Community: Seeking safety in an insecure world*, Cambridge: Polity Press.

Bauman, Z. (2003) *Liquid love: On the frailty of human bonds*, Cambridge: Polity Press.

Bayley, M. (1997) 'Empowering and relationships', in P. Ramcharan (ed) *Empowerment in everyday life: Learning disability*, London: Jessica Kingsley.

Bechtel, W. and Abrahamsen, A. (1991) *Connectionism and the mind: An introduction to parallel processing in networks*, Oxford: Blackwell.

Beirens, H., Hughes, N., Hek, R. and Spicer, N. (2007) 'Preventing social exclusion of refugees and asylum seeking children: building new networks', *Social Policy and Society*, vol 6, pp 219–29.

Belenky, M. (1986) *Women's way of knowing: The development of self, voice and mind*, New York, NY: Basic Books.

Bell, C. and Newby, H. (1971) 'Community studies, community power and community conflict', in C. Bell and C. Newby (eds) *Community studies*, London: George Allen and Unwin.

Bell, J. (1992) *Community development team work: Measuring the impact*, London: Community Development Foundation.

Benson, J.K. (1975) 'The inter-organisational network as a political economy', *Administrative Science Quarterly*, vol 20, pp 229–49.

Bentley, T. (2005) *Everyday democracy – why we get the politicians we deserve*, London; Demos.

Bhavnani, R., Mirza, H.S. and Meetoo, V. (2006) *Tackling the roots of racism: Lessons for success*, Bristol: The Policy Press.

Biddle, W. W. and Biddle, L. J. (1965) *The community development process*, New York, NY: Holt, Rinehart and Winston.

Black Radley (2007) *Lozells disturbance summary report*, Birmingham: Black Radley.

Blake, G., Diamond, J., Foot, J., Gidley, B., Mayo, M., Shukra, K. and Yarnit, M. (2008) *Governance and diversity – fluid communities, solid structures*, York: Joseph Rowntree Foundation.

Blaxter, L., Farnell, R. and Watts, J. (2003) 'Difference, ambiguity and the potential for learning – local communities working in partnership with local government', *Community Development Journal*, vol 38, pp 130–9.

Blokland, T. (2003) *Urban bonds: Social relationships in an inner-city neighbourhood*, Cambridge: Polity Press.

Blunkett, D. (2001) *Politics and progress: Renewing democracy and civil society*, London: Demos, Politico's Publishing.

Boeck, T. and Fleming, J. (2005) 'Social policy – a help or a hindrance to social capital?' *Social Policy and Society*, vol 4, pp 259–70.

Boeck, T., Fleming, J. and Kemshall, H. (2006) 'The context of risk decisions: does social capital make a difference?', *Forum: Qualitative Social Research*, vol 7, no 1.

Boeck, T. and McCulloch, P. (2001) *Social capital survey: Saffron Lane estate*, Leicester: De Montfort University.

Boeck, T., Gage, M., Adamason, J., Cheney, J. and Pye, S. (2007) *Social capital and stronger communities in Leicestershire*, Leicester: CVS Community Partnership.

Böhm, D. (1994) *Thought as a system*, London: Routledge.

Böhm, D. (1996) *On dialogue*, London: Routledge.

Boissevain, J. (1974) *Friends of friends: Networks, manipulators and coalitions*, Oxford: Blackwell.

Bollobás, B. (2001) *Random graphs* (2nd edn), Cambridge: Cambridge University Press.

Borgatti, S. P., Everett, M. G. and Freeman, L. C. (2002) *Ucinet for Windows: Software for social network analysis*, Harvard: Analytic Technologies.

Bott, E. (1957) *Family and social networks*, London: Tavistock.

Bourdieu, P. (1986) 'The forms of capital', in J. G. Richardson (ed) *Handbook of theory and research for the sociology of education*, New York, NY: Greenwood Press.

Bourke, J. (1994) *Working class cultures in Britain, 1890–1960*, London: Routledge.

Bowen, G. A. (2008) 'An analysis of citizen participation in anti-poverty programmes', *Community Development Journal*, vol 43, pp 65–78.

Bowles, M. (2008) *Democracy: The contribution of community development to local governance and democracy*, London: Community Development Foundation.

Boyle, D., Clark, S. and Burns, S. (2006) *Hidden work: Co-production by people outside paid employment*, York: New Economics Foundation and Joseph Rowntree Foundation.

BRAC (1980) *The net: Power structure in ten villages*, Dacca: Bangladesh Rural Advancement Committee.

Bradley, D. (2004) *Participatory approaches: A facilitator's guide*, London: Voluntary Services Overseas.

Brah, A. (2007) 'Non-binarised identities of similarity and difference', in M. Wetherell, M. Lafleche and R. Berkeley (eds) *Identity, ethnic diversity and community cohesion*, London: Sage Publications.

Brannan, T., John, P. and Stoker, G. (2006) 'Active citizenship and effective public services and programmes: how can we know what really works?' *Urban Studies*, vol 43, pp 993–1008.

Brannan, T., John, P. and Stoker, G. (eds) (2007) *Re-energising citizenship: Strategies for civil renewal*, Basingstoke: Palgrave Macmillan.

Brent, J. (2009) *Searching for community: Representation, power and action on an urban estate*, Bristol: The Policy Press.

Briggs, X. (1997) 'Social capital and the cities: advice to change agents', *National Civic Review*, vol 86, pp 111–17.

Briner, R., Poppleton, S., Owens, S. and Kiefer, T. (2008) *The nature, causes and consequences of harm in emotionally demanding occupations*, Norwich: HMSO, Health and Safety Executive.

Brindle, D. (2008) *Care and support: A community responsibility?* York: Joseph Rowntree Foundation.

Brown, M.E. (2001) 'Ethnic and internal conflicts: causes and implications', in C.A. Crocker, F.O. Sampson and P. Aall (eds) *Turbulent peace: The challenges of managing international conflict*, Washington, DC: United States Institute of Peace, pp 209-226.

Bruegel, I. (2005) 'Social capital and feminist critique', in J. Franklin (ed) *Women and social capital*, working paper no 12, London: South Bank University.

Bryant, R. (1997) 'The road to nowhere: the Barton by-pass campaign', *Community Development Journal*, vol 32, pp 77–86.

Bubb, S. and Davidson, H. (2004) *Only connect: A leader's guide to networking*, London: ACEVO.

Buchanan, M. (2003) *Nexus: Small worlds and the ground breaking theory of networks*, New York: Norton Books.

Bunch, C. with Antrobus, P., Frost, S. and Reilly, N. (2001) 'International networking for women's human rights', in M. Edwards and J. Gaventa (eds) *Global citizen action*, Boulder, CO: Lynne Rienner Publishers.

Buonfino, A. and Hilder, P. (2007) *Neighbouring in contemporary Britain*, York: Joseph Rowntree Foundation.

Buonfino, A. with Thomson, L. (2007) *Belonging in contemporary Britain*, London: Young Foundation.

Burgess, P., Hall, S., Mawson, J. and Pearce, G. (2001) *Devolved approaches to local governance: Policy and practice in neighbourhood management*, York: Joseph Rowntree Foundation.

Burkett, I. and Bedi, H. (2006) *What in the world … Global lessons, inspirations and experiences in community development*, Falkland, Fife: International Association for Community Development.

Burns, D. (2007) *Systemic action research*, Bristol: The Policy Press.

Burns, D., Williams, C.C. and Windebank, J. (2004) *Community self help*, Basingstoke: Palgrave.

Burt, R. (2000) 'The network structure of social capital', in B.M. Staw and R.I. Sutton (eds) *Research in Organizational Behavior*, New York: Elsevier.

Burton, P. (2004) 'Power to the people?', *Local Economy*, vol 19, pp 193–8.

Burton, P., Goodlad, R. and Croft, J. (2006) 'How would we know what works? Context and complexity in the evaluation of community involvement', *Evaluation*, vol 12, pp 294–312.

Butcher, H. (1993) 'Introduction: some examples and definitions', in H. Butcher, A. Glen, P. Henderson and J. Smith (eds) *Community and public policy*, London: Pluto Press.

Butcher, H., Glen, A., Henderson, P. and Smith, J. (eds) (1993) *Community and public policy*, London: Pluto Press.

Butt, J. (2001) 'Partnership and power: the role of black and minority ethnic voluntary organisations in challenging racism', in S. Balloch and M. Taylor (eds) *Partnership working: Policy and practice*, Bristol: The Policy Press.

Byrne, D. (1998) *Complexity theory and the social sciences*, London: Routledge.

Byrne, D. (2005) 'Complexity, Configurations and Cases', *Theory, Culture & Society*, vol 22, pp 95–111.

Cacioppo, J.T. and Patrick, B. (2008) *Loneliness: Human nature and the need for social connection*, New York: W.W. Norton and Company.

Cahn, E. (2000) *No more throwaway people: The co-production imperative*, Washington, DC: Essential Books.

Cantle, T. (2001) *Community cohesion: A report of the independent review team*, London: Home Office.

Cantle, T. (2008) *Community cohesion: A new framework for race and diversity* (2nd edn), Basingstoke: Palgrave Macmillan.

Capra, F. (1996) *The web of life: A new synthesis of mind and matter*, London: HarperCollins.

Capra, F. (2004) 'Living networks', in H. McCarthy, P. Miller and P. Skidmore (eds) *Network logic: Who governs in an inter-connected world?* London: Demos.

Carnegie, D. (1937) *How to win friends and influence people*, Sydney: Angus and Robertson.

Castells, M. (1996) *The rise of the network society: The information age: Economy, society and culture*, Oxford: Blackwell.

Castells, M. (2001) *The Internet galaxy*, New York, NY: Oxford University Press.

Cattell, V. (2001) 'Poor people, poor places and poor health: the mediating role of social networks and social capital', *Social Sciences and Medicine*, vol 52, pp 1501–16.

CD Challenge group (2006) *The Community Development Challenge report*, London: Department for Communities and Local Government.

CDF (Community Development Foundation) (2008a) *Funding single identity groups – summary of findings,* London: CDF.

CDF (2008b) *Community development's role in empowerment*, London: CDF.

CDP (Community Development Project) (1974) *Inter-project report*, London: Community Development Project Information Intelligence Unit.

CDP (1977) *Gilding the ghetto: The state and the poverty experiment*, London: Community Development Project Information Intelligence Unit.

CDX (Community Development Exchange) (2006) *What is community development?* Sheffield: CDX.

CENI (Community Evaluation Northern Ireland) (2006) *Toolkit to measure the added value of voluntary and community based activity*, Belfast: Voluntary Sector Unit, Department for Social Development.

Chambers, R. (1983) *Rural development: Putting the last first*, Harlow: Longman.

Chanan, G. (1992) *Out of the shadows*, Dublin: European Foundation for the Improvement of Living and Working Conditions.

Chanan, G. (2003) *Searching for solid foundations: Community involvement and urban policy*, London: ODPM.

Chanan, G. (2004) *Measures of community*, London: ODPM.

Chappell, N., Funk, L., Carson, A., MacKenzie, P. and Stanwick, R. (2006) 'Multi-level health promotion: how can we make it work?' *Community Development Journal*, vol 42, pp 352–66.

Chauhan, V. (2009) *Creating spaces: Community development approaches to building stronger communities*, London: Community Development Foundation.

Chayko, M. (2002) *Connecting: How we form social bonds and communities in the Internet age*, Albany, NY: State University of New York Press.

Christian, M. (1998) 'Empowerment and black communities in the UK', *Community Development Journal*, vol 33, pp 18–31.

Church, C. (2008) *Better places, better planet*, London: Community Development Foundation.

Cialdini, R.B. (1993) *Influence: The psychology of persuasion*, New York, NY: William Morrow.

Cilliers, P. (1998) *Complexity and post-modernism*, London: Routledge.

Clark, G. and Greenfields, M. (eds) (2006) *Here to stay*, Hatfield: University of Hertfordshire Press.

Clarke, S., Hoggett, P. and Thompson, S. (eds) (2006) *Emotions, politics and society*, Basingstoke: Palgrave Macmillan.

Clarke, S., Gilmour, R. and Garner, S. (2007) 'Home, identity and community cohesion', in M. Wetherell, M. Lafleche and R. Berkeley (eds) *Identity, ethnic diversity and community cohesion*, London: Sage Publications.

Clarke, T. (1963) *Working with communities*, London: National Council of Social Services.

Clegg, S. (1989) *Frameworks of power*, London: Sage Publications.

CLG (Communities and Local Government) (2008) *Communities in control – real people, real power*, London: Department for Communities and Local Government.

CLG (2009) *Guidance on meaningful interaction – how encouraging positive relationships between people can build community cohesion*, London: CLG with the National Community Forum.

Coates, T. (2007) *Building the plane as you fly it: Community development systems in New Orleans*, unpublished Masters dissertation in Public Policy at the John F. Kennedy School of Government, Harvard University. Accessed at: http://belfercenter.ksg.harvard.edu/publication/18739/building_the_plane_as_you_fly_it.html

Cobble, D.S. (2004) *The other women's movement: Workplace justice and social rights in modern America*, Princeton: Princeton University Press.

Coffé, H. and Geys, B. (2007) 'Toward an Empirical Characterization of Bridging and Bonding Social Capital', *Nonprofit and Voluntary Sector Quarterly*, vol 36, pp 121–39.

Cohen, A. (1985) *The symbolic construction of community*, London: Routledge.

Cohen, J. and Stewart, I. (1994) *The collapse of chaos: Discovering simplicity in a complex world*, New York, NY: Viking.

Cohn, M. (2008) *Trust – self interest and the common good*, Oxford: Oxford University Press.

CoIC (Commission on Integration and Cohesion) (2007) *Our shared future*, London: Communities and Local Government.

Coker, E.M. (2008) 'Religion, ethnicity, and community mental health: service provision and identity politics in an unplanned Egyptian community', *Community Development Journal*, vol 43, pp 79–92.

Cole, K.C. (1984) *Sympathetic vibrations: Reflections on physics as a way of life*, New York, NY: Bantam Books.

Coleman, J. (1990) *Foundations of social theory*, Cambridge, MA: Harvard University Press.

Community Alliance (2007) *An ever-evolving story: How community anchor organisations are making a difference*, London: Community Alliance.

Connolly, P. (2003) *Liveable London: The need for a walkable neighbourhood: Older and disabled people have their say*, London: Living Streets.

Considine, M. (2003) 'Networks and inter-activity: making sense of front-line governance in the United Kingdom, the Netherlands and Australia', *Journal of European Public Policy*, vol 10, pp 46–58.

Cook, K., Burt, R.S. and Lin, N. (2001) *Social capital: Theory and practice*, Edison, NJ: Aldine Transaction.

Cooke, B. and Kothari, U. (eds) (2001) *Participation: The new tyranny?* London: Zed Books.

Cornwall, A. (2008) 'Unpacking "participation": models, meanings and practices', *Community Development Journal*, vol 43, pp 269–83.

Corrigan, P. and Leonard, P. (1978) 'Community work and politics', in P. Corrigan and P. Leonard (eds) *Social work practice under capitalism: A Marxist approach*, London: Macmillan.

Cowley, J. (1977) 'The politics of community organising', in J. Cowley (ed) *Community or class struggle?* London: Stage One.

Cox, E. (2006) *Empowering neighbourhoods: Going beyond the double devolution deal*, London: Local Government Information Unit.

Craig, G. (2007) 'Something old, something new …', *Critical Social Policy*, vol 38, pp 335–59.

Craig, G. and Mak, H.W. (2007) *The Hong Kong Declaration: Building democratic institutions and civil society through community development, in the Asia-Pacific Region*, Hong Kong: IACD.

Craig, G. and Mayo, M. (eds) (1995) *Community and empowerment: A reader in participation and development*, London: Zed Books.

Craig, G., Gorman, M. and Vercseg, I. (2004) 'The Budapest declaration: building civil society through community development', *Community Development Journal*, vol 39, pp 423–9.

Craig, G., Burchardt, T. and Gordon, D. (2008) *Social justice and public policy*, Bristol: The Policy Press.

Creasy, S., Gavelin, K. and Potter, D. (2008) *Everybody needs good neighbours? A study of the link between public participation and community cohesion*, London: Involve.

Crow, G. (2002) *Social solidarities*, Buckingham: Open University Press.

Crow, G. and Allan, G. (1994) *Community life*, Hemel Hempstead: Harvester Wheatsheaf.

CRU (2005) *Firm foundations: The government's strategy for community capacity building*, London: Civil Renewal Unit, Home Office.

Cuff, D. (2005) 'Enduring proximity: the figure of the neighbour in suburban America', *Postmodern Culture*, vol 15, no 2, http://muse.jhu.edu/journals/postmodern_culture/v015/15.2cuff.html.

Curtis, R.L. and Zurcher, L.A. (1973) 'Stable resources of protest movements: the multi-organisational field', *Social Forces*, vol 52, pp 53–61.

Dale, A. and Sparkes, J. (2008) 'Protecting ecosystems: network structure and social capital mobilization', *Community Development Journal*, vol 43, pp 143–56.

Damasio, A. (2006) *Descartes' error: Emotion, reason and the human brain*, London: Vintage.

Datta, D. (2007) 'Sustainability of community-based organisations of the rural poor: learning from CONCERN's rural development projects, Bangladesh', *Community Development Journal*, vol 42, pp 47–62.

Davies, W. (2003) *You don't know me but …: Social capital and social software*, London: The Work Foundation.

Day, G. (2006) *Community and everyday life*, Abingdon: Routledge.

de Groot, A.D. (1965) *Thought and choice in chess*, The Hague: Mouton.

Dekker, P. and Uslaner, E.M. (eds) (2001) *Social capital and participation in everyday life*, London; Routledge.

Demos (2003) *Inside out – rethinking inclusive communities*, London: Demos.

Dench, G., Gavron, K. and Young, M. (2006) *The new East End: Kinship, race and conflict*, London: Profile.

Dennett, D. (1991) *Consciousness explained*, London: Little Brown.

Department for International Development (DFID) (1999) *Better health for poor people*, London: DFID.

Derrett, R. (2003) 'Making sense of how festivals demonstrate a community's sense of place', *Event Management,* vol 8, pp 49–58.

Derricourt, N. and Dale, J. (1994) 'Mapping the community work minefield', in S. Jacobs and K. Popple (eds) *Community work in the 1990s,* Nottingham: Spokesman.

Dharamsi, F., Edmonds, G., Filkin, E., Headley, C., Jones, P., Naish, M., Scott, I., Smith, H. and Williams, J. (1979) *Community work and caring for children,* Ilkley: Owen Wells.

Difonzo, N. (2008) *The watercooler effect: A psychologist explores the extraordinary power of rumours,* New York: Avery Publishing.

Dines, N. and Cattell, V. with Gesler, W. and Curtis, S. (2006) *Public spaces, social relations and well-being in east London,* Bristol: The Policy Press.

Dinham, A. (2005) 'Empowered or over-powered? The real experiences of local participation in the UK's New Deal for Communities', *Community Development Journal,* vol 40, pp 301–12.

Dinham, A. (2007) 'Raising expectations or dashing hopes? Well-being and participation in disadvantaged areas', *Community Development Journal,* vol 42, pp 181–93.

Dinham, A., Furbey, R. and Lowndes, V. (eds) (2009) *Faith in the public realm – controversies, policies and practices,* Bristol: The Policy Press.

Dominelli, L. (1995) 'Women in the community: feminist principles and organising in community work', *Community Development Journal,* vol 30, pp 133–43.

Dominelli, L. (2006) *Women and community action* (2nd edn), Bristol: The Policy Press.

Donelson, A. (2004) 'The role of NGOs and NGO networks in meeting the needs of US *colonias*', *Community Development Journal,* vol 39, pp 332–44.

Dorsner, C. (2008) 'Implementing the Yaounde Declaration: practical issues on participatory processes in community development projects', *Community Development Journal,* vol 43, pp 413–27.

Doucet, A. (2000) '"There's a huge gulf between me as a male carer and women": gender domestic responsibility and the community as an institutional arena', *Community, Work and Family,* vol 3, no 3, pp 163–84.

Douglass, F. (1857) 'No progress without struggle!', An address on West Indian Emancipation (4 August).

Dreyfus, H.L. and Dreyfus, S.E. (1986) *Mind over machine: The power of intuition and expertise in the era of the computer,* New York, NY: The Free Press.

Duck, S. (1992) *Human relationships,* London: Sage Publications.

Dunbar, R. (1996) *Grooming, gossip and the evolution of language*, London: Faber and Faber.

Durkheim, E. (1893) *The division of labour in society*, London: Macmillan.

du Toit, A.-M. (1998) 'Building cultural synergy and peace in South Africa', *Community Development Journal*, vol 33, no 2, pp 80–90.

Dutton, W. and Helsper, E.J. (2007) *The Internet in Britain*, Oxford: University of Oxford.

Eade, D. (1997) *Capacity building: An approach to people-centred development*, Oxford: Oxfam.

Eckert, P. and McConnell-Ginet, S. (1998) 'Communities of practice: where language, gender and power all live', in J. Coates (ed) *Language and gender: A reader*, Oxford: Blackwell.

Edwards, M. and Gaventa, J. (eds) (2001) *Global citizen action*, Boulder, CO: Lynne Rienner Publishers.

Edwards, R., Hadfield, L., Lucey, H. and Mauthner, M. (2006) *Sibling identity and relationships: Brothers and sisters*, London: Routledge.

Eguren, I.R. (2008) 'Moving up and down the ladder: community-based participation in public dialogue and deliberation in Bolivia and Guatemala', *Community Development Journal*, vol 43, pp 312–28.

Eksted, M. and Fagerberg, I. (2005) 'Lived experiences of the time preceding burnout', *Journal of Advanced Nursing*, vol 49, no 1, pp 59–67.

Elsdon, K., Reynolds, J. and Stewart, S. (1995) *Voluntary organisations: citizenship, learning and change*, Leicester: National Institute of Adult and Community Education.

Elworthy, S. (1996) *Power and sex: A book about women*, Shaftesbury: Element Books.

Emery, F.E. and Trist, E.L. (1965) 'The causal texture of organisational environments', *Human Relations*, vol 18, pp 21–31.

Erikson, K. (1979) *In the wake of the flood*, London: Allen and Unwin.

Estrella, M. and Gaventa, J. (1998) *Who counts reality? Participatory monitoring and evaluation: A literature review*, Brighton: Institute of Development Studies, University of Sussex.

Etzioni, A. (1993) *The spirit of community*, New York, NY: Crown Books.

Evans, S. (2009) *Community and ageing – maintaining quality of life in housing with care settings*, Bristol: The Policy Press.

Evers, A. (2003) 'Social Capital and Civic Commitment: on Putnam's way of understanding', *Social Policy and Society*, vol 2, pp 13–22.

Evison, I. (2008) *Faith communities pulling together*, London: Community Development Foundation.

Fairfax, P., Green, E., Hawran, H., South, J. and Cairns, L. (2002) *Well-connected! – A self-assessment tool on community involvement for organisations*, Bradford: Bradford Health Action Zone and Bradford Building Communities Strategy.

Farrar, M. (2001) *The struggle for 'community' in a British multi-ethnic inner-city area: Paradise in the making*, Lampeter: Edwin Mellor Press.

FCDL (Federation for Community Development Learning) (2009) *Draft national occupational standards for community development practice*, available at: www.fcdl.org.uk.

Fearon, K. (1999) *Women's work: The study of the Northern Ireland Women's Coalition*, Belfast: Blackstaff Press.

Fehr, B. (1996) *Friendship processes*, London: Sage Publications.

Ferguson, K. (1984) *The feminist case against bureaucracy*, Philadelphia, PA: Temple University Press.

Fernet, C., Guay, F. and Senecal, C. (2004) 'Adjusting to job demands; the role of work self determination and job control in predicting burnout', *Journal of Vocational Behavior* (online), vol 65, pp 39–56.

Ferree, M.M. (1992) 'The political context of rationality: rational choice theory and resource mobilisation', in A.D. Morris and C. McClurg Mueller (eds) *Frontiers in social movement theory*, New Haven, CT: Yale University Press.

Field, J. (2003) *Social capital*, London: Routledge.

Fieldhouse, E. (2008) 'Social capital and ethnic diversity', in N. Johnson (ed) *Citizenship, cohesion and solidarity*, London: The Smith Institute.

Fineman, S. (1993) 'Organisations as emotional arenas', in S. Fineman (ed) *Emotions in organisations*, London: Sage Publications.

Finnegan, R. (1989) *The hidden musicians*, Cambridge: Cambridge University Press.

Finney, N. and Simpson, L. (2009) *Sleepwalking to segregation? Challenging myths about race and migration*, Bristol: The Policy Press.

Fischer, C. (1982) *To dwell amongst friends: Personal networks in town and city*, Chicago, IL: University of Chicago Press.

Flam, H. and King, D. (eds) (2005) *Emotions and social movements*, London: Routledge.

Flecknoe, C. and McLellan, N. (1994) *The what, how and why of neighbourhood community development* (3rd edn), London: Community Matters.

Flint, J. and Robinson, D. (2008) *Community cohesion in crisis? New dimensions of diversity and difference*, Bristol: The Policy Press.

Foley, M. and Edwards, B. (1999) 'Is it time to dis-invest in social capital?' *Journal of Public Policy*, vol 19, pp 141–73.

Forrest, R. and Kearns, A. (2001) *Social cohesion, social capital and neighbourhood change*, Bristol/York:The Policy Press/Joseph Rowntree Foundation.

Forster, E.M. (1910) *Howards end*, London: Edward Arnold.

Foth, M. (2006) 'Analysing the factors influencing the successful design and uptake of interactive systems to support social networks in urban neighbourhoods', *International Journal of Technology and Human Interaction*, vol 2, pp 65–79.

Foth, M. (2008) 'Networking serendipitous social encounters in urban neighbourhoods', in E. Eyob (ed) *Social implications of data mining and information privacy: Interdisciplinary frameworks and solutions*, Hershey, PA: IGI Global.

Foth, M. and Hearn, G. (2007) 'Networked individualism of urban residents: Discovering the communicative ecology in inner-city apartment buildings', *Information, Communication & Society*, vol 10, pp 749–72.

Foucault, M. (1977) *Discipline and punishment*, Harmondsworth: Penguin.

Frances, J., Levacic, R., Mitchell, J. and Thompson, G. (1991) 'Introduction', in G.Thompson, J. Frances, R. Levacic and J. Mitchell (eds) *Markets, hierarchies and networks: The co-ordination of social life*, London: Sage Publications.

Francis, D., Henderson, P. and Thomas, D. (1984) *A survey of community development workers in the United Kingdom*, London: NISW.

Francis, D., Grayson, J. and Henderson, P. (2002) *Rich seam: Community development in coalfield communities*, London: Community Development Foundation.

Frankenberg, R. (1966) *Communities in Britain: Social life in town and country*, Harmondsworth: Penguin.

Fraser, E., Thirkell, A. and McKay, A. (2003) *Tapping into existing social capital – rich networks, poor connections*, London: Department for International Development.

Fraser, H. (2005) 'Four different approaches to community participation', *Community Development Journal*, vol 40, pp 286–300.

Freeman, J. (1973) *The tyranny of structurelessness*, New York, NY: Falling Wall Press.

Freeman, L. (2000) 'Visualising social networks', *Journal of Social Structure*, vol 1, no 1.

Freire, P. (1972) *Pedagogy of the oppressed*, Harmondsworth: Penguin.

Fujimoto, I. (1992) 'Lessons from abroad in rural community revitalisation; the one village, one product', *Community Development Journal*, vol 27, pp 10–20.

Fukuyama, F. (1996) *Trust: The social virtues and the creation of prosperity*, London: Hamilton.

Furbey, R., Dinham, A., Farnell, R., Finneron, D. and Wilkinson, G. with Howarth, C., Hussain, D. and Palmer, S. (2006) *Faith as social capital: Connecting or dividing?* Bristol: The Policy Press.

Gabriel, Z. and Bowling, A. (2004) 'Quality of life from the perspectives of older people', *Ageing and Society*, vol 24, pp 675–91.

Gaetner, S. and Dovidio, J. (2000) *Reducing intergroup bias: The common ingroup identity model*, Hove: Psychology Press.

Gamble, C. (1999) *The paleolithic societies of Europe*, Cambridge: Cambridge University Press.

Garland, C., Hume, F. and Majid, S. (2002) 'Re-making connections: refugees and the development of emotional capital in therapy groups', *Psychoanalytical Psychotherapy*, vol 16, no 3, pp 197–214.

Geertz, C. (1973) *The interpretation of cultures*, New York: Basic Books.

Giarchi, G. (2001) 'Caught in the nets: a critical examination of the use of the concept of "networks" in community development studies', *Community Development Journal*, vol 36, pp 63–71.

Gibson, T. (1996) *The power in our hands: Neighbourhood-based world shaking*, Charlbury: Jon Carpenter.

Gilchrist, A. (1994) *Report and evaluation of the Bristol Festival Against Racism*, Bristol: Avon Race Equality Unit.

Gilchrist, A. (1995) *Community development and networking*, London: Community Development Foundation.

Gilchrist, A. (1998a) '"A more excellent way": developing coalitions and consensus through informal networking', *Community Development Journal*, vol 33, no 2, pp 100–8.

Gilchrist, A. (1998b) 'Connectors and catalysts', *SCCD News*, no 18, pp 18–20.

Gilchrist, A. (1999) 'Serendipity and the snowflakes', *SCCD News*, no 19, pp 7–10.

Gilchrist, A. (2000) 'The well-connected community: networking to the "edge of chaos"', *Community Development Journal*, vol 35, pp 264–75.

Gilchrist, A. (2001) 'Strength through diversity: a networking approach to community development', unpublished PhD thesis, University of Bristol.

Gilchrist, A. (2003) 'Linking partnerships and networks', in S. Banks, H. Butcher, P. Henderson and J. Robertson (eds) *Managing community practice*, Bristol: The Policy Press.

Gilchrist, A. (2004) *Community cohesion and community development: Bridges or barricades?* London: Community Development Foundation.

Gilchrist, A. with Rauf, T. (2005) *Community development and networking* (2nd edn), London: Community Development Foundation.

Gilchrist, A. (2006a) 'Partnership and participation: power in process', *Public Policy and Administration*, vol 21, pp 70–85.

Gilchrist, A. (2006b) 'Community development and networking for health', in J. Orme, M. Grey, T. Harrison, J. Powell and P. Taylor (eds) *Public health for the 21st century: Policy, participation and practice*, Basingstoke: Open University Press/McGraw Hill Education.

Gilchrist, A. (2007) *Equalities and communities: Challenge, choice and change*, London: Community Development Foundation.

Gilchrist, A. and Taylor, M. (1997) 'Community networking: developing strength through diversity', in P. Hoggett (ed) *Contested communities: Experiences, struggles, policies*, Bristol: The Policy Press.

Gill, O. and Jack, G. (2007) *The child and family in context: Developing ecological practice in disadvantaged communities*, Lyme Regis: Russell House Publishing.

Gilligan, C. (1982) *In a different voice: Psychological theory and women's development*, Cambridge, MA: Harvard University Press.

Gittings, C. and Harris, K. (2008) *Older people and neighbouring: The role of street parties in promoting community cohesion*, Bristol: Streets Alive Ltd.

Gladwell, M. (2000) *The tipping point: How little things can make a big difference*, London: Little Brown.

Gleick, J. (1987) *Chaos: Making a new science*, New York, NY: Viking.

Glen, A., Henderson, P., Humm, J. and Meszaros, H. with Gaffney, M. (2004) *A survey of community development workers in the UK*, London: Community Development Foundation/SCCD.

Gluckman, M. (ed) (1952) *Order and rebellion in tribal Africa*, London: Cohen and West.

Godfrey, M., Townsend, J. and Denby, T. (2004) *Building a good life for older people in local communities: The experience of ageing in time and place*, York: Joseph Rowntree Foundation.

Goetschius, G.W. (1969) *Working with community groups*, London: Routledge and Kegan Paul.

Goffman, E. (1959) *The presentation of self in everyday life*, New York, NY: Doubleday.

Goldstein, N.J., Martin, S.M. and Cialdini, R.B. (2008) *Yes! 50 scientifically proven ways to be persuasive*, Cambridge: Simon and Schuster.

Gordon, G. (1999) *The Internet: A philosophical inquiry*, London: Routledge.

Gramsci, A. (1971) *Selections from the prison notebooks*, London: Lawrence and Wishart.

Granovetter, M. (1973) 'The strength of weak ties', *American Journal of Sociology*, vol 78, pp 1360–80.

Granovetter, M. (1974) *Getting a job: A study of contacts and careers*, Cambridge, MA: Harvard University Press.

Granovetter, M. (1978) 'Threshold models of collective behaviour', *American Journal of Sociology*, vol 78, pp 1420–43.

Granovetter, M. (1985) 'Economic action and social structure: the problem of embeddedness', *American Journal of Sociology*, vol 9, pp 481–510.

Gratton, L. (2008) *Hot spots: Why some companies buzz with energy and innovation – and others don't*, Harlow: Pearson Educational.

Gray, A. (2003) *Towards a conceptual framework for studying time and social capital*, London: South Bank University.

Green, A. and White, R.J. (2007) *Attachment to place: Social networks, mobility and prospects of young people*, York: Joseph Rowntree Foundation.

Greenfield, S. (2008) *ID: The quest for identity in the 21st century*, London: Sceptre.

Griffiths, H. (1981) 'Community work in the 80s: paid and voluntary action', in G. Poulton (ed) *Community work issues and practice in the 80s*, Southampton: Southern Council for Community Work Training.

Guijt, I. and Shah, M.K. (1998) *The myth of community – gender issues in participatory development*, London: Intermediate Technology Publications.

Gunaratne, R. (2005) 'International and regional implications of the Sri Lankan Tamil insurgency', in R. Soysa (ed) *Peace in Sri Lanka: Obstacles and opportunities*, London: World Alliance for Peace in Sri Lanka (WAPS).

Hall, P. (2000) 'Social capital in Britain', *British Journal of Politics*, vol 29, pp 417–61.

Hall, S. (1990) 'Cultural identity and diaspora', in J. Rutherford (ed) *Identity: Community, culture, difference*, London: Lawrence and Wishart.

Halpern, D. (2005) *Social capital*, Cambridge: Polity Press.

Hampton, K. (2003) 'Grieving for a lost network: collective action in a wired suburb', *The Information Society*, vol 19, no 5, pp 1–13.

Hampton, K. (2007) 'Neighbourhoods in the network society: the e-neighbours study', *Information, Communication and Society*, vol 10, pp 714–48.

Handy, C. (1988) *Understanding voluntary organisations*, Harmondsworth: Penguin.

Hanifan, L.J. (1916) 'The rural school community centre', *Annals of the American Academy of Political and Social Science*, vol 67, pp 130–8.

Hanley, L. (2007) *Estates: An intimate history*, London: Granta.

Harbor, B., Morris, P. and McCormack, I. (eds) (1996) *Learning to disagree*, London/Dublin: UNISON/IMPACT.

Hargreaves, D. (2004) 'Networks, knowledge and innovation', in H. McCarthy, P. Miller and P. Skidmore (eds) *Network logic: Who governs in an inter-connected world?* London: Demos.

Harper, R. (2001) *Social capital: A review of the literature*, London: Office for National Statistics.

Harris, K. (2003) 'Keep your distance: remote communication, face-to-face and the nature of community', *The Journal of Community Work and Development*, vol 1, no 4, pp 5–28.

Harris, K. (2006) *Respect in the neighbourhood: Why neighbourliness matters*, Lyme Regis: Russell House Publishing.

Harris, K. (2008) *Neighbouring and older people: An enfolding community?* London: Community Development Foundation.

Harris, M. and Young, T. (2009) *Bridging community divides: Impact of grassroots bridge building activities*, London: Institute for Voluntary Action Research (IVAR).

Harrow, J. and Bogdanova, M. (2006) *Sink or SWIM: Towards a 21st century community sector*, London: bassac.

Hastings, C. (1993) *The new organisation: Growing the culture of organizational networking*, Maidenhead: McGraw-Hill.

Hay, S. (2008) *Developing active networks in local communities: a review of Local Links, a pilot programme in West Yorkshire*, York: Joseph Rowntree Foundation.

Heald, T. (1983) *Networks: Who we know and how we use them*, London: Hodder and Stoughton.

Hedstrom, P. (2005) *Dissecting the social: On the principles of analytical sociology*, Cambridge: Cambridge University Press.

Helgesen, S. (1990) *The female advantage: Women's ways of leadership*, New York, NY: Doubleday.

Helliwell, J. and Putnam, R. (2006) 'The social context of well-being', in F. Huppert, N. Baylis and B. Keverne (eds) *The science of well-being*, Oxford: Oxford University Press.

Help the Aged (2008) *Towards common ground: The Help the Aged manifesto for lifetime neighbourhoods*, London: Help the Aged.

Henderson, P. (2000) 'An historical perspective on community development in the UK – power, politics and radical action', in P. Ashton and A. Hobbs (eds) *Communities developing for health*, Liverpool: Health for All.

Henderson, P. (2005) *Including the excluded: From practice to policy in European community development*, Bristol: The Policy Press.

Henderson, P. and Glen, A. (2006) 'From recognition to support: community development workers in the United Kingdom', *Community Development Journal*, vol 41, pp 277–92.

Henderson, P. and Salmon, H. (1998) *Signposts to local democracy: Local governance, communitarianism and community development*, London: Community Development Foundation.

Henderson, P. and Salmon, H. (2001) *Social exclusion and community development*, London: Community Development Foundation.

Henderson, P. and Thomas, D.N. (1980) *Skills in neighbourhood work* (1st edn), London: Allen and Unwin.

Henderson, P. and Thomas, D.N. (1987) *Skills in neighbourhood work* (2nd edn), London: Allen and Unwin.

Henderson, P. and Thomas, D.N. (2002) *Skills in neighbourhood work* (3rd edn), London: Routledge.

Henning, C. and Leiberg, M. (1996) 'Strong ties or weak ties? Neighbourhood networks in a new perspective', *Scandinavian Housing and Planning Research*, vol 13, no 1, pp 3–26.

Herath, S. (2008) 'Disasters in Sri Lanka: the relevance of the concept of well-being', Paper presented to conference on Human well-being, hosted by Sarvodaya and Durham University Project Sri Lanka, Colombo, February 2008.

Heraud, B. (1975) 'The new towns: a philosophy of community', in P. Leonard (ed) *The sociology of community action*, Keele: Sociological Review.

Hero, R.E. (2007) *Racial diversity & social capital: Equality & community in America*, Cambridge: Cambridge University Press.

Heron, J. (1996) *Co-operative inquiry: Research into the human condition*, London: Sage Publications.

Hewstone, M., Tausch, N., Hughes, J. and Cairns, E. (2007) 'Prejudice, inter-group contact and identity: do neighbourhoods matter?' in M. Wetherell, M. Lafleche and R. Berkeley (eds) *Identity, ethnic diversity and community cohesion*, London: Sage Publications.

Hickey, S. (2004) *Participation: From tyranny to transformation exploring new approaches to participation in development*, London: Zed Books.

Hiller, H. and Franz, T. (2004) 'New ties, old ties and lost ties: the use of the Internet in diaspora', *New Media & Society*, vol 6, pp 731–52.

Hillery, G. (1955) 'Definitions of community: areas of agreement', *Rural Sociology*, vol 20, pp 111–23.

Hindess, B. (1996) *Discourse of power: From Hobbes to Foucault*, Oxford: Blackwell.

Hoerr, J. (1993) 'Solidaritas at Harvard: organising in a different voice', *The American Prospectus*, vol 14, pp 67–82.

Hoggett, P. (2006) 'Pity, compassion, solidarity' in S. Clarke, P. Hoggett and S. Thompson (eds.) *Emotions, politics and society*, Basingstoke: Palgrave Macmillan.

Hoggett, P. (2009) *Politics, identity and emotion*, Boulder, CO: Paradigm.

Hoggett, P. and Miller, C. (2000) 'Working with emotions in community organisations', *Community Development Journal*, vol 35, pp 352–64.

Hoggett, P., Mayo, M. and Miller, C. (2008) *The dilemmas of development work*, Bristol: The Policy Press.

Holland, C., Clark, A., Katz, J. and Peace, S. (2007) *Social interactions in urban public spaces*, Bristol: The Policy Press.

Homans, G.C. (1950) *The human group*, London: Routledge and Kegan Paul.

Hope, A., Timmell, S. and Hodzi, C. (2000) *Training for transformation: A handbook for community development workers*, Sterling, VA: Stylus Publications.

Hosking, D.-M. and Morley, I.E. (1991) *A social psychology of organising: People, processes and contexts*, London: Harvester Wheatsheaf.

Hothi, M. with Bacon, N., Brophy, M. and Mulgan, G. (2008) *Neighbourliness + Empowerment = Well being: Is there a formula for happy communities*, London: Young Foundation/IDeA.

Hudson, M., Phillips, J., Ray, K. and Barnes, H. (2007) *Social cohesion in diverse communities*, York: Joseph Rowntree Foundation.

Huisman, M. and van Duijn, M.A.J. (2005) 'Software for social network analysis', in P.J. Carrington, J. Scott and S. Wasserman (eds) *Models and methods in social network analysis*, Cambridge: Cambridge University Press.

Humphries, B. and Martin, M. (2000) 'Unsettling the learning community: from "dialogue" to "difference"', *Community, Work and Family*, vol 3, pp 279–95.

Hunter, A. and Staggenborg, S. (1988) 'Local communities and organised action', in C. Milofsky (ed) *Community organisations: Studies in resource mobilisation and exchange*, New York, NY: Oxford University Press.

Hunter, F. (1953) *Community power structure*, Chapel Hill, NC: University of North Carolina Press.

Hussein, D. (2007) 'Identity formation among British Muslims', in M. Wetherell, M. Lafleche and R. Berkeley (eds) *Identity, ethnic diversity and community cohesion*, London: Sage Publications.

Hustedde, R. and King, B. (2002) 'Rituals: emotions, community faith in soul and the messiness of life', *Community Development Journal*, vol 37, pp 338–48.

Innerarity, F. (2003) *Gender dimensions of social capital in the Caribbean*, Kingston, Jamaica: University of West Indies Press.

Innes, M. and Jones, V. (2006) *Neighbourhood security and urban change: Risk, resilience and recovery*, York: Joseph Rowntree Foundation.

Isen, A. and Levin, P. (1972) 'Effect of feeling good on helping: cookies and kindness', *Journal of Personality and Social Psychology*, vol 21, pp 384–8.

Jacobs, J. (1961) *The death and life of great American cities*, London: Cape.

James, M. (2007) *FCCB evaluation report*, London: Community Development Foundation.

Jantsch, E. (1980) *The self-organising universe*, Oxford: Pergamon Press.

Jaworski, J. (1996) *Synchronicity: The inner path of leadership*, San Francisco, CA: Berrett-Köhler.

Jeffers, S., Hoggett, P. and Harrison, L. (1996) 'Race, ethnicity and community in three localities', *New Community*, vol 22, pp 111–26.

Jirasinghe, R.C. (2007) *The rhythm of the sea*, Hambantota, Sri Lanka: Hambantota Chamber of Commerce.

Johnson, N. (2007) *Two's company, three is complexity*, Oxford: Oneworld.

Johnson, S. (2001) *Emergence: The connected lives of ants, brains, cities and software*, New York: Scribner.

Jones, T. (2007) *Utopian dreams: In search of the good life*, London: Faber and Faber.

Kagan, C. (2006) *Making a difference: Participation and wellbeing*, Manchester: RENEW Intelligence Report.

Kane, L. (2008) 'The World Bank, community development and education for social justice', *Community Development Journal*, vol 43, pp 194–209.

Kanter, R. (1983) *The changemasters*, New York, NY: Simon and Schuster.

Karl, M. (ed) (1999) *Measuring the immeasurable: Planning, monitoring and evaluation of networks*, New Dehli: Women's Feature Service, NOVIB.

Kauffman, S. (1995) *At home in the universe: The search for the laws of complexity*, London: Penguin.

Kawachi, I. (1996) 'A prospective study of social networks in relation to total mortality and cardiovascular disease in the USA', *Journal of Epidemiology and Community Health*, vol 50, pp 245–91.

Kay, A. (2006) 'Social capital, the social economy and community development', *Community Development Journal*, vol 41, pp 160–73.

Kelly, C. and Breinlinger, S. (1996) *The social psychology of collective action: Identity, justice and gender*, London: Taylor and Francis.

Kennedy, J., Livesley, M., Poll, C. and Sanderson, H. (2008) *Standards in community connecting*, Birmingham: In Control.

Khan, O. (2007) 'Policy, identity and community cohesion', in M. Wetherell, M. Lafleche and R. Berkeley (eds) *Identity, ethnic diversity and community cohesion*, London: Sage Publications.

King, M.L. (1968) *Chaos or community? Where do we go from here?*, London: Hodder and Stoughton.

Klandermans, B. (1997) *The social psychology of protest*, Oxford: Blackwell.

Klein, J. (1973) *Training for the new helping professions*, London: Goldsmiths College.

Klinenberg, E. (2002) *Heat wave: A social autopsy of disaster in Chicago*, Chicago: University of Chicago Press.

Knoke, D. (1990a) *Organising for collective action: The political economies of association*, New York, NY: Aldine de Gruyter.

Knoke, D. (1990b) *Political networks: The structural perspective*, Cambridge: Cambridge University Press.

Kolb, D. (1992) 'Women's work: peacemaking in organisations', in D. Kolb and J.M. Bartunek (eds) *Hidden conflict in organisations: Uncovering behind the scenes disputes*, Newbury Park, CA: Sage Publications.

Korsching, P. and Allen, J. (2004) 'Locality-based entrepreneurship: a strategy for community economic vitality', *Community Development Journal*, vol 39, pp 385–400.

Kottegoda, S. (2004) *Negotiating household politics: Women's strategies in urban Sri Lanka*, Colombo: Social Scientists' Association.

Kretzmann, J. and McKnight, J. (1993) *Building communities from the inside out: A path toward finding and mobilizing a community's assets*, Evanston, IL: Institute for Policy Research, Northwestern University.

Krishnamurthy, A., Prime, D. and Zimmeck, M. (2001) *Voluntary and community activities: Findings from the British Crime Survey 2000*, London: ACU research team, Home Office.

Kubisch, A.C., Brown, P., Chaskin, R., Fullbright-Anderson, K. and Hamilton, R. (2002) 'Strengthening the connexions between communities and external resources', in A.C. Kubish (ed) *Voices from the field 2: Reflections on comprehensive community change*, Washington: The Aspen Institute.

Kumar, N. (2005) *The effectiveness of World Bank support for community development: An OED evaluation*, Washington, DC: World Bank.

Kurki, L. (2003) 'Evaluating restorative justice practices', in A. von Hirsch, J. Roberts, A.E. Bottoms, K. Roach and M. Schiff (eds) *Restorative justice and criminal justice: Competing or reconcilable paradigms?* Oxford: Hart.

Kuzwe, C.N. (1998) 'The role of NGOs in democratisation and education in peacetime Rwanda', *Community Development Journal*, vol 33, pp 174–7.

Laguerre, M.S. (1994) *The informal city*, Basingstoke: Macmillan.

Laslett, P. (1956) 'The face-to-face society', in P. Laslett (ed) *Philosophy, politics and society*, Oxford: Blackwell.

Laumann, E. and Pappi, F. (1976) *Networks of collective action: A perspective on community influence systems*, New York, NY: Academic Press.

Laurence, J. and Heath, A. (2008) *Predictors of community cohesion: Multi-level modelling of the 2005 Citizenship Survey*, London: Department for Communities and Local Government.

Layard, R. (2005) *Happiness: Lessons from a new science*, London: Penguin.

Lederach, J. (2005) *The moral imagination*, Oxford: Oxford University Press.

Ledwith, M. (1997) *Participating in transformation: Towards a working model of community empowerment*, Birmingham: Venture Press.

Ledwith, M. (2006) *Community development*, Bristol: The Policy Press/BASW.

Ledwith, M. and Asgill, P. (2000) 'Critical alliance: black and white women working together for social justice', *Community Development Journal*, vol 35, pp 290–9.

Ledwith, M. and Springett, J. (2009) *Participatory practice: Community-based action for transformative change,* Bristol: The Policy Press.

Lees, R. and Mayo, M. (1984) *Community action for change*, London: Routledge and Kegan Paul.

Leissner, A. (1975) 'Models for community work and community and youth workers', *Social Work Today*, vol 5, no 22, pp 669–75.

Lewin, R. (1993) *Complexity: Life on the edge of chaos*, London: Phoenix.

Lewis, M. (2005) *Asylum: Understanding public attitudes*, London: IPPR.

LEWRG (London Edinburgh Weekend Return Group) (1979) *In and against the state*, London: Pluto Press.

LGA (Local Government Association) (2002) *Guidance on community cohesion*, London: LGA.

Liebler, C. and Ferri, M. (2004) 'NGO networks: building capacity in a changing world', Paper presented to the Office of Private and Voluntary Co-operation for USAID.

Lifelong Learning UK (2009) *National occupational standards for community development work* (revised), available at: www.lluk.org

Lin, N. (2002) *Social capital: A theory of social structure and action*, Cambridge: Cambridge University Press.

Lingayah, S. (2001) *Prove it! Measuring impacts of renewal: Findings and recommendations*, London: New Economics Foundation.

Livingstone, M., Bailey, N. and Kearns, A. (2008) *People's attachment to place: The influence of neighbourhood deprivation*, York: Joseph Rowntree Foundation.

Loney, M. (1983) *Community against government*, London: Heinemann.

Longstaff, B. (2008) *Strategies − local strategic approaches to community development*, London: Community Development Foundation.

Loader, B. and Keeble, L. (2004) *A literature review of community informatics initiatives*, York: Joseph Rowntree Foundation

Lovelock, J. (1979) *Gaia*, Oxford: Oxford University Press.

Lowndes, V. (2000) 'Women and social capital: a comment on Hall's "social capital in Britain"', *British Journal of Politics*, vol 30, pp 533–40.

Lowndes, V. and Sullivan, H. (2004) 'Like a horse and carriage or a fish on a bicycle: how well do local partnerships and public participation go together?' *Local Government Studies*, vol 30, pp 51–73.

Lowndes, V., Pratchett, L. and Stoker, G. (2006) *Locality matters: Making participation count in local politics*, London: Institute for Public Policy Research.

Lownsbrough, H. and Beunderman, J. (2007) *Equally spaced? Public space and interaction between diverse communities*, London: Demos.

Lukes, S. (1974) *Power: A radical view*, Basingstoke: Macmillan.

Lupton, R. (2004) *Poverty Street: The dynamics of neighbourhood decline and renewal*, Bristol: The Policy Press.

Lyford, J. (2001) *Women's networking: A practical guide*, Produced and printed on behalf of the Women's Decision Making Network, Derby: Derby City Council.

Lyons, J. (2007) *Place-shaping: A shared ambition for the future of local government*, London: HMSO.

McCarthy, H. (2004) 'The old girls network', in H. McCarthy, P. Miller and P. Skidmore (eds) *Network logic: Who governs in an inter-connected world?* London: Demos.

McDonnell, B. (2002) *A social capital framework – evaluating community and voluntary sector activity – briefing paper no. 1*, Belfast: CENI.

McInroy, N. (2004) 'Working with complexity: the key to effective regeneration', *Local Work*, Working paper no 60, Manchester: CLES.

McKenzie, K. and Harphan, T. (eds) (2006) *Social capital and mental health*, London: Jessica Kingsley.

MacLean, D. and McIntosh, R. (2003) 'Complex adaptive systems: towards a theory for practice', in E. Mitleton-Kelly (ed) *Complex systems and evolutionary perspectives on organisations: the application of complexity theory to organisations*, pp 149–66, London: Pergamon.

Madanipour, A. (2003) *Public and private spaces of the city*, London: Routledge.

Maffesoli, M. (1996) *The time of the tribes: The decline of individualism in mass society*, London: Sage Publications.

Marriott, P. (1997) *Forgotten resources? The role of community buildings in strengthening local communities*, York: Joseph Rowntree Foundation.

Marwell, G. and Oliver, P. (1993) *The critical mass in collective action: A micro-social theory*, Cambridge: Cambridge University Press.

Maslach, C. (1982) *Burnout: The cost of caring*, Englewood Cliffs, NJ: Prentice Hall.

Mathers, J., Parry, J. and Jones, S. (2008) 'Exploring resident (non-) participation in the UK New Deal for Communities regeneration programme', *Urban Studies*, vol 45, pp 591–606.

Maturana, H.R. and Varela, F.J. (1987) *The tree of knowledge: The biological roots of human understanding*, Boston, MA: Shambhala.

May, J., Rogerson, C. and Vaughn, A. (2000) 'Livelihoods and assets', in J. May (ed) *Poverty and inequality in South Africa: Meeting the challenge*, pp 229–56, London: Zed Books.

May, N. (1997) *Challenging assumptions: Gender considerations in urban regeneration in the UK*, York: Joseph Rowntree Foundation.

Mayo, M. (ed) (1977) *Women in the community*, London: Routledge and Kegan Paul.

Mayo, M. (1979) 'Radical politics and community action', in M. Loney and M. Allen (eds) *The crisis in the inner-city*, London: Macmillan.

Mayo, M. (2000) *Cultures, communities, identities: Cultural strategies for participation and empowerment*, London: Palgrave.

Mayo, M. (2005) *Global citizens: Social movements and the challenge of globalization*, London: Zed Books.

Mayo, M. (2008) 'Community development, contestations, continuities and change', in G. Craig, K. Popple and M. Shaw (eds) *Community development in theory and practice: An international reader*, Nottingham: Spokesman.

Mayo, M. and Rooke, A. (2006) *Evaluation of the active learning for active citizenship*, London: Department of Communities and Local Government.

Mayo, M. and Taylor, M. (2001) 'Partnership and power in community regeneration', in S. Balloch and M. Taylor (eds) *Partnership working*, Bristol: The Policy Press.

Mead, G.H. (1938) *The philosophy of the act* (ed C.W. Morris), Chicago, IL: Chicago University Press.

Medd, W. (2001) 'Making (dis)connections: complexity and the policy process?' *Social Issues*, vol 1, no 2.

Meikle, S. (2002) 'The urban context and poor people', in R. Rakodi and T. Lloyd-Jones (eds) *Urban livelihoods: A people-centred approach to reducing poverty*, pp 37–51, London: Earthscan Publications.

Mellor, M. and Stephenson, C. (2005) 'The Durham miners' gala and the spirit of community', *Community Development Journal*, vol 40, pp 343–51.

Melucci, A. (1996) *Challenging codes: Collective action in the information age*, Cambridge: Cambridge University Press.

Middleton, A., Murie, A. and Groves, R. (2005) 'Social capital and neighbourhoods that work', *Urban Studies*, vol 42, pp 1711–38.

Milgram, S. (1967) 'The small world problem', *Psychology Today*, vol 2, pp 60–7.

Milgram, S. (1977) *The individual in a social world*, Reading, MA: Addison-Wesley.

Mill, J.S. (1848) *Principles of political economy with some of their applications to social philosophy* (ed W.J. Ashley), London: Longmans, Green and Co.

Miller, J. (1974) *Aberfan: A disaster and its aftermath*, London: Constable.

Miller, J.B. (1976) *Towards a new psychology of women*, Boston, MA: Beacon Press.

Miller, K. and Rasco, L. (2004) *The mental health of refugees: Ecological approaches to healing and adaptation*, Mahwah, NJ: Lawrence Erlbaum Associates.

Miller, M. (1958) 'A comparative study of decision making in English and American cities', in C. Bell and C. Newby (eds) *Community studies*, London: George Allen and Unwin.

Miller, P. (2004) 'The rise of network campaigning', in H. McCarthy, P. Miller and P. Skidmore (eds) *Network logic: Who governs in an inter-connected world?* London: Demos.

Milofsky, C. (1987) 'Neighbourhood-based organisations: a market analogy', in W.W. Powell (ed) *The non-profit sector: A research handbook*, New Haven, CT: Yale University Press.

Milofsky, C. (1988a) 'Introduction: networks, markets, cultures and contracts: understanding community organisations', in C. Milofsky (ed) *Community organisations: Studies in resource mobilisation and exchange*, New York, NY: Oxford University Press.

Milofsky, C. (1988b) 'Structure and process in community self-help organisations', in C. Milofsky (ed) *Community organisations: Studies in resource mobilisation and exchange*, New York, NY: Oxford University Press.

Mingers, J. (1995) *Self-producing systems: Implications and applications of autopoiesis*, New York, NY: Plenum Press.

Misztal, B. (2000) *Informality: Social theory and contemporary practice*, London: Routledge.

Mitchell, J.C. (ed) (1969) *Social networks in urban situations: Analyses of personal relationships in central African towns*, Manchester: Manchester University Press.

Mitchell, W.J. (2003) *Me++: The cyborg self and the networked city*, Cambridge, MA: MIT Press.

Mitleton-Kelly, E. (ed) (2003) *Complex systems and evolutionary perspectives on organisations: The application of complexity theory to organisations*, London: Pergamon.

Modood, T. (2003) 'New forms of Britishness: post-immigration ethnicity and hybridity in Britain', in R. Sackmann, B. Peters and T. Faust (eds) *Identity and integration: Migrants in Western Europe*, Aldershot: Ashgate.

Modood, T. (2007) *Multiculturalism – a civic idea*, Cambridge: Polity Press.

Morgan, G. (1989) *Creative organisation theory: A resource book*, London: Sage Publications.

Morrissey, J. (2000) 'Indicators of citizen participation: lessons from learning teams in rural EZ/EC communities', *Community Development Journal*, vol 35, no 1, pp 59–74.

Morrissey, M. and Smyth, M. (2002) *Northern Ireland after the Good Friday Agreement: Victims, grievance and blame*, London: Pluto Press.

Morrissey, M., Healy, K., McDonnell, B., Harbison, J. and Kelly, J. (2006) *Development of a methodology to map community infrastructure and inform public investment in geographic communities*, Belfast: Community Evaluation Northern Ireland.

Moser, C. (2008) 'Assets and livelihoods: a framework for asset-based social policy', in C. Moser and A. Dani (eds) *Assets, livelihoods and social policy*, Boston: World Bank.

Mowlam, A. and Creegan, C. (2008) *Modern-day social evils: The voices of unheard groups*, York: Joseph Rowntree Foundation.

Mubangizi, B.C. (2003) 'Drawing on social capital for community economic development: Insights from a South African rural community', *Community Development Journal*, vol 38, pp 140–50.

Mulgan, G. (1997) *Connexity: How to live in a connected world*, London: Chatto and Windus.

Mulgan, G. (2004) 'Connexity revisited', in H. McCarthy, P. Miller and P. Skidmore (eds) *Network logic: Who governs in an inter-connected world?* London: Demos.

Mulgan, G. and Ali, R. (2007) 'Belonging – local and national', in N. Johnson (ed) *Britishness: Towards a progressive citizenship*, London: The Smith Institute.

Mumford, K. and Power, A. (2003) *East Enders: Family and community in east London*, Bristol: The Policy Press.

Murray, M. and Murtagh, B. (2003) 'Exploring equity, diversity and inter-dependence through dialogue and understanding in rural Northern Ireland', *Community Development Journal*, vol 38, pp 287–97.

Nakaya, U. (1954) *Snow crystals: Natural and artificial*, Boston: Harvard University Press.

Nalder, G. and Dallas, A. (2006) 'Personalized profiling and self-organization as strategies for the formation and support of open m-learning communities', in *Across generations and cultures, Proceedings of the 5th World Conference on Mobile Learning*, Banff: Athabasca University.

Narayan, D. (2002) *Empowerment and poverty reduction: A source book*, Washington, DC: World Bank.

Narayan, D. and Pritchett, L. (1997) *Cents and sociability: Household income and social capital in rural Tanzania*, Social Development and Development Research Group, Policy Research Paper No 1796, Washington, DC: World Bank.

Narayan, D., Patel, R., Schafft, K., Rademacher, A. and Koch-Schullem, S. (2000a) *Voices of the poor – can anyone hear us?* Oxford: Oxford University Press.

Narayan, D., Chambers, R., Shah, M. and Petesch, P. (2000b) *Voices of the poor – crying out for change*, Oxford: Oxford University Press.

Nash, V. and Christie, I. (2003) *Making sense of community*, London: IPPR.

Navarro, A. (2006) *Refugee integration and cohesive communities: Community development in practice*, London: Community Development Foundation.

Nelson, C., Dickinson, S., Beetham, M. and Batsleer, J. (2000) 'Border crossings/translations: resources of hope in community work with women in Greater Manchester', *Community, Work and Family*, vol 3, pp 349–62.

Newcomb, T.M. (1961) *The acquaintance process*, New York, NY: Holt, Rinehart and Winston.

Newman, I. and Geddes, M. (2001) 'Developing local strategies for social inclusion', Paper presented to Local Authorities and Social Exclusion programme, Local Government Centre, Warwick University, March.

Newman, J., Barnes, M., Sullivan, H. and Knops, A. (2004) 'Public participation and collaborative governance', *Journal of Social Policy*, vol 33, pp 203–23.

Nietzsche, F. (1878) *Thus Spake Zarathustra*, trs A. Tille (1960), London: J.M. Dent and Sons.

Nisbet, R.A. (1953) *The quest for community*, Oxford: Oxford University Press.

Northmore, S., Sampson, R. and Harland, S. (2006) 'Involving the voluntary and community sector', in D. Pilch (ed) *Neighbourliness*, London: Smith Institute.

Obama, B. (2004) *Dreams from my father* (2nd edn), New York: Three Rivers Press.

O'Brien, C. (2007) 'Integrated community development/conflict resolution strategies as peace-building in South Africa and Northern Ireland', *Community Development Journal*, vol 42, pp 114–30.

Office of the Third Sector (2007) *The future role of the third sector in social and economic regeneration: Final report*, Cm 7189, Norwich: HM Treasury and the Cabinet Office.

Ohmer, M. and Beck, E. (2006) 'Citizen participation in neighbourhood organizations in poor communities and its relationship to neighbourhood and organizational collective efficacy', *Journal of Sociology and Social Welfare*, vol 33, no 1, pp 179–202.

Ohri, A. (1998) *The world in our neighbourhood*, London: Development Education Association.

Ohri, A. and Manning, B. (eds) (1982) *Community work and racism*, London: Association of Community Workers.

Oladipo Fiki, C., Amupitan, J., Dabi, D. and Nyong, A. (2007) 'From disciplinary to interdisciplinary community development: the Joss-McMaster drought and rural water use project', *Journal of Community Practice*, vol 15, pp 147–70.

Oldenberg, R. (1991) *The great good place: Cafes, coffee shops, community centres, beauty parlours, general stores, bars, hangouts, and how they get you through the day*, New York, NY: Paragon House.

Oliver, B. (2006) 'Identity and change: youth working in transition', in *Youth & Policy*, no 93, pp 5–19.

Oliver, B. (2007) *Connected identities: Youth working in transition*, unpublished Ed.D thesis, University of Sussex.

Oliver, M. (1996) *Understanding disability*, London: Macmillan.

O'Malley, J. (1977) *The politics of community action: A decade of struggle in Notting Hill*, Nottingham: Spokesman.

Opare, S. (2007) 'Strengthening community-based organisations for the challenge of rural development', *Community Development Journal*, vol 42, pp 251–64.

Ouchi, W.G. (1980) 'Markets, bureaucracies and clans', *Administrative Science Quarterly*, vol 25, pp 129–41.

Packham, C. (2008) *Active citizenship and community learning*, Exeter: Learning Matters.

Packard, N. (1988) *Adaptation Toward the Edge of Chaos*, Urbana-Champaign: University of Illinois, Center for Complex Systems Research.

Pahl, R. (2000) *On friendship*, Cambridge: Polity Press.

Parekh, B. (2000) *The future of multi-racial Britain*, London: Profile Books.

Parekh, B. (2007) 'Reasoned identities: a committed relationship' in M. Wetherell, M. Lafleche and R. Berkeley (eds) *Identity, ethnic diversity and community cohesion*, London: Sage Publications.

Park, R. (ed) (1925) *The city*, Chicago, IL: University of Chicago Press.

Park, R. (1929) *Human communities: The city and human ecology*, Glencoe, IL: Free Press.

Passy, F. (2003) 'Social networks matter. But how?', in M. Diani and D. McAdam (eds) *Social movements and networks: Relational approaches to collective action*, Oxford: Oxford University Press.

Payne, M. (1982) *Working in teams*, London: Macmillan.

Percy-Smith, B. and Matthews, H. (2001) 'Tyrannical spaces: young people, bullying and urban neighbourhoods', *Local environment*, vol 6, pp 49–63.

Perkins, D.D., Brown, B.B. and Taylor, R.B. (1996) 'The ecology of empowerment', *Journal of Social Issues*, vol 52, pp 85–110.

Perrow, C. (1992) 'Small firm networks', in N. Nohria and R. Eccles (eds) *Networks and organisations*, Boston, MA: Harvard Business School Press.

Phelps, R., Adams, R. and Bessant, J. (2007) 'Life cycles of growing organizations: a review with implications for knowledge and learning', *International Journal of Management Reviews*, vol 9, pp 1–30.

Phillips, C. (2007) 'Ethnicity, identity and community cohesion in prison', in M. Wetherell, M. Lafleche and R. Berkeley (eds) *Identity, ethnic diversity and community cohesion*, London: Sage Publications.

Phillips, R. (2005) *Community indicators measuring systems*, Aldershot: Ashgate.

Phillips, S. (2002) 'Social capital, local networks and community development', in R. Rakodi and T. Lloyd-Jones (eds) *Urban livelihoods: A people-centred approach to reducing poverty*, pp 133–50, London: Earthscan Publications.

Phillipson, C., Allan, G. and Morgan, D.H.J. (2004) *Social networks and social exclusion: Sociological and policy perspectives*, Aldershot: Ashgate Publishing.

Pilch, D. (ed) (2006) *Neighbourliness*, London: Smith Institute.

Pitchford, M. (2008) *Making spaces for community development*, Bristol: The Policy Press.

PIU (Performance and Innovation Unit) (2002) *Social capital: A discussion paper*, London: Cabinet Office.

Plowden, B.H. (1967) *Children and their schools*, London: HMSO.

Popple, K. (1995) *Analysing community work*, Buckingham: Open University Press.

Powell, W. (1990) 'Neither market, nor hierarchy: network forms of organisation', *Research in Organisational Behaviour*, vol 12, pp 295–336.

Power, A. (2007) 'Neighbourhood renewal, mixed communities and social integration', in J. Hills, J. LeGrand and D. Piachaud (eds) *Making social policy work*, Bristol: The Policy Press.

Power Inquiry (2006) *Power to the people: An independent inquiry into Britain's democracy*, York: Power Inquiry.

Prendergast, J. (2008) *Disconnected citizens – is community empowerment the solution*, London: Social Market Foundation.

Purcell, R. (2005) *Working in the community: perspectives for change,* North Carolina: Lulu Press.

Purdue, D. (2001) 'Neighbourhood governance: leadership, trust and social capital', *Urban Studies*, vol 38, no 12, pp 2211–24.

Purdue, D. (2007) 'A learning approach to community empowerment', in T. Gossling, L. Oerlemans and R. Jansen (eds) *Inside networks*, Cheltenham: Edward Elgar.

Purdue, D., Razzaque, K., Hambleton, R. and Stewart, M. (2000) *Community leadership in urban regeneration*, Bristol/York: The Policy Press/Joseph Rowntree Foundation.

Putnam, R. (1993) 'The prosperous community', *The American Prospect*, vol 13, pp 11–18.

Putnam, R. (1995) 'Bowling alone: America's declining social capital', *Journal of Democracy*, vol 6, pp 65–78.

Putnam, R. (2000) *Bowling alone: The collapse and revival of American community*, London: Simon and Shuster.

Putnam, R. (2001) 'Social capital: measurement and consequences', *Isuma – Canadian Journal of Policy Research*, vol 2, pp 41–52.

Putnam, R. (2007) '*E Pluribus Unum*: diversity and community in the twenty-first century', *Scandinavian Political Studies*, vol 30, pp 137–74.

Raco, M. (2003) 'New Labour, community and the future of Britain's urban renaissance', in R. Imrie and M. Raco (eds) *Urban renaissance? New Labour, community, and urban policy*, pp 239–49, Bristol: The Policy Press.

Rahman, H. (2006) *Empowering marginal communities with information networking*, Hershey, PA: Idea Group Publishers.

Rahman, M.A. (1990) 'The case of the Third World: people's self-development', *Community Development Journal*, vol 25, pp 307–13.

Rahman, M.A. (1993) *People's self-development: Perspectives on participatory action research: A journey through experience*, London: Zed Books.

Rai, D.P., Duggal, I. and Singh, Y.K. (2007) *Community development*, New Delhi: Shree Publishing.

Rai, S. (2008) *Routes and barriers to citizen governance*, York: Joseph Rowntree Foundation.

Rattansi, A. (2002) *Who's British? Prospect and the new assimilation: Cohesion, community and citizenship*, London: Runnymede Trust.

Ray, K., Savage, M., Tampubolon, G., Warde, A., Longhurst, M. and Tomlinson, M. (2003) 'The exclusiveness of the political field: networks and political mobilisation', *Social Movement Studies*, vol 2, pp 37–60.

Redcliffe-Maud, J. (1969) *Report of the Royal Commission on Local Government in England 1966–1969*, London: HMSO.

Rees, S. (1991) *Achieving power: Practice and policy in social welfare*, London: Allen and Unwin.

Rheingold, H. (2002) *Smart mobs: The next social revolution*, Cambridge, MA: Basic Books.

Richardson, L. (2008) *DIY community action: Neighbourhood problems and community self-help*, Bristol: The Policy Press.

Riedel, B. (2008) *The search for Al Qaeda: Its leadership, ideology and future*, Washington: Brookings Institution Press.

Riley, E. and Wakely, P. (2005) *Communities and communication: Building urban partnerships in Colombo*, Rugby: ITDG Publishing.

Roberts, M. and Roche, M. (2001) 'Quantifying social capital: measuring the intangible in the local policy context', *Radical Statistics*, vol 76, pp 15–28.

Robertson, D., Smyth, J. and McIntosh, I. (2008) *Neighbourhood identity: Effects of time, location and social class*, York: Joseph Rowntree Foundation.

Robertson, S. (2005) *Youth clubs, association, participation, friendship and fun!*, Lyme Regis: Russell House Publishing.

Robinson, D. (2004) *Unconditional leadership: A principle-centred approach to developing people, building teams and maximizing results*, London: Community Links.

Robinson, R. and Reeve, K. (2006) *Neighbourhood experiences of new immigration: Reflections from the evidence base*, York: Joseph Rowntree Foundation.

Rogaly, B. and Taylor, B. (2007) 'Welcome to 'Monkey Island': identity and community in three Norwich estates', in M. Wetherell, M. Lafleche and R. Berkeley (eds) *Identity, ethnic diversity and community cohesion*, London: Sage Publications.

Rogers, B. and Robinson, E. (2004) *The benefits of community engagement: A review of the evidence*, London: Active Citizenship Centre.

Rogers, P., Hasci, T., Petrosino, A. and Huebner, T. (eds) (2000) *Program theory in evaluation: Challenges and opportunities*, San Francisco, CA: Josey-Bass.

Rose, S. (1998) *From brains to consciousness*, London: Allen Lane.

Rural Development Foundation (2006) *Village statistical profiles – 50 villages in Vavuniya District*, Vavuniya, Sri Lanka: RDF/USAID.

Russell, H. (2005) *National evaluation of local strategic partnerships – issues paper: voluntary and community sector engagement in local strategic partnerships*, London: Office of the Deputy Prime Minister.

Ryberg, T. and Larsen, M.C. (2008) 'Networked identities: understanding relationships between strong and weak ties in networked environments', *Journal of Computer Assisted Learning*, vol 24, pp 103–15.

Sampson, R. (2004) 'Networks and neighbourhoods', in H. McCarthy, P. Miller and P. Skidmore (eds) *Network logic: Who governs in an interconnected world?*, London: Demos.

Sampson, R., Morenoff, J. and Gannon-Rowley, T. (2002) 'Assessing neighbourhood effects: social processes and new directions in research', *Annual Review of Sociology*, vol 28, pp 443–78.

Sayyid, B. and Zac, L. (1998) 'Political Analysis in a World Without Foundations', in E. Scarborough and E. Tanenbaum (eds.) *Research strategies in the social sciences: A guide to new approaches*, pp 249–67, Oxford: Oxford University Press.

SCCD (Standing Conference for Community Development) (2001) *Strategic framework for community work*, Sheffield: SCCD.

SCCD (2003) *Resource pack to promote networking for community development*, Sheffield: SCCD.

Schilderman, T. and Ruskulis, O.E. (2005) *Building bridges with the grassroots: Scaling-up through knowledge sharing*, Bourbon-on-Dunsmore: ITDG Publishing.

Schneiderman, L. (1988) *The psychology of social change*, New York, NY: Human Sciences Press.

Schön, D. (1990) *The reflective practitioner: How professionals think in action*, Aldershot: Avebury.

Scott, J. (2000) *Social network analysis: A handbook* (2nd edn), London: Sage Publications.

Scott, S., Houston, D. and Sterling, R. (2002) *Working together, learning together: An evaluation of the national training programme for social inclusion partnerships*, Glasgow: Department of Urban Studies, University of Glasgow.

Scott, W.R. (1992) *Organisations: Rational, natural and open systems*, Englewood Cliffs, NJ: Prentice Hall.

Seabeck, A., Rogers, B. and Srikandarajah, D. (2007) 'Living together: diversity and identity in contemporary Britain', in N. Pearce and J. Margo (eds) *Politics for a new generation: The progressive moment*, Basingstoke: Palgrave Macmillan.

Searle, B. (2008) *Well-being: In search of a good life*, Bristol: The Policy Press.

Seebohm, F. (1968) *Report of the Committee on Local Authority and Allied Personal Social Services*, London: HMSO.

Seebohm, P. and Gilchrist, A. (2008) *Connect and include: An exploratory study of community development and mental health*, London: National Social Inclusion Partnership/Community Development Foundation.

Seidler, V.J. (2009: forthcoming) *Embodying identities: Culture, differences and social theory*, Bristol: The Policy Press.

Sen, A. (2006) *Identity and violence: The illusion of destiny*, London: Allen Lane.

Seyfang, G. (2001) 'Money that makes a change: community currencies North and South', in C. Sweetman (ed) *Gender, development and Money*, Oxford: Oxfam.

Seyfang, G. (2003) 'With a little help from my friends: evaluating time banks as a tool for community self-help', *Local Economy*, vol 18, pp 257–64.

Seyfang, G. and Smith, K. (2002) *The time of our lives: Using time banking for neighbourhood renewal and community capacity building*, London: New Economics Foundation.

Shankland, A. (2000) *Analysing poverty for sustainable livelihoods*, Brighton: Institute of Development Studies, University of Sussex.

Shaw, A. (2002) *Kinship and continuity – Pakistani families in Britain*, Amsterdam: Harwood Academic Press.

Shaw, M. (2008) 'Community development and the politics of community', *Community Development Journal*, vol 43, pp 24–36.

Shaw, M. and Martin, I. (2000) 'Community work, citizenship and democracy: remaking the connections', *Community Development Journal*, vol 35, no 4, pp 401–13.

Shiva, V. (2002) 'Paradigmatic shift: rebuilding true security in an age of insecurity', *Resurgence*, no 214, September/October, pp 36–7.

Shuftan, C. (1996) 'The community development dilemma: what is really empowering?' *Community Development Journal*, vol 31, pp 260–4.

Shukra, K. (1995) 'From black power to black perspectives: the reconstruction of a black political identity', *Youth and Policy*, vol 49, pp 5–17.

Shutte, A. (2001) *Ubuntu: An ethic for a new South Africa*, Pietermaritzburg: Cluster Publications.

Sieh, E.W. (2005) *Community corrections and human dignity*, Sudbury, MA: Jones and Bartlett.

Singer, P. (2007) 'Give us a smile: the glow of goodwill should be a state priority. It's a cheap and effective way to improve lives', *The Guardian*, 18 April.

Sivanandan, A. (1990) 'All that melts into air is solid: the hokum of New Times', *Race and Class*, vol 31, pp 1–30.

Skeffington, A.M. (1969) *People and planning: Report of the Committee on Public Participation in Planning*, London: HMSO.

Skidmore, P. (2004) 'Leading between', in H. McCarthy, P. Miller and P. Skidmore (eds) *Network logic: Who governs in an inter-connected world?*, London: Demos.

Skidmore, P. and Bound, K. (2008) *The everyday democracy index*, London: Demos.

Skidmore, P. and Craig, J. (2005) *Start with people: How community organisations put citizens in the driving seat*, London: Demos.

Skidmore, P., Bound, K. and Lownsbrough, H. (2006) *Community participation: Who benefits?*, York: Joseph Rowntree Foundation.

Skinner, S. and Church, C. (2007) *ChangeCheck: A practical guide to assessing the impact of your community centre*, London: bassac.

Skinner, S. and Wilson, M. (2002) *Assessing community strengths*, London: Community Development Foundation.

Smith, G. (1999) 'IT rams CD', *SCCD News*, no 21, Autumn, pp 9–16.

Smith, K. (2005) *Yes we can: A practical guide to timebanking*, London: Timebanks UK.

Smock, C. (2004) *Democracy in action: Community organising and urban change*, Chichester, NY: Columbia University Press.

Somerville, P. (2005) 'Community governance and democracy', *Policy and Politics*, vol 33, pp 117–44.

Somerville, P. (2009) '"The feeling's mutual": respect as the basis for co-operative interaction', in A. Millie (ed) *Securing respect: Behavioural expectations and anti-social behaviour in Britain,* Bristol: The Policy Press.

Sotarauta, M. (2003) *Building knowledge-based core competencies and leadership in the flowing world*, Tampere, Finland: University of Tampere, Finland.

Spratt, E. with Miller, S. (2008) *Cohesion and access to local services: An evaluation of connecting communities plus, community grants*, London: Community Development Foundation.

Sprigings, N. and Allen, C. (2005) 'The communities we are re-gaining but need to lose', *Community, Work and Family*, vol 8, pp 389–411.

Stack, C. (1974) *All our kin: Strategies for survival in a black community*, New York, NY: Harper and Row.

Stackman, R.W. and Pinder, C.C. (1999) 'Context and sex effects on personal work networks', *Journal of Social and Personal Relationships*, vol 16, pp 39–64.

Stein, M.R. (1960) *The eclipse of community: An interpretation of American studies*, Princeton, NJ: Princeton University Press.

Stephens, L., Ryan-Collins, J. and Boyle, D. (2008) *Co-production: A manifesto for growing the core economy*, London: New Economics Foundation.

Stephenson, K. (1999) 'Networks', in R. Dorf (ed) *The technology management handbook*, Boca Raton, FL: CRC Press.

Stephenson, K. (2004) 'Towards a theory of government', in H. McCarthy, P. Miller and P. Skidmore (eds) *Network logic: Who governs in an inter-connected world?*, London: Demos.

Stephenson, M. (2007) 'Developing community leadership through the arts in Southside, Virginia: social networks, civic identity and civic change', *Community Development Journal*, vol 42, pp 79–96.

Stewart, M. (2000) 'Community governance', in H. Barton (ed) *Sustainable communities: The potential for community neighbourhoods*, London: Earthscan.

Stone, C. (2001) *Networking: The art of making friends*, London: Vintage Press.

Strogatz, S. (2004) *Sync: The emerging science of spontaneous order*, Harmondsworth: Penguin Books.

Sullivan, H. and Stewart, M. (2006) 'Who owns the theory of change?', *Evaluation*, vol 12, pp 179–99.

Sullivan, H. and Taylor, M. (2007) 'Themes of neighbourhood in urban policy', in I. Smith, E. Lepine and M. Taylor (eds) *Disadvantages by where you live? Neighbourhood governance in contemporary urban policy*, Bristol: The Policy Press.

Sullivan, H., Downe, J., Entwistle, T. and Sweeting, D. (2006) 'The three challenges of community leadership', *Local Government Studies*, vol 32, pp 489–508.

Surowiecki, J. (2004) *The wisdom of crowds: Why the many are smarter than the few and how collective wisdom shapes business, economies, societies and nations*, London: Random House.

Symons, B. (1981) 'Promoting participation through community work', in L. Smith and D. Jones (eds) *Deprivation, participation and community action*, London: Routledge and Kegan Paul.

Szreter, S. and Woolcock, M. (2004) 'Health by association? Social capital, social theory, and the political economy of public health', *International Journal of Epidemiology*, vol 33, pp 1–18.

Tajfel, H. (1981) *Human groups and social categories: Studies in social psychology*, Cambridge: Cambridge University Press.

Tam, H. (2007) 'Civil renewal: the agenda for empowering citizens', in T. Brannan, P. John and G. Stoker (eds) *Re-energising citizenship: Strategies for civil renewal*, Basingstoke: Palgrave Macmillan.

Tarrow, S. (1994) *Power in movement: Social movements, collective action and politics*, Cambridge: Cambridge University Press.

Tarrow, S. (2005) *The new transnational activism*, Cambridge: Cambridge University Press.

Tasker, L. (1975) 'Politics, theory and community work', in D. Jones and M. Mayo (eds) *Community work two*, London: Routledge and Kegan Paul.

Taylor, J. (2004) 'The information utility', in H. McCarthy, P. Miller and P. Skidmore (eds) (2004) *Network logic: Who governs in a network society?*, London: Demos.

Taylor, M. (1996) 'Between public and private: accountability in voluntary organisations', *Policy & Politics*, vol 24, pp 57–72.

Taylor, M. (1997) *The best of both worlds: The voluntary sector and local government*, York: Joseph Rowntree Foundation.

Taylor, M. (2000) 'Communities in the lead: power, organisational capacity and social capital', *Urban Studies*, vol 37, pp 1019–35.

Taylor, M. (2003) *Public policy in the community*, Basingstoke: Palgrave Macmillan.

Taylor, M. (2007) *Neighbourhood management and social capital*, London: Department for Communities and Local Government.

Taylor, M. (2008) *Transforming disadvantaged places: Effective strategies for places and people*, York: Joseph Rowntree Foundation.

Taylor, M., Barr, A. and West, A. (2000) *Signposts to community development* (2nd edn), London: Community Development Foundation.

Taylor, M., Wilson, M., Purdue, D. and Wilde, P. (2007) *Changing neighbourhoods: Lessons from the JRF Neighbourhoods Programme*, Bristol: The Policy Press.

Temple, B. (2005) *Learning to live together: Developing communities with dispersed refugee people seeking asylum*, York: Joseph Rowntree Foundation.

Thake, S. (2001) *Building communities, changing lives: The contribution of large independent neighbourhood regeneration organisations*, York: Joseph Rowntree Foundation.

Thake, S. (2009) 'Individualism and community', in Joseph Rowntree Foundation (ed) *Contemporary social evils*, Bristol: The Policy Press.

Theis, J. and Grady, H.M. (1991) *Participatory rural appraisal for community development*, London: International Institute for Environment and Development/Save the Children Fund.

Theodore, N. and Martin, N. (2007) 'Migrant civil society: new voices in the struggle over community development', *Journal of Urban Affairs*, vol 29, pp 269–78.

Thomas, D. (1976) *Organising for social change: A study in the theory and practice of community work*, London: Allen and Unwin.

Thomas, D. (1983) *The making of community work*, London: Allen and Unwin.

Thomas, D. (1995) *Community development at work*, London: Community Development Foundation.

Tindall, D. (2007) 'From metaphors to mechanisms: critical issues in networks and social movements', book review, *Social Networks*, vol 29, pp 160–8.

Tönnies, F. (1887) *Community and association*, London: Routledge and Kegan Paul.

Too, L. (1997) *Feng shui fundamentals: Networking*, Shaftesbury: Element Books.

Traynor, B. (2008) 'Community building: limitations and promise', in J. Defillipis and S. Saegert (eds), *The community development reader*, London: Routledge.

Trevillion, S. (1992) *Caring in the community: A networking approach to community partnership*, Harlow: Longmans.

Trevillion, S. (1999) *Networking and community partnership*, Aldershot: Ashgate.

Twelvetrees, A. (1982) *Community work* (1st edn), Basingstoke: Macmillan.

Twelvetrees, A. (2008) *Community work* (4th edn), Basingstoke: Palgrave Macmillan.

Twine, F. (1994) *Citizenship and social rights: The interdependence of self and society*, London: Sage Publications.

United Nations (1955) *Social progress through community development*, New York: United Nations.

Uphoff, N. and Wijayaratna, C.M. (2000) 'Demonstrated benefits from social capital: the productivity of farmer organisations in Gal Oya, Sri Lanka', *World Development*, vol 28, pp 1825–90.

Veale, A.M. (2000) 'Dilemmas of "community" in post-emergency Rwanda', *Community, Work and Family*, vol 3, pp 233–9.

Völker, B., Flap, H. and Lindenberg, S. (2007) 'When are neighbourhoods communities? Community in Dutch neighbourhoods', *European Sociological Review*, vol 23, pp 99–114.

Waddington, D., Wykes, K. and Critcher, C. (1991) *Split at the seams? Community, continuity and change after the 1984–5 coal dispute*, Milton Keynes: Open University Press.

Wakefield, S.E.L. and Poland, B. (2005) 'Family, friend or foe: critical reflections on the relevance and role of social capital in health promotion and community development', *Social Science and Medicine*, vol 60, pp 2819–32.

Walker, P., Lewis, J., Lingayah, S. and Sommer, F. (2000) *Prove it! Measuring the effects of neighbourhood renewal on local people*, London: New Economics Foundation.

Walljasper, J. (2007) *The great neighbourhood book: A do-it-yourself guide to placemaking*, London: New Society.

Warburton, D. (1998) 'A passionate dialogue: community and sustainable development', in D. Warburton (ed) *Community and sustainable development: Participation in the future*, London: Earthscan.

Ward, C. (1973) *Anarchy in action*, London: Allen and Unwin.

Warne, T. and Howarth, M. (2009) *Explicating the role of partnerships in changing the health and well-being of local communities: A review of the literature and development of the Warnwarth conceptual framework for partnership evaluation*, Salford: University of Salford.

Warner, W.L. and Lunt, P.G. (1942) *The status system of a modern community*, New Haven, CT: Yale University Press.

Warren, M. (2001) *Dry bones rattling*, Princeton, NJ: Princeton University Press.

Wasserman, S. and Faust, K. (1994) *Social network analysis*, Cambridge: Cambridge University Press.

Watt, S., Lea, M. and Spears, M. (2002) 'How social is Internet communication? A reappraisal of bandwidth and anonymity effects', in S. Woolgar (ed) *Virtual society? Technology, cyberbole and reality*, Oxford: Oxford University Press.

Watts, B. (2008) *What are today's social evils? The results of a web consultation*, York: Joseph Rowntree Foundation.

Watts, D.J. (2003) *Six degrees: The new science of networks*, London: W.W. Norton.

Watts, D.J. (2004) *Small worlds: The dynamics of networks between order and randomness*, Princeton, NJ: Princeton University Press.

WCAN (Warwickshire Community Action Network) (2002) *Networking or not working: A training resource pack*, Leamington Spa: Community Action Forum (Warwick District).

Webb, S. and Animashaun, H. (2007) *Using technology for community groups*, London: Community Sector Coalition/Community Development Foundation.

Webber, M.M. (1963) 'Order in diversity: community without propinquity', in W.J. Lowdon (ed) *Cities and space: The future use of urban land*, Baltimore, MD: Johns Hopkins Press.

Weber, M. (1947) *The theory of social and economic organisation*, New York, NY: Free Press.

Weeks, J. (2000) *Making sexual history*, Cambridge: Polity Press.

Wellman, B. (1979) 'The community question: the intimate networks of East Yorkers', *American Journal of Sociology*, vol 84, pp 1201–31.

Wellman, B. (2000) 'Network capital in a multi-level world: getting support from personal communities', in L. Nan, K. Cook and R. Burt (eds) *Social capital: Theory and research*, Chicago, IL: Aldyne de Gruyter.

Wellman, B. (2002) 'Little boxes, glocalization, and networked individualism', in M. Tanabe, P. van den Besselaar and T. Ishida (eds) *Digital cities II*, Berlin: Springer-Verlag.

Wellman, B. (ed) (2006) *Personal networks in the 21st century*, special issue of *Social Networks*, vol 28.

Wellman, B. and Haythornthwaite, C. (eds) (2002) *The Internet in everyday life*, Oxford: Blackwell.

Wenger, E., McDermott, R. and Snyder, W.M. (2002) *Cultivating communities of practice*, Boston: Harvard Business School Press.

Werbner, P. (1988) 'Taking and giving: working women and female bonds in a Pakistani immigrant neighbourhood', in S. Westwood and P. Bhachu (eds) *Enterprising women: Ethnicity, economy and gender relations*, London: Routledge.

Werbner, P. (1990) *The migration process: Capital, gifts and offerings among British Pakistanis*, Oxford: Berg.

Wetherell, M., Lafleche, M. and Berkeley, R. (eds) (2007) *Identity, ethnic diversity and community cohesion*, London: Sage Publications.

Wharf Higgins, J., Naylor, P.-J. and Day, M. (2008) 'Seed funding for health promotion: sowing sustainability or scepticism?', *Community Development Journal*, vol 43, pp 210–21.

Wheatley, M.J. (1992) *Leadership in the new science: Learning about organisation from an orderly universe*, San Francisco, CA: Berrett-Koehler Publishers.

Wheeler, W.M. (1928) *Emergent evolution and the development of societies*, New York, NY: WW Norton.

White, H.C. (1963) *An anatomy of kinship*, Englewood Cliffs, NJ: Prentice-Hall.

White, L.E. (1950) *Community or chaos*, London: National Council for Social Service.

White, L. (2001) 'Effective governance: complexity thinking and management science', *Systems Research and Behavioural Science*, vol 18, pp 241–57.

Williams, C. and Windebank, J. (2000) 'Helping each other out? Community exchange in deprived neighbourhoods', *Community Development Journal*, vol 35, pp 146–56.

Williams, C. and Windebank, J. (2003) *Poverty and the third way*, London: Routledge.

Williams, C., Lee, R., Leyshon, A. and Thrift, N. (2001) *Bridges into work: An evaluation of Local Exchange Trading Schemes (LETS)*, Bristol: The Policy Press.

Williams, G. (1973) 'Ways in for a community development worker', *Talking Point*, no 10, Newcastle-upon-Tyne: ACW.

Williams, P. (2002) 'The competent boundary spanner', *Public Administration*, vol 80, pp 103–24.

Williams, R. (1976) *Keywords: A vocabulary of culture and society*, Glasgow: Collins.

Williamson, O.E. (1975) *Markets and hierarchies: Analysis and anti-trust implications*, New York, NY: Free Press.

Wilson, E.O. (1998) *Consilience: The unity of knowledge*, London: Little, Brown and Company.

Wilson, M. and Wilde, P. (2001) *Building practitioner strengths*, London: Community Development Foundation.

Wollebaek, D. and Selle, P. (2002) 'Does participation in voluntary associations contribute to social capital? The impact of intensity, scope and type', *Nonprofit and Voluntary Sector Quarterly*, vol 31, pp 32–61.

Womankind Worldwide (2000) 'Exchanging skills and experiences', Newsletter, Winter.

Woodward, V. (2005) 'Engaging civil society, civil renewal and active learning for active citizenship', *The Development Education Journal*, vol 12, pp 9–11.

Woolcock, M. (1998) 'Social capital and economic development: towards a theoretical synthesis and policy framework', *Theory and Society*, vol 27, pp 151–208.

Woolcock, M. (2001) 'The place of social capital in understanding social and economic outcomes', *ISUMA Canadian Journal of Policy Research*, vol 2, pp 11–17.

Worpole, K. and Knox, K. (2007) *The social value of public spaces*, York: Joseph Rowntree Foundation.

Wrench, J. (2007) *Diversity management and discrimination: Immigrants and ethnic minorities in the EU*, Aldershot: Ashgate.

Young, F. and Glasgow, N. (1998) 'Voluntary social participation and health', *Research on Aging*, vol 20, pp 339–62.

Young, M. and Willmott, P. (1957) *Family and kinship in East London*, London: Routledge and Kegan Paul.

Younghusband, E. (1968) *Community work and social change: A report on training*, London: Longman.

Zeldin, T. (1994) *An intimate history of humanity*, London: Sinclair-Stevenson.

Zetter, R., Griffiths, S. and Nando, S. (2005) 'Social capital or social exclusion? The impact of dispersal on UK refugee organisations', *Community Development Journal*, vol 40, pp 169–81.

Zetter, R., Griffiths, D. and Sigona, M. (2006) *Immigration, social cohesion and social capital: What are the links?*, York: Joseph Rowntree Foundation.

Zipf, G.K. (1965) *Human behavior and the principle of least effort*, New York, NY: Hafner.

Index